Explanation in Archaeology

Social Archaeology

General Editor
Ian Hodder, University of Cambridge

Advisory Editors
Margaret Conkey, University of California
at Berkeley
Mark Leone, University of Maryland
Alain Schnapp, U.E.R. d'Art et d'Archaeologie, Paris
Stephen Shennan, University of Southampton
Bruce Trigger, McGill University, Montreal

Published

In preparation

Explanation
in Archaeology

Guy Gibbon

Basil Blackwell

British Library Cataloguing in Publication Data

Gibbon, Guy, *1939–*
    Explanation in archaeology. – (Social
    Archaeology).
    1. Archaeology. Theories
    q. Title   II. Series
    930.1′01

    ISBN 0−631−16802−8
    ISBN 0−631−16931−8 (Pbk)

Library of Congress Cataloging in Publication Data

Gibbon, Guy E., 1939–
    Explanation in archaeology/Guy Gibbon.
       p. cm. − −(Social archaeology)
    Bibliography: p.
    Includes index.
    ISBN 0−631−16802−8. − − ISBN
    0−631−16931−8 (pbk.)
    1. Archaeology− −Philosophy.   2. Archaeology− −Methodology.
    I. Title.   II. Series.
    CC72.G53 1989
    930.′01− −dc19

Typeset in Garamond on 10.5/12 pt
by Setrite Typesetters
Printed in Great Britain by T.J. Press (Padstow) Ltd, Padstow, Cornwall.

Contents

Preface

This book is a study of strategies of knowing in one discipline, archaeology. It is intended, however, as a contribution to a broader on-going discussion of knowing in history, the social sciences and the humanities. Among the questions raised in this broader arena of discussion are: What is knowledge? Is it indubitably certain or in some sense hypothetical? How does it differ from belief? Is there a scientific method? How should substantive disciplines interpret philosophies of science and of social science? What role does the social context of knowledge play in its construction, if any? How do our inherent potentialities as a biological species (e.g. the nature of our sense organs and the structure of our brain) affect our knowledge claims?

I have tried to approach questions like these from an open and flexible stance, for it remains uncertain at this time whether or not we shall ever be able to establish indubitably secure knowledge, identify *the* scientific method or transcend (in some as yet unspecified way) the limitations of our senses. What we do need is sustained interdisciplinary investigation of a broad array of questions about knowing. In this book, I suggest the rubric 'anthropology of knowledge' for this area of interdisciplinary enquiry, for anthropology, at least in North America, includes cultural, biological, linguistic and archaeological subdivisions. These subdivisions encompass, for example, the biological basis of knowing, the sociocultural context of learning, the generation of human-sized linguistic categories, and the evolutionary development of the human condition.

Viewed from this perspective, *Explanation in Archaeology* is an anthropological enquiry, not an enquiry within the philosophy of science or of social science or the sociology of knowledge. Its goal is not to demand yet another revolution in archaeology, but to explore how and why certain concepts of research are adopted and adapted in archaeology, and to determine in what manner archaeological research is rule governed. Although the focus of this enquiry is the New Archaeology movement of the 1960s and early 1970s, similar enquiries could and should be made of interpretative archaeology (contextual, structural, postprocessual archaeology), traditional archaeology (the archaeology in the Americas of the 1930s to the 1950s) and other archaeological research programmes. It is an essential quest, for it concerns why we do what we do as archaeologists.

I would like to dedicate the book to David A. Baerreis, my graduate advisor, and to John Watkins, who took me under his wing during my studies at the London School of Economics.

Guy Gibbon

Acknowledgements

I should like to express my gratitude to the many people who helped in the preparation of this book: the librarians of Heidelberg and Mannheim universities in West Germany, where the research and first draft of the manuscript were completed; Professor Harald Hauptmann of the Institut für Ur-und Früh-Geschichte at Heidelberg University for access to the library of the institute; Hermine Heimburger for a pleasant working environment in Mannheim; Phyllis and Eugene Grolla for an equally pleasant working environment at Big Sandy Lake, Minnesota, where the manuscript was completed; my mother, Mildred Gibbon, who provided critical financial support that off-set the dwindling value of the dollar. Special gratitude is also due Ian Hodder and an unnamed reviewer for their constructive criticism of an earlier draft of the manuscript.

1

Introduction

New Archaeology was a reform movement launched by a handful of archaeologists in departments of anthropology in North America in the mid-1960s. It rose to a peak of intellectual vogue in the late 1960s and early 1970s, and gradually faded in popularity in the mid-1970s. In recent years only the movement's most ardent supporters still argue for the validity of the set of assumptions upon which it was based.

If New Archaeology is out of favour today, why devote time and energy to its study? There are many reasons: it is a fascinating example of the encounter between archaeology and the philosophy of science; it continues to influence all methodological discussions in North American archaeology; it remains fuzzily understood, even by many of its supporters; its form as well as its substance still emerge in what are said to be 'revised' formats.

While all these are sufficient grounds for studying New Archaeology, there is a still more fundamental reason why this particular movement should be of special interest to anthropological archaeologists. To be an archaeologist is to engage in a systematic social practice governed by rules which provide a standard and a set of goals. Although we may not be explicitly aware of them, it is these rules which underpin our ability to communicate effectively with one another. Though much of the literature of New Archaeology may be familiar to the reader, I believe that it takes on a rather different meaning when viewed from this perspective. As a form of social practice, what were the rules that governed New Archaeology? How were they understood? Why were they adopted and abandoned when they were? How did they constrain archaeology? Since New Archaeology and its social context are still fresh in our memories, I believe that its study will enable us to explore answers to questions like these with greater assurance and in greater detail than is possible for earlier movements and schools.[1] Even though we might never agree on answers to 'anthropological' questions like these, the effort itself should prove stimulating and bring about new conceptions of how we know and understand the archaeological record.

An important argument in this book can be quickly summarized: a few archaeologists in the 1960s adopted a logical empiricist conception of science in order to reform their discipline by making it 'explicitly scientific'; the movement was doomed to failure from its inception by inherent flaws in this conception of science. Although a seemingly straightforward argument, it conceals decisions of which the reader should be aware. There are a variety of conceptions, for instance, of what logical empiricism, a form of positivism, is or was, and New Archaeology itself has been only vaguely defined. If the nature of the impact of logical empiricism on New Archaeology is to be explored, then definitions are necessary – and have been made here in some detail. The definitions chosen, however, determine to a degree greater than might be wished the nature of the impact that is found, opening any discussion like this to charges of circularity and curmudgeonry. The reader should be aware of this dilemma from the start.[2] As a consequence, this book is necessarily only an interpretation – a reading – of the significance of the adoption and adaptation of logical empiricism in archaeology.

A thesis of this book is that both New Archaeology and logical empiricism display the characteristics of research programmes. Since the concept is used here as a heuristic to demonstrate just how archaeology is rule governed, it seems appropriate to introduce some of its features in this introductory chapter.

The concept of a research programme applied here is loosely based

---

[1] An important source of information, of course, is those individuals who participated in the New Archaeology research programme, a concept to be developed below. This is an appropriate place to stress that this book is not an attack on New Archaeology or on those who attempted to introduce it into archaeology with so much ardour. There are no villains here. Many New Archaeologists were and continue to be among the most productive and innovative persons in the discipline. The study of New Archaeology as a social phenomenon within archaeology is too important to become lost in the sterility of 'point scoring' or in acrimonious squabbling between proponents of different programmes.

[2] There is still little agreement on what logical empiricism and, more broadly, positivism are or were, what the task of the philosophy of science is and so forth. This does not mean that there are not a large number of people who will define them exactly, only that there are so many conflicting positions that they certainly cannot all be right. For this reason, it is necessary to learn to compare readings of methodological issues in archaeology rather than to accept one because it appears in a text and is forcefully or authoritatively stated.

on the idea of a methodology of scientific research programmes introduced by Karl Popper, Imre Lakatos and their colleagues and students.[3]
We could just as well have referred to plan of study or research
strategy, project, or approach. However, the research programme concept as developed by Popper and Lakatos explicitly focuses on the
underlying or key assumptions that inform a programme or plan of
study, and on the commitments that an archaeologist, in our case, must
make in applying that strategy to the archaeological record.[4] Archaeologists have always debated the most appropriate methods for dealing
with their subject matter. When stripped to their essentials, these debates have been and are debates over assumptions, interests and purposes. The concept of a research programme is, then, a device for
organizing these underlying principles and for making our understanding
of them explicit.

A research programme is composed of a network of presuppositions
and of rules or prescriptions for research that follow from these presuppositions. Archaeologists today generally share a tacit agreement

[3] For an introduction to the methodology of scientific research programmes, see
Lakatos, 'Falsification and the methodology of scientific research programmes', in
Lakatos and Musgrave (eds), 1970, pp. 91–196; and 'History of science and its
rational reconstruction', in Buck and Cohen (eds), 1971, pp. 91–136; Popper, *The
Logic of Scientific Discovery*, 1959; Howson (ed.), *Method and Appraisal in the
Physical Sciences*, 1976; Urbach, 'Progress and degeneration in the "I.Q. Debate"',
pp. 99–135, 235–59; Watkins et al., 'Criteria of scientific progress: a critical
rationalist view, 1975; Zahar, 'Why did Einstein's programme supersede Lorentz's?
pp. 95–123, 223–62. Full use of Lakatos's detailed analysis of the structure of
research programmes is not made here, although its use would strengthen the
argument. Here a set of presuppositions is regarded as the defended core of a
programme and the interpretations of these presuppositions as the band of auxiliary
assumptions that can be altered without changing the programme itself. Examples
are given in chapter 2. While I do agree that research programmes 'develop'
through time, I do not accept Lakatos's view that the adoption and abandonment of
a programme are purely internal logical affairs based upon pragmatic considerations.
Unlike a Kuhnian paradigm, a research programme does not necessarily dominate a
discipline but may be only one of several options (see Kuhn, *The Structure of
Scientific Revolutions*, 1970). In addition there is no reason why scholars cannot
participate in more than one programme. Stated another way, one is only a New
Archaeologist when one is following the rules of the New Archaeology research
programme.
[4] Lakatos thought that the sign of a mature discipline was the presence of well-
developed and consistent research programmes. His examples are taken from the
natural sciences, for, he argued, mature research programmes are largely absent in
the social sciences (which is also the conclusion that Kuhn reached with regard to
paradigms). That research may be poorly formulated and draw on assumptions
belonging to different research programmes or just be based on an incomplete
programme (lacking, say, an adequate epistemology) are, then, obvious possibilities.

about certain conventions, or rules of activity or practice, without which no serious thinking about archaeological assemblages could be carried on. These primary presuppositions are required if any systematic activity akin to archaeology as we understand it most broadly is to be possible at all. Examples are: 'Archaeological assemblages are the material remains of past human activity' (and not deliberately planted as a joke by fun-loving aliens), and 'We can learn about the history of the human species by studying archaeological remains'. Corresponding presuppositions in the natural sciences are: 'Nature is not chaotic; hence all phenomena are governed by laws, if only statistical', and 'Like causes produce like effects' (which justifies the conviction that objects have stable dispositions). These presuppositions can be regarded as the ultimate justifications of archaeology, and they lead directly to general methodological directives such as 'Preserve and examine archaeological sites and materials!'

Denial of the primary presuppositions of archaeology, perhaps precipitated by a stunning interstellar message confessing the joke, would entail the collapse of archaeology as we know it. Here, however, we are interested in what might be called secondary presuppositions, i.e. presuppositions which are supplementary or subsidiary to the primary set and whose denial would not entail the collapse of archaeology.

Secondary presuppositions serve as heuristics in the research process. They motivate the choice of research strategies and bias researchers' expectations concerning the types of answers that will explain or make understandable their subject matter. Hence they may be field specific and even differ within fields. Examples of secondary presuppositions in the natural sciences are: 'All regularities in nature can be represented mathematically' (therefore all properties are quantifiable), and 'Nature is in certain respects simple' (hence scientists should prefer the simplest of alternative hypotheses). Examples in archaeology are: 'An archaeological assemblage is a mirror image of past human activity', and 'Culture is an extrasomatic adaptive system'. Rejection of any one of these assumptions would lead to a shift in research strategy and probably to a shift in the kinds of questions asked about the archaeological record. Yet their rejection would not mean the end of archaeology as we know it. For instance, archaeologists who reject the idea that archaeological assemblages are mirror images of past human activity would still carry on research in a recognizably similar manner to other archaeologists, even though they would conceive of the task of interpreting archaeological assemblages differently.

Research cannot proceed by the haphazard recording of data or by idle musing over a problem. Some set of assumptions is required which defines just what data are worth collecting, just what should be done with the collected data, just what would be an acceptable explanation of the data and so on. In archaeology these assumptions provide the rules that we mentioned earlier. We call these necessary sets of assumptions research programmes.

Once a research programme has been adopted, however, its philosophical presuppositions serve to organize and structure research. They do this by generating research problems which participants work on, by providing grounds for recognizing which observations are relevant and which pose problems, and, for example, by defining what counts as an adequate solution to a problem. A research programme is able to serve these multiple purposes because it presupposes or even explicitly highlights an ontology, epistemology and methodology. Its ontology defines what entities, processes or, more broadly, 'things' can be said really to exist; its epistemology defines the nature, limits and validity of knowledge about these 'things'; its methodology defines appropriate procedures or methods for gaining this knowledge. Like a scientific theory, a research programme is accepted because it solves some problems, eliminates others and provides a guide to further research. It is abandoned when it no longer provides this guidance or when people come to believe that an alternative programme meets these criteria better.

Since research programmes in the social sciences tend to be somewhat diffuse, their interpretation and analysis raise problems. These are compounded by the tendency to leave core presuppositions unstated. As a result, their discovery must depend on the analysis of symptoms, such as the problems thought to be important, attempted solutions to problems, what practitioners are or were willing to accept as models, references to philosophies of science and the like. However, once these presuppositions have been identified, we can ask the following questions. How did the working out of the 'logic' of its presuppositions influence the history of the programme? Were the presuppositions tightly networked or loose and inconsistent? How did they influence or constrain research? Was research consistent with the implications of the programme? Was the programme abandoned because internal problems could not be resolved? Which substantive research results in the discipline in question are consistent with the programme and which are not? The imaginative reader can easily add to the list.

The core presuppositions that define logical empiricism and the New Archaeology as research programmes are identified in chapters 2 and 4; some criticisms of these programmes are summarized in chapters 3 and 5. Readers might be tempted to scan or skip entirely chapters 2 and 3, which provide an introduction to the logical positivist/empiricist philosophy of science. This would be a mistake. Logical empiricism provided the philosophical underpinnings of New Archaeology and strongly structured its development. As I will argue throughout the book, philosophical perspectives and substantive research are inextricably interwoven; to view them as separate spheres of discourse is but one result of our having adopted a positivist philosophy of science in archaeology. It is principally for this reason that in chapters 2–5 we concentrate on the relationship between positivist philosophy and North American archaeology, and not solely upon the internal development of New Archaeology within archaeology itself.

Some of the reasons why a positivist philosophy of science was adopted by archaeologists and why New Archaeology took the form it did are explored in chapter 6. A different theory of science – realism – is introduced in chapter 7 to demonstrate to those archaeologists who insist that we have no choice but to remain positivist that viable alternatives exist within the philosophy of science. A series of general questions concerning the history and methodology of archaeology, and the relationship between archaeology, the philosophy of science and the anthropology of knowledge are raised in the final chapter.

This book has two goals. The first is to provide the reader with a brief overview of the conceptual foundation of New Archaeology. The second and more basic is to introduce some of the many issues involved in adopting a research programme. Since all research is guided by one research programme or another, these issues should concern every archaeologist. Perhaps their importance can be made more vivid through a series of questions. What should archaeology be about? What is the subject matter of archaeology? What is the importance in archaeology of past peoples, environments and cultures? What special problems arise out of archaeological research itself? What is the relationship of archaeology to anthropology? To history? To the natural sciences? Which methods and techniques should be applied in the pursuit of archaeological knowledge? When? Why? What are the roles of explanation, model building, prediction, theory construction, story-telling, taxonomies and observation in archaeology? Is archaeology a science? A social science? A human science? A historical discipline? A humanistic enterprise? Can archaeologists avoid answering, if only implicitly, questions like these without reference to a research programme?

Research is as much about the epistemologies and ontologies that archaeologists adopt as it is about the substantive 'stuff' of archaeological assemblages, and as much about the assumptions that are made about the research process, the world and people as about the potsherds and other artefacts that form in part an archaeological assemblage. Such commonly encountered phrases as 'Only those things that are in principle observable can be said to exist' or 'Data relating to an entire extinct cultural system are present in the archaeological record' are as much a part of research as are field survey methods and excavation procedures. The fact that sincere intelligent people can disagree, often quite vigorously, over the most appropriate ontology, epistemology and methodology for archaeology suggests that archaeology is not the straightforward and progressive study of the past that textbooks would have us believe.

2

The Philosophical Foundations:
Logical Positivism and Logical Empiricism

It would not be an exaggeration to claim that positivism has been one of the most influential philosophies of the human sciences in the western world since Auguste Comte introduced the term 'positive' philosophy in the mid-nineteenth century. Like rationalism, idealism and other philosophies with long histories, however, it has meant and continues to mean different things to different people. Indeed, few positivists, whether philosophers or scientists, seem ever to have agreed on the presuppositions of the programme. At best they have tended to have somewhat similar responses to questions of knowing like: What is scientific knowledge? What kinds of things or processes exist in the world? How can we best gain knowledge of these things and processes? Is it necessary to use fundamentally different methods to gain knowledge of natural and human phenomena? These responses have tended to share three basic assumptions: (1) experience of the senses is the only source of knowledge (empiricism); (2) all phenomena can be explained in terms of natural causes and laws without attributing spiritual, supernatural or other metaphysical significance to them (Naturalism); (3) the natural sciences offer a privileged model of rationality. Positivist research programmes are elaborations of this very basic core of agreed assumptions.

The roots of positivism extend back to early arguments concerning the most appropriate assumptions to adopt in 'empirical' investigations. Francis Bacon and Thomas Hobbes made significant contributions to this tradition in the seventeenth century, as did David Hume and Bishop Berkeley in the eighteenth century, and Comte and John Stuart Mill in the first half of the nineteenth century. By the 1860s, positivist assumptions had been widely adopted by researchers in both the natural and human sciences. Some of these assumptions have continued to dominate the methodological framework of the behavioural and social sciences until the present time, although their interpretation has varied among positivists and schools of positivist philosophy.[1]

Here we are interested in a form of positivism called logical positivism and its later maturer phase called logical empiricism. In the first section of this chapter logical positivism and logical empiricism are treated as a developing research programme organized around seven core assumptions.[2] Other common uses of the term 'positivism' are reviewed in the second section, for discussions of positivism, assessments of its impact on the human sciences and its present status obviously depend upon just how the term is defined. A few of the implications for the social sciences of adopting the logical positivist/empiricist (LP/E) research programme are summarized in the third section, for it was the maturer logical empiricist phase of the programme which profoundly influenced the social sciences in the 1950s and 1960s.

This chapter should not be mistaken for a comprehensive and balanced survey of positivist thought. Its sole purpose is to introduce some of the flavour of this philosophy and, more specifically, those elements of the LP/E research programme that apparently proved attractive to researchers in the social sciences in the 1950s and 1960s. Readers interested in more detailed discussions of positivism in its many guises are referred to the references in the footnotes in this and the following chapter.

---

[1] For an introduction to positivism and its history, see Achinstein and Barker (eds), *The Legacy of Logical Positivism*, 1969; Ayer, *Language, Truth and Logic*, 1946; Ayer (ed.), *Logical Positivism*, 1959; Bergmann, *The Metaphysics of Logical Positivism*, 1967; Feigl, 'Logical empiricism', in Runes (ed.), 1947, pp. 406–8, and 'Some major issues and developments in the philosophy of science of logical empiricism', in Fiegl and Scriven (eds), 1956, vol. 1, pp. 3–37; Friedrichs, *A Sociology of Sociology*, 1970; Hanfling, *Logical Positivism*, 1981; Joergensen, *The Development of Logical Empiricism*, 1951; Keat and Urry, *Social Theory as Science*, 1975, particularly pp. 4–26; Kolakowski, *The Alienation of Reason: A History of Positivist Thought*, 1968, and *Positivist Philosophy*, 1972; von Mises, *Positivism: A Study in Human Understanding*, 1951; Passmore, *A Hundred Years of Philosophy*, 1968, particularly pp. 367–93; Polkinghorne, *Methodology of the Human Sciences*, 1983, pp. 15–91; Reichenbach, *The Rise of Scientific Philosophy*, 1951; Simon, *European Positivism in the Nineteenth Century*, 1963; Walsh, 'Varieties of positivism', in Filmer *et al.* (eds), 1972, pp. 37–55.

[2] For the characteristics of a research programme, see Lakatos, 'Falsification and the methodology of scientific research programmes', in Lakatos and Musgrave (eds), 1970, pp. 91–196, and 'History of science and its rational reconstruction', in Buck and Cohen (eds), 1971, pp. 91–136. Few methodological approaches (compared with scientific theories) have been treated as research programmes, although the term 'programme' or even 'research programme' is commonly used in conjunction with them. See Brown, *Perception, Theory and Commitment: The New Philosophy of Science*, 1977, p. 26, for another explicit treatment of logical empiricism as a research programme.

The Logical Positivist/Empiricist Research Programme

The positivist philosophy known as logical positivism was the product of a Thursday evening discussion group of philosophically minded mathematicians and scientists organized by the physicist and philosopher Moritz Schlick at the University of Vienna in the late 1920s and early 1930s.[3] Among the more significant members over the years of this Vienna Circle, as they called themselves, were Rudolf Carnap, Herbert Feigl, Phillip Frank, Kurt Gödel, Hans Han, Karl Menger, Otto Neurath and Friedrich Waisman. Their philosophy was called 'logical' positivism, because it united strong antimetaphysical or anti-speculative tendencies and the empiricism of Hume, Ernst Mach and the early Einstein with a conception of symbolic logic or axiomatics developed through the work of Leibnitz, Frege, Hilbert, Whitehead and Russell. Logical positivists felt that the true task of philosophy was to make knowledge statements clear and unambiguous through logical analysis. Their unique synthesis of the 'new logic' and empiricism in carrying out this task constituted, in their view, 'an altogether decisive turning point in philosophy'.[4]

As so often happens in the early stages of a research programme, premature enthusiasm led certain logical positivists to issue statements which now seem highly presumptuous and naive, if not fanatical. A more sophisticated, less radically empiricist positivist stance, however, emerged between the mid-1930s and the mid-1950s. In contrast with the Vienna Circle with its, for the most part, talented amateurs, this 'second generation' consisted of professional philosophers of science. Among the most prominent were A.J. Ayer, Richard Braithwaite, Rudolf

---

[3] Joergensen, *Development of Logical Empiricism*; Kraft, *The Vienna Circle*, 1953; Feigl, 'The origin and spirit of logical positivism', in Achinstein and Barker (eds), 1969, pp. 3–24. The logical positivism of the Vienna Circle was not an isolated movement but part of a widespread trend in western philosophy and science. For example, the Berlin group (formed in 1928, and including Reichenbach, Alexander Herzberg, Walter Dubislav and Carl Hempel), the Munster group and the Ernst Mach Society in Germany, the Lvov–Warsaw group in Poland (of which Alfred Tarski was an important member), the Uppsala School in Sweden, and operationalists (such as Percy Bridgman) and pragmatists (like William James) in North America developed positions which were similar in many respects to those of the Vienna Circle. There were also French positivists (e.g. Pierre Laffiette and Emile Littre) and Latin American positivists, particularly in Brazil (e.g. Nisia Floresta, Benjamin Constant and Luis Pereira Barreto). See Joergensen, *Development of Logical Empiricism*, pp. 48–60, and the articles on positivism in Philip P. Wiener (ed.), *Dictionary of the History of Ideas*, vol. 3, 1973, for related movements and individuals.

[4] Schlick, 'The turning point in philosophy', in Ayer (ed.), 1959, p. 54.

Carnap, Herbert Feigl, Carl Hempel, Israel Scheffler, Ernest Nagel and May Brodbeck.[5] It was logical empiricism, the mature phase of the LP/E research programme, that profoundly influenced the social sciences in western academia in the 1950s and 1960s. Attacks on this programme today commonly point to extreme statements by logical positivists and dismiss the entire programme. However, these attacks overlook the dynamic nature of the programme. Like many similar methodological programmes, it has proceeded from initial insight and overenthusiasm, to mature examination and reformulation, and, as we shall see in chapter 3, to a quagmire of contradictions and unsolved − if not unsolvable − problems. Throughout this process, however, the core assumptions or commitments of the programme persisted, although their interpretation underwent change. When the assumptions themselves were eventually abandoned or severely altered in the 1960s, the programme itself degenerated as a philosophy of science, although positivism as a general philosophical movement continues today in other forms.

In this chapter our concern is the programme's core assumptions and their interpretation up to the 1950s and 1960s, the period of their

[5] Logical empiricists were interested in a much wider variety of issues than those discussed here. The work of Carnap, Tarski and others on linguistic analysis is one example. See Carnap, *The Logical Syntax of Language*, 1937, *Introduction to Semantics*, 1942, *Formalization of Logic*, 1942, and *Meaning and Necessity: A Study in Semantics and Modal Logic*, 1947; Tarski, *Logic, Semantics, Metamathematics*, 1956. Ayer, Carnap and Hempel are considered uncompromisingly positivist, but others are more difficult to classify. Unlike these individuals, for example, neither Braithwaite nor Nagel was ever associated with positivist organizations like the Vienna Circle, and both have been more cautious in their statements than most logical empiricists. Popper's position remains controversial. Ayer wrote in 1959 that 'the affinities between him and the positivists whom he criticizes appear more striking than the divergences', see Ayer, *Logical Positivism*, p. 6. Popper himself, however, has never regarded himself as a positivist and vigorously attacked the Vienna Circle in the 1930s; see Popper, *Unended Quest*, 1976, p. 87. Unlike the logical positivism of the Vienna Circle, a unified logical empiricist view never crystallized during the 1950s and 1960s. The principles of logical empiricism are presented by Hempel, *Aspects of Scientific Explanation and Other Essays in the Philosophy of Science*, 1965, and *Philosophy of Natural Science*, 1966; Nagel, *The Structure of Science 1961*; Braithwaite, *Scientific Explanation*, 1959; Rudner, *Philosophy of Social Science*, 1966; Bhaskar, *The Possibility of Naturalism*, 1979, pp. 129−32. See Schilpp (ed.), *The Philosophy of Rudolf Carnap*, 1963, and Hintikka (ed.), *Rudolf Carnap, Logical Empiricist*, 1975, for guides to the work of Carnap. The founding document of logical empiricism is generally considered to be Carnap's 'Testability and meaning' in which an argument is presented for the liberalization of the logical positivists' theory of meaning (Carnap, 'Testability and meaning', *Philosophy of Science* 3, 419−71, 1936, and 1−40, 1937; reprinted with omissions in Feigl and Brodbeck (eds), 1953, pp. 47−92).

greatest influence. Unlike the Vienna Circle, logical empiricists neither prepared a group statement nor were suffused with a high degree of unity, perhaps because they were more geographically scattered and the simple solutions of their predecessors had proved no longer acceptable. As a result, the partial description of logical empiricism that follows is to be regarded as 'representative' rather than the view of any particular logical empiricist. Likewise, the core assumptions of the LP/E research programme presented below should be considered a simplified reconstruction — a reconstruction, however, which is sufficient for our purposes, for, as I will argue later, the subtleties of the arguments among logical empiricists were largely ignored by those social scientists who adopted their views. Instead, the position of individual logical empiricists, such as Hempel or Nagel, were simply taken as unproblematic expositions of the programme.

With these words of caution, then, the LP/E research programme, as reconstructed here, is defined by the following seven core presuppositions.

1 *Only those things of which we can be absolutely certain can be counted as knowledge.* A central theme of western philosophy has been the quest for infallibility, and a key expression of this theme is the presupposition that knowledge must be infallible.[6] This means that only those things of which we are absolutely certain can be counted as knowledge. The positivist conception of science has its roots in this tradition. In addition to this assumption, positivists also equated true certain knowledge with scientific and mathematical knowledge. Knowledge claims derived from other areas of enquiry, such as metaphysics, theology or ethics, were not considered legitimate human knowledge because they failed the test, according to the positivist criterion (see assumption 2 below), of certain truth.

This assumption must be understood within the broader intellectual context of the emergence of positivism. At its birth, a priori and eternal truths were widely thought to exist, 'vital forces' and Hegel's Absolute were popular concepts and divine revelation was considered an unquestionable source of knowledge by many people. Positivists adopted what they considered a strong antispeculative attitude and set out to

---

[6] Since its early beginnings in Greece, western thought has remained strongly committed to an intellectual tradition which requires certainty of science. The most characteristic form of scepticism about knowledge is presented in the assumption that we ought not to claim knowledge about anything unless we are absolutely sure about it — unless there is no possibility that we might be wrong. This standard of apodictic knowledge — absolute indubitable certainty — has been accepted in general by western epistemologists, and epistemology has become the search for methods and foundations which enable us to be assured of the truth of our beliefs. For a brief review, see Polkinghorne, *Methodology for the Human Sciences*, pp. 9–13.

expose metaphysical—speculative claims like these as both cognitively meaningless and devoid of explanatory power. Statements about the contents and properties of the world are, according to this view, only contingently true; that is they are not known to be true until they are subjected to empirical control in the world of experience. Since questions concerning values, theology and metaphysics are not testable in this sense, it was claimed that they must be abandoned as cognitively meaningless: the world cannot be known through arguments of logical necessity or other a priori means.

2 *Observation is the only source of sure and certain knowledge.* The foundation on which positivists grounded their claims of certainty was the empiricists' realm of sense data.[7] In the extreme form adopted by logical positivists (phenomenalism and physicalism), the only meaningful statements are logical tautologies or those that can be tested by comparison with sense data or experience.[8] A question commonly asked by logical positivists in attacking other programmes was: What are the empirical consequences of believing this or that to be true? The meaning of concepts and sentences was clarified by reducing them to statements about observables, facts, experience and the immediately 'given' or to statements derivable from these. Sentences that went beyond the realm of the observable, such as 'the first cause of the world is the Unconscious', were eliminated as meaningless.

Empiricism, then, is concerned with the epistemological foundations of scientific claims. By claiming that internal sense experience (not to be confused with projected external objects) provides a certain ground — an experiential 'given' — which cannot be doubted, positivists provided 'epistemological guarantees' for science. It was this assumptive weapon that allowed positivists to deny the existence of synthetic a priori knowledge about the world and to undercut metaphysics and traditional

---

[7] Various foundations have been proposed upon which to anchor claims of certainty. Plato's realm of ideas, Descartes' clear and distinct ideas in consciousness and the rationalists' realm of logic and mathematical truths are examples. Rationalists have been inclined to a view whereby knowledge is obtained through a process of deducing true propositions from a few fundamental axioms. Empiricists have been inclined more to the view that knowledge is obtained through a process whereby truth is induced from experiential observations of particular facts and their connections. There is a whole metaphysics behind the privilege granted to observation in positivist methodology whose roots are fascinating to explore. For general reviews, see Yolton (ed.), *Theory of Knowledge*, 1965, and Hamlyn, *The Theory of Knowledge*, 1971.

[8] Carnap in *The Logical Structure of the World* (1967; first published in German in 1928) provides an account of the whole apparatus of empirical discourse. See also Anscombe, 'On brute facts', 1957—8, pp. 69—72.

rationalism. By eliminating statements that were neither analytical (tautological or 'logical') nor synthetic (empirical) from our knowledge system, positivists hoped to be able to provide a sounder base for the growth of knowledge; they aimed to rebuild knowledge from a foundation of the truth of facts — the facts of sense data.

Therefore priority was given in the LP/E research programme to an observation language that was regarded as epistemologically and ontologically privileged. By epistemologically privileged was meant (1) that the truth or falsity of observational statements could be known independent of the truth or falsity of theoretical statements (i.e. that observational statements were theory neutral), and (2) that the truth or falsity of observational statements could be known with greater degree of certainty than those containing theoretical terms. Being ontologically privileged meant that reality could be attributed only to observable phenomena and that only terms in the observational language actually referred to what could properly be said to exist.

For the positivist, the independent existence of an observational realm, of immediately observed data independent of theory and of an observational language independent of theory was assumed and was not considered problematic. One result of this assumption was an agreement among positivists that, to be meaningful, scientific terms, sentences and theories must be grounded in the secure observational base. Familiar attempts to accomplish this aim are described by the terms 'verification', 'falsification', 'testability' and 'operationalization'. One eventual effect of this extreme empiricist position was the postulation in positivist science of a number of fundamental dichotomies, such as fact/value, observation term/theoretical term and fact/theory. Another effect was the thesis of atomism, i.e. the thesis that (1) facts are the ultimate base and building blocks of science, and (2) every fact is ontologically distinct from every other fact (i.e. the existence or non-existence of any fact is completely independent of the existence or non-existence of any other fact). This means that the fundamental units of meaningful language in science must correspond to facts, for facts are the fundamental units of experience, the ultimate existents. None the less, scientific knowledge itself consists, as we shall see, in generalizations from experience or the facts. Finally, the stress on observability also led logical positivists to a belief in the methodological unity of all scientific endeavour — to a belief, as Otto Neurath first expressed it, in the 'unity of science'.

3 *The primary tool for the analysis of science is formal logic.* A central quest of logical positivists and empiricists was the identification of an infallible means of reasoning from a set of premises to a certain conclusion. This was one expression of the more general goal in western philosophy of attaining true knowledge (assumption (1)). Logical positivists thought that the formal deductive logic of Bertrand Russell and

A.N. Whitehead's *Principia Mathematica* (1910–13)[9] could fulfil this quest in the philosophy of science, for the strength of deductive logic is the necessary connection between premises and conclusion in a valid (logically correct) argument. A standard example is as follows: if all men are mortal and Socrates is a man, than it necessarily follows (logically) that Socrates is mortal. Therefore the adoption of the principles of deductive logic proved attractive to logical positivists and empiricists because they promised to replace fallible human beings in the decision-making process by a set of logical algorithms much like the strict unambiguous rules of arithmetic. This set of algorithms would provide standards to which reasoning ought to conform. Furthermore, since logic is a normative discipline, it should also be capable of providing the foundations of a normative philosophy of science. The primary objection to historically based philosophy of science, i.e. a philosophy of science based on descriptions of past scientific activities, was that validly deduced normative statements concerning how science should be carried out can no more be derived (it was assumed) from descriptions of how it has been carried out than a moral 'ought' can be derived from an 'is'.

The paradigmatic role that the deductive logic of *Principia Mathematica* played in LP/E is evident in familiar assumptions associated with the programme. Examples are (1) the major task of the philosophy of science is the logical analysis of propositions, (2) philosophers should be concerned only with logical questions, and (3) all scientific statements must be formulable in the notation of principia logic. Like other deep-seated presuppositions, the privileged status of the deductive logic of *Principia Mathematica* as the fundamental tool for the analysis of science was not questioned. This meant that any theorem of symbolic logic was assumed to be capable in principle of throwing light on the nature of science (and thus worthy of discussion) and that symbolic logic itself should be developed (as Carnap in particular attempted to do). Interestingly, the clear straightforward writing style of many logical empiricists was one outcome of this focus on unambiguous logical reasoning.

The reliance of logical empiricists upon the techniques and concepts of formal logic will become evident below in their analysis of explanation as a form of logical argument, their definition of theoretical terms through formal correspondence rules, their attempts to specify the logical relationships involved in the testing of theories and their concept of 'the logic of science'.

4 *There is a discoverable logic to science.* The assumption that there was a 'logic of science' played a key role in the LP/E attempt (1) to

[9] Russell and Whitehead, *Principia Mathematica*, 1910–13.

cleanse the sciences and philosophy of vague generalizations and metaphysical content and (2) to establish true results which will stand forever. In addition, it was the framework which was to integrate the natural sciences, philosophy and the social sciences into the single 'unified science' that was a positivist ideal. In this process philosophy itself was to be radically restructured by reducing it to the 'logic of science', i.e. to the philosophy of science and the logic of mathematics discussed above.

The idealized concept of science that eventually resulted from this endeavour is now known as the deductive − nomological model, the nomological or deductive model, or simply the orthodox model. The theses and assumptions of this model have been variously described.[10] For our purposes, it is sufficient to mention the following.

i) *The (linguistic) theory of meaning that underlies the fact/value distinction.* A typical and early claim of the LP/E research programme was that only 'meaningful statements' are to be accorded the status of knowledge claims. Meaningfulness (or cognitive significance) was strictly defined, following core assumption (2) above, as being attributable only to those statements which are either analytical (tautologies or self-contradictions) or synthetic (factual statements which may be verified or falsified by evidence). It was these statements that provided an objective foundation for science. According to this definition, metaphysical statements are neither true nor false − how could we know if the Unconscious is the First Cause of the world? − but only meaningless.[11] Being neither analytical nor synthetic, they cannot be permitted scientific consideration, although they might express emotional stances or 'general attitudes towards life' that are otherwise interesting.

[10] For a brief review, see Caldwell, *Beyond Positivism*, 1982, pp. 19−35; Polkinghorne, *Methodology for the Human Sciences*, pp. 59−91; Keat and Urry, *Social Theory as Science*, pp. 9−26. For more extended discussions, see Hempel, *Philosophy of Natural Science*, and Nagel, *Structure of Science*.

[11] Schlick, for example, comments that: 'The denial of the existence of a transcendent external world would be as much a metaphysical statement as its affirmation. Hence the consistent empiricist does not deny the transcendent world, but shows that both its denial and affirmation are meaningless.' He continues in the following paragraph: 'This last distinction is of the greatest importance. I am convinced that the chief opposition to our view derives from the fact that the distinction between the falsity and the meaningless of a proposition is not observed. The proposition "Discourse concerning a metaphysical external world is meaningless" does *not* say: "There is no external world", but something altogether different. The empiricist does not say to the metaphysician "what you say is false", but "what you say asserts nothing at all!" He does not contradict him, but says "I don't understand you". From this perspective, then, the range of meaningful propositions is limited by the range of possible sense impressions.' See Schlick, 'Positivism and realism', in Ayer (ed.), 1959, p. 197.

The distinction between analytical and synthetic statements was fairly clear. Carnap, Ayer, Popper, Hempel and others, however, devoted much effort during the 1930s and 1940s to the development of an objective criterion — a criterion of cognitive significance — for distinguishing legitimate synthetic statements from metaphysical assertions. This criterion was modified considerably over the years, but almost all these efforts at specifying a criterion of cognitive significance relied heavily on observational evidence. That is, the truth of a statement was to be determined by its correspondence with the facts. If, on testing, a statement did not correspond to the facts, it was false; if it did, it was true.

The most conservative and dogmatic of the early logical positivists supported a strict demand for complete verification. That is, they argued that a knowledge claim is true only if it is possible to demonstrate a strict logical relationship between a synthetic statement and observations. However, Carnap admitted in 1935 that presumed synthetic statements (like laws) cannot be strictly verified. He proposed instead the concept of 'gradually increasing confirmation' through tests of single instances: 'If in the continued series of such testing experiments no negative instance is found but the number of positive instances increases then our confidence in the law will grow step by step.'[12] Much effort was also expended later on trying to define what counts as a confirming instance, on attempting to make the notion 'degree of confirmation of a hypothesis' more concrete, in searching for an inductive logic based on probability theory, on developing a 'logic of confirmation' based upon the calculus of probabilities and on trying to resolve a number of 'paradoxes of confirmation'.[13]

Eventually the emphasis of positivist theorists shifted from a focus on distinguishing legitimate knowledge statements from meaningless metaphysical utterances to the evaluation of competing theories by such criteria as formal simplicity, explanatory and predictive power, and degree of confirmation relative to available evidence.[14] None the less, the key assumption that scientific propositions receive their justification from some form of direct confirmation by experience remained, and the project to find an algorithm on the basis of which it was possible to

---

[12] Carnap, 'Testability and meaning', p. 425. This move in effect rejected the logical positivist thesis that the sentence is the fundamental unit of meaning for an older Humean concern with the meaning of terms. The strict verificationist theory of meaning would have had the effect, if maintained, of eliminating just those segments of science which its proponents took to be paradigmatic of all knowledge. For a review, see Ashby, 'Verifiability principle', in Edwards (ed.), 1967, pp. 240–7.

evaluate scientific theories still existed. The assumption was that, even if it was not possible to prove the final truth of a hypothesis, a set of rules which would allow us to determine the degree to which a hypothesis has been confirmed by available evidence could be produced.

ii) *The operationalist – instrumentalist interpretation of theoretical concepts* The positivist insistence on the primacy of physical data raised considerable problems concerning the status of theoretical terms such as 'atom', 'entropy', 'magnetic field', 'gene', 'virus', and 'electron', which do not (or at least did not at the time) appear to refer to observables and were often not even amenable to explicit definition in terms of observables, as are non-theoretical terms like 'stone', 'wood', and 'grey'. The problem was: if we assume that scientific theories contain true statements about the world, then how do theoretical terms in these statements receive their meaning?

Mach, whose conception of science had strongly influenced logical positivists, had adopted a strong phenomenalist position according to which theoretical entities were only handy fictions. Since these entities had no independent existential status of their own, they had no meaning in a strict sense. Their function in science was to help us to resolve puzzling situations. As these puzzles were resolved, fictional terms were to be eliminated from the objective language of science.[15] In this

---

[13] See Hempel, 'Studies in the logic of confirmation', 1945, pp. 1–26, 97–121, for an early statement; the first paradox, the 'paradox of the raven', was introduced by Hempel in this paper. Work on the paradoxes of confirmation intensified in the 1960s. See also Hempel, 'A purely syntactical definition of confirmation', 1943, pp. 122–43; Carnap, *Logical Foundations of Probability, 1950, and The Continuum of Inductive Methods*, 1952; Carnap and Jeffrey (eds), *Studies in Inductive Logic and Probability*, 1971. For reviews, see Swinburne, 'The paradoxes of confirmation – a survey', 1971, 318–30, and *An Introduction to Confirmation Theory*, 1973; Brown, *Perception, Theory and Commitment*, pp. 25–36. Eventually even the viability of the analytical – synthetic distinction was cast in doubt. See Hempel, 'The Empiricist criterion of meaning', in Ayer (ed.), 1959, pp. 108–29; Quine, *From a Logical Point of View*, 1953, pp. 20–46; Suppe, 'Critical introduction', in Suppe (ed.) 1977, pp. 67–80. We can see here two of the central problems of logical empiricism: (1) the nature of the confirmation relation that holds between a scientific law and the observation statements which confirm or disconfirm it, and (2) the problem of how scientific terms acquire their meaning. See Popper, *The Logic of Scientific Discovery*, 1959, for a different, falsificationist, approach to the problem of how empirical evidence can be used to evaluate theories or hypotheses.

[14] Hempel, 'Empiricist criterion of meaning', p. 129.

[15] For a statement of this view, see Mach, *Popular Scientific Lectures*, 1895, p. 206. Scheffler has characterized the position as 'eliminative fictionalism'; see Scheffler, 'The fictionalist view of scientific theories', in Brody (ed.), 1970, pp. 211–22. For somewhat related views, see Russell's discussion of 'inferred entities' in *Mysticism and Logic*, p. 150, and Bridgman's discussion of 'operationism' in *The Logic of Modern Physics*, 1927, p. 7.

view scientific theories are merely instruments (thus instrumentalism), for they lack empirical content. They cannot be true or false but only useful or not. However, Mach's view, among other consequences, would drastically limit the possibility of extending concepts into new areas of research. This consequence was regarded as too constraining by logical positivists.

By the early 1930s the dominant positivist view was that theoretical terms receive their meaning by being reducible to assertions about phenomena in the observation language or thing-language through 'correspondence rules'.[16] However, in 1958 Hempel drew attention to a dilemma which arises if theoretical terms are defined in terms of observations: if they are, they cannot function as explanations; if they are not, then they cannot be said to have empirical support.[17] Attempts to resolve the problem of theoretical terms culminated in the notion of theories as hypothetico-deductive systems which are provided with a 'dictionary' or an 'interpretation system'. The dictionary does not actually contain definitions, 'but statements to the effect that a theoretical sentence of a certain kind is true if and only if a corresponding empirical sentence of a specified kind is true'.[18] In this view theoretical terms of hypothetical constructs gain meaning either explicitly by being connected to observations through correspondence rules or a dictionary, or implicitly through their systematic relations to other terms in the theory. Thus, even though some scientific terms may not be directly expressible in an observation language, they can be accorded cognitive significance just because they are embedded in a successfully confirmed theory. Even though they themselves cannot be directly tested, they can gain some degree of confirmation through the positive test of other statements in the theory. This also meant that, in science, theories as a whole are to be tested and not isolated hypotheses.

---

[16] See Hempel, 'The theoretician's dilemma', in Feigl et al. (eds), 1958, pp. 37–98; Carnap, 'The methodological character of theoretical concepts', in Feigl and Scriven (eds), 1956, pp. 38–76; Feigl, 'The orthodox view of theories', in Radner and Winokur (eds). 1970. pp. 3–16; Braithwaite, Scientific Explanation, p. 51. For an early formulation of this resolution of the problem of the empirical significance of theoretical terms, see Campbell, Physics: The Elements, 1920. For different attempts to characterize observational terms, see Spector, 'Theory and observation', 1967, pp. 1–20, 89–104, and for different types of correspondence rules see Shapere (ed.), Philosophical Problems of Natural Science, 1965, 'Introduction'. See Nagel, The Structure of Science, for a discussion of 'theoretical' and 'observational' languages.
[17] Hempel, 'theoretician's dilemma'.
[18] Hempel, p. 72. 'Theoreticians dilemma', Campbell first used the term 'dictionary' in this general sense in his Physics.

This shift in emphasis amounted to a general loosening of earlier demands for the empirical translatability of theoretical terms. However, there still remained a strong commitment among logical empiricists to the view that theoretical terms must be anchored as firmly as possible in phenomenal reality. The main point here, however, is that no matter how theoretical terms are defined, they are intended to refer in principle to the thing-world. They are instruments for talking about phenomenal reality and are not to be interpreted as referring to 'essences' or other metaphysical 'objects' or 'forces' that lay at the back of, so to speak, phenomenal reality.

iii) *The view that scientific theories are primarily systems of logically arranged statements.* Logical empiricists strongly supported the hypothetico-deductive (HD) model of the structure of a theory that emerged in the writings of Carnap, Hempel and others in the 1940s and 1950s. As well as laying out the structure of a theory, the model also provided answers to uncertainties concerning the status and function of theories. In the model the formal structure of a theory is an HD system or calculus which contains 'primitive' sentences, or axioms, and 'derivative' statements, or theorems. Higher-level hypotheses or statements, such as axioms, more frequently refer to theoretical entities, while lower-level statements, most often derivative theorems, tend to describe observable phenomena. The theory gains empirical meaningfulness only when some of its statements, usually the derived ones, are translated into the observation language by means of interpretation sentences in the dictionary. In archaeology, for example, a theory might include the term 'intensive agriculture'. Although the term is most frequently defined with reference to observable human behaviour, archaeologists must provide an interpretation in terms of archaeological 'observables' such as irrigation ditches, for, as archaeologists, they cannot directly observe past human behaviour but only its byproducts. These 'translations' are necessary, for it is the propositions expressed in these translated sentences which are tested against reality for the purposes of evaluating theories in archaeology.[19]

According to Hempel, theories serve many useful functions in science: (1) they allow generality in the specification of scientific laws; (2) they possess a certain formal simplicity which allows the use of powerful and elegant mathematical machinery; (3) they can serve the practical function of allowing the scientist to discover interdependences among observables; (4) they are convenient and fruitful heuristic devices, often serving an explanatory function of their own.[20]

---

[19] Gibbon, *Anthropological Archaeology*, 1984, pp. 49–59.
[20] Hempel, 'Theoretician's dilemma', pp. 67–77.

With reference to the status of theories, some logical empiricists, such as Nagel, argued that either a realist or instrumentalist interpretation of the cognitive status of theories is consistent with the HD model of theoretical structures.[21] The main difference between these two interpretations is that realists claim that theoretical terms refer to real entities and therefore that theories can be judged as true or false, while instrumentalists remain agnostic on the point, claiming that theories are only heuristic instruments which prove either adequate or not. Whichever interpretation is adopted, however, the goal of a strict logical empiricist should be the elimination of theories, for the sole function of science is the discovery of constant relations between observation statements; theories only function as intermediaries in this process.[22]

iv) *The covering-law model of explanation.* The most widely adopted and discussed model of scientific explanation associated with the LP/E programme in the 1950s and 1960s was the covering-law model or deductive pattern developed and elaborated by Hempel.[23] At the root of the model is the belief that all sufficient explanations involve the deductive subsumption of events to be explained under propositions consisting of hypothetically assumed general laws of nature and initial or antecedent conditions. Hempel maintained that all such deductive−nomological explanations should assume a logical form in which a particular event or lower-level law must necessarily follow from the conjunction of general laws and initial conditions. For an explanation to be sound, i.e. empirically adequate, the sentences forming the laws and initial conditions must be true (Hempel's criterion of empirical adequacy). If these conditions are satisfied, then the form of the deductive argument ensures the logical certainty of the conclusion. It should not be surprising, given the commitment of the programme to principia logic, that the problem of analysing scientific explanations was formulated as a logical problem (and, it should be added, one which can be formulated in the symbolism of principia logic) and that the basic pattern of scientific explanation itself was considered to be that of deductive logic.

Hempel also developed an inductive-probabilistic (IP) covering-law model to describe those explanations in science that make use of statistical laws. In this model the laws (now statistical laws) and the initial

---

[21] Nagel, *Structure of Science*, p. 152.
[22] See note 15.
[23] The classic statement is Hempel and Oppenheim, 'Studies in the logic of explanation', 1948, pp. 135−75. See also Hempel, 'The function of general laws in history', 1942, pp. 35−48, 'Deductive−nomological vs. statistical explanation', in Feigl and Maxwell (eds), 1962, pp. 98−169; and *Aspects of Scientific Explanation*. Similar views are expressed by Popper, *Logic of Scientific Discovery*, p. 59.

conditions only confer a high logical or inductive probability upon the event to be explained: 'Unlike a deductive explanation, a statistical explanation does not show that given the premises, the phenomenon to be explained necessarily occurs, but only that it is highly probable, or, perhaps, almost certain.'[24] He also maintained that these two covering-law models adequately described almost all legitimate explanations that might occur in the natural and social sciences, including 'motivational explanations' of human behaviour.[25] Scientific explanations, like scientific theories, then, are also primarily systems of logically arranged statements that must be given empirical interpretation to gain empirical meaningfulness.

v) *The belief that explanation and prediction are logically symmetrical and represent the principal aim of science.* Early positivists, such as Comte and Mach, gave no role to explanation in science, as we understand the word. The dominant view held that theories do not explain phenomena but are instead only economical and eventually eliminable tools for the organization of complexes of sensations; establishing correlations (laws) among phenomena is all that science can and should do (Comte). This view was eventually challenged by Hempel and others. Hempel rejected the 'naive' view that theories can only describe but not explain phenomena, and asserted, instead, that the goal of science is explanation. The so-called symmetry thesis of explanation and prediction was also one of Hempel's assertions. The structural symmetry of explanation and prediction is a result of the logical form of deductive-nomological explanation: if the event E has already occurred, then the formal structure of sentences 'explains' the event; if the event has yet to occur, then the structure 'predicts' the event. This implies, of course, that every explanation is a potential prediction.[26] None the less, a 'prediction criterion' proposed by Hempel and Oppenheim to resolve a logical problem in their deductive model ensured the primacy of prediction. This was in keeping with the claim in empiricist philosophy that the primary function of scientific knowledge is the prediction of observables.

If we assume that observational languages are theory neutral and that, to be meaningful, scientific statements must have empirical consequences, then it makes sense to stress the evaluation of theoretical statements by their predictive success. For this reason, positivists have tended to emphasize the predictive performance of theories and hypotheses rather than the reality of their assumptions or their explanatory power.

[24] Hempel, *Aspects of Scientific Explanation*, p. 383, and 'Explanation and prediction by covering laws', in Baumrin (ed.), 1963, pp. 107–33.
[25] Hempel and Oppenheim, Studies in the logic of explanation', p. 325; Hempel, *Aspects of Scientific Explanation*, p. 448.
[26] Hempel and Oppenheim, 'studies in the logic of explanation', p. 323.

vi) *The search for laws.* A dominant theme of the LP/E research programme which was pregnant with implication for the task of the scientist was the claim that there can be no scientific explanation without generalization. The conceptions of generalization usually adopted by positivists have been closely tied to the Humean analysis of causation. According to Hume, a claim of causal connection between an event A and an event B requires the general claim that events of the second kind invariably follow (or accompany) events of the first kind. A causal statement, or law, in this sense, then, is only a claim of constant conjunction in time, and is not a claim that, in some commonsense way, one event 'caused' or 'resulted in' the occurence of another.[27]

The normal procedure proposed for converting a proposed law (a theoretical proposition) into a real, i.e. highly confirmed, law was to test the theory in which it was embedded in the manner already discussed. That is, a set of 'hypotheses' derived from the theory was to be given an empirical interpretation and compared with empirical observations; if the predicted and disclosed observations were the same, the hypotheses were provisionally accepted and the theory was 'confirmed'. Even if the hypotheses tested were not derived from all the axioms in the theory, they acquired some degree of confirmation by being a component of the theory. Confidence in the 'law' increased the more tests the theory survived.

Laws can either have a universal form (whenever A, then B) or be of a statistical nature (whenever A, then B at known probability *p*). Laws having a universal form are to be preferred, for they ensure the logical necessity of deductive-nomological explanations.[28] The concept of a 'general law', however, was not unproblematic, and a number of positivist philosophers offered alternative formulations of the concept.[29] Ideally, though, a law remained a universal highly confirmed statement about regular contingent relationships in nature.

vii) *The hypothetico-deductive approach.* Like other theses of the 'logic of science', logical empiricists have provided different interpretations of the HD approach or method.[30] Basically, however, the HD approach is a view of the process of theory formulation and evaluation — a blueprint of basic scientific procedure. A scientist begins a project by formulating a hypothesis (a statement of constant conjunction

[27] Hume, *A Treatise of Human Nature*, 1975, pp. 73–94.

[28] Hempel and Oppenheim, 'Studies in the logic of explanation', p. 338.

[29] Hempel and Oppenheim, 'Studies in the logic of explanation', pp. 337–50; Ayer, 'What is a law of nature?', in Brody (ed.), 1970, pp. 39–34; Popper, *Logic of Scientific Discovery*, 3; Nagel, *Structure of Science*, 4; Jobe, 'Discussion: some recent work on the problem of law', 1967, pp. 363–81.

[30] Braithwaite, *Scientific Explanation*, pp. 12–21. The HD model first emerged in the writings of Carnap and Hempel.

between two or more variables), or a provisional theory, and proceeds to test the hypothesis or theory through the process of the logic of confirmation discussed earlier, i.e. the process that 'secures' the relation between a hypothesis and an observation report. Logical empiricists generally maintained that there is no 'logic of discovery' by which we can arrive at hypotheses and theories from observations; their formulation is purely a matter of conjecture. Still, logical empiricists have argued over the preferred form and ideal properties of a hypothesis.[31] In an influential argument Popper has even claimed that in science it makes no sense simply to 'observe' and collect data without reference to a hypothesis or theory, for, he argues, how would one know what to look for?[32]

5 *All sciences share the same methodological and substantive base.* The stress on observability also led logical positivists and empiricists to assert the methodological unity of all scientific endeavour − to assert, as mentioned earlier, the 'unity of science'. The main claims of this thesis are that the natural and social sciences share not only the same fundamental aims and methods (methodological unity) but also the same substantive base (substantive unity), no matter how seemingly diverse their subject matter. The postulation of an experiential given had already provided an epistemological basis for the unity of science thesis; by implication, the social sciences no less than the natural sciences are concerned with observable phenomena and, since all phenomena belong to the same natural world, they share the same base.

According to one popular interpretation of this thesis, substantive unity could be achieved by the reduction of the statements of all sciences to reports of sensations about the experiential 'given' in one basic master science, usually considered to be mathematical physics. The actual procedure for carrying out this reductive process was to involve the derivation of the concepts and laws of one discipline from those of a more fundamental discipline through a step-by-step process: for instance, of the social from the ecological, of the ecological from the biological and so on. When considered as a separate doctrine, the unity of science thesis is identical with the philosophical doctrine of methodological naturalism. According to this doctrine, the same general kinds of procedures are appropriate to all the sciences.

Carnap attributed the unity of science thesis to the new logic employed

---

[31] This emphasis follows, again, from the commitment of the programme to the analysis in terms of *principia* logic; only completed theories were to be analysed, since incomplete theories were not yet amenable to such analysis.

[32] See, for example, Popper, *Objective Knowledge*, 1972, p. 259.

by the logical positivists. The following quotation is representative of this argument:

> Thus, with the aid of the new logic, logical analysis leads to a *unified science*. There are not different sciences with fundamentally different methods or different sources of knowledge, but only *one* science. All knowledge finds its place in this science and, indeed, is knowledge of basically the same kind; the appearance of fundamental differences between the sciences are the deceptive result of our using different sub-languages to express them.[33]

Belief in this thesis led Neurath and Carnap in the 1930s to explore the possibilities of developing a physicalist language in which metaphysical propositions would by definition be non-existent. Carnap's later work on the semantics of empirical languages is directly tied to this effort. The unity of science thesis was instrumental in justifying the introduction of positivist concepts and assumptions into the social sciences, for positivism in the form of logical positivism developed originally as a philosophy of the natural sciences (even though some logical positivists such as Neurath were social scientists).[34] If the assumption that all sciences share the same fundamental aims and methods (methodological unity) is accepted, then disciplines such as history and the humanities could not claim special intersubjective and communicative ways of knowing (e.g. the hermeneutic) or explanation by reference to a person's reasons or motives for doing something ('reason-giving' explanations).[35]

---

[33] Carnap, 'The old and the new logic', in Ayer (ed.), 1959, p. 144.

[34] Kraft, *The Vienna Circle*, 1953.

[35] The assumption that no significant difference exists between the situations in which the natural and social sciences operate was defended on one of two grounds. First, since 'subjective meanings', intentions, motives and similar 'internal' experiences are not accessible to observation, they ought to be left out of scientific study, whose only legitimate object is observable behaviour. Second, it was claimed that subjective factors presented no methodological problem of their own since they could be fully reduced to external phenomena that were amenable to normal scientific treatment. Thus the subjective aspect of social life was either assumed to present no special problem to scientific study or − in as much as it did − it ought to be left where it belongs, in the domain of poetry (i.e. outside science). For a review of the early debates, see Polkinghorne, *Methodology for the Human Sciences*, pp. 15−57; Cassirer, *The Philosophy of the Enlightenment*, 1951; and Gay, *The Enlightenment: An Interpretation*, vols 1 and 2, 1966, 1969. Note that the claim that the natural and social sciences share a common logical and methodological foundation does not mean that they necessarily use the same procedures or methods, for different subject matters require, pragmatically, rather different methods of inquiry.

To rely on such devices was to engage in metaphysical speculation.[36]

The implications of the unity of science thesis were numerous and relatively clear for the social scientist. For instance, it was and still is generally accepted that the exact natural sciences (and particularly mathematical physics) are considerably more advanced than the social sciences. If the unity of method is to be taken seriously, it then makes sense to emulate the methods of the natural sciences. This can be accomplished by seeking guidance from the philosophy of science, for philosophers of science were in the process of defining the principles that, or so it was assumed, constituted this universally applicable scientific method that the unity of science thesis presupposes. Furthermore, once discovered, these principles could serve as a measure of the relative degree of maturity of individual social science disciplines by indicating just where and to what extent they lagged in scientific development.

The unity of science thesis had implications other than the justification of the normative role of the philosophy of science and the emulation of the natural sciences. By accepting the naturalist position, the assumption that science is the only legitimate form of human knowledge could be strongly defended. In addition, the thesis was an expression of a spirit of cooperation among scientists and philosophers. Together they hoped to be able to break down disciplinary boundaries and to create a unified science composed of all true knowledge.[37]

6 *Science is value free and objective.* The sixth core assumption is sociological relativism with respect to norms, particularly ethical norms. Logical positivists and empiricists were interested in what exists in the world and, as scientists, not in what ought to exist. Therefore they characteristically divorced science from questions of value, for value statements cannot be deduced from scientific statements alone. Science was to be value free, objective, subject to the control of the immediately given and not subject to the control of normative judgements. The goal of science was to produce systems of generalizations whose truth or falsity was to be judged only or at least primarily by the conformity of predictions with experience.

7 *Science must be socially valuable.* The final core assumption is that science should be pragmatic and aid people in their day-to-day lives. In part the thesis of the practical applicability of science had its

---

[36] As Ayer has expressed it: 'the scale and diversity of the phenomena with which the social sciences dealt made them less successful in establishing scientific laws, but this was a difficulty of practice, not of principle: they too were concerned in the end with physical events' (*Logical Positivism*, p. 21).

[37] One result of this goal was the publication of the logical positivist/empiricist *International Encyclopedia of Unified Science* series by the University of Chicago Press.

roots in eighteenth-century industrial Europe. Widespread changes had produced an intellectual movement whose goal was to understand social, moral and intellectual life — and to control it if possible. According to Comte, a new order of society could be developed through scientific approaches that would alleviate the suffering and chaos caused by social systems built upon speculative systems of philosophy. If scientists could discover the laws — the regularities — of social behaviour, then human beings would be able to establish a perfect society based on these laws.[38] By discovering the laws of 'social physics', science would ensure social order and progress.

It is precisely for many of these same reasons (and especially the emphasis upon the control of society) that Marxist philosophers have criticized LP/E as a tool of capitalism.[39] The assumption of the practical applicability of science did, however, influence the practice of positivist science. Most importantly it placed an emphasis on working with solvable problems and on adopting procedures or approaches that would improve scientists' ability to make useful empirical predictions.

Other Definitions of Positivism

LP/E has been interpreted here as a vigorous research programme within the tradition of positivist philosophy. The terms positivism, logical positivism and logical empiricism have been defined, however, in a variety of other ways. It is necessary in discussing the present status of positivist philosophy or the nature of its impact on the social sciences in the 1950s and 1960s to keep this diversity of meanings firmly in mind.

Positivism has often been identified with only one or only some of the basic assumptions of the LP/E research programme reconstructed here. For example, von Wright along with other philosophers and theorists identifies positivism with the unity of science thesis.[40] Hume

---

[38] See Mandelbaum, *History, Man, and Reason: A Study in Nineteenth-Century Thought*, 1971; Sutton, *Nationalism, Positivism, and Catholicism: The Politics of Charles Maurras and the French Catholics, 1890–1914*, 1982; and Hawthorn, *Enlightenment and Despair: A History of Sociology*, 1976, for discussions of the nineteenth-century intellectual setting within which Comte's ideas were formulated.

[39] See, for example, the arguments in Boeselager, *The Soviet Critique of Neopositivism*, 1975.

[40] von Wright, *Explanation and Understanding*, 1971, p. 4. Mitchell and Rosen interpret the thesis as 'the belief that the natural sciences offer a privileged model of rationality'; see Mitchell and Rosen, *The Need for Interpretation: Contemporary Conceptions of the Philosopher's Task*, 1983, p. 3.

argued strongly for the view of causation and the antimetaphysical doctrine later adopted by logical positivists and empiricists, but he would have rejected the reduction of philosophy to the logic of science and sociological relativism with respect to norms. Comte and Durkheim were positivists who believed, among other disagreements with the full research programme, in the irreducibility of the social to the psychological or physical. Comte argued that there is a social level of phenomena with its own distinctive features and laws. He also regarded society as a basic reality and rejected all theories which suggested that the only real human phenomena are individual people.[41] Others accepted positivism as a philosophy of science but did not reject values and ethics as forms of knowledge; they simply regarded them as forms of knowledge having no role in science. Still others have taken the extreme position that anyone with a strong aversion to speculative thinking is a positivist.

In addition, each core assumption of the programme, as we have seen, is capable of multiple interpretations. For instance, not all positivists adopted the HD model of science which is, after all, only one interpretation of the fourth core assumption. Spencer, Comte and other early positivists argued that the scientific method was that of induction.[42] There are, then, both inductivist and deductivist reconstructions of the logic of science, and logical empiricists considerably modified most of the logical positivists' solutions to such key problems as the status of theoretical terms, the structure, function and status of theories, and the form and relevance of scientific explanation. Peter Halfpenny, David Walsh and others have provided instructive lists which provide some idea of the diversity of meanings that the term positivism has had for different people.[43]

Clearly there are diverse conceptions of what the term positivism represents, and these conceptions in their diversity are more widely used than that of LP/E as a research programme. The existence of a variety of 'positivist' viewpoints introduces a certain tension into discussions of positivism that is difficult to avoid. Debate naturally occurs over whether positivism is a defunct philosophy or whether someone like Popper, who holds some but not all of the core assumptions of the

---

[41] For an introduction to Comte's positivist philosophy, see Lenzer (ed.), *Auguste Comte and Positivism: The Essential Writings*, 1975.

[42] See, for example, Keat and Urry, *Social Theory as Science*, p. 24. For general reviews, see Kockelmans (ed.), *Philosophy of Science: The Historical Background*, 1968; Giere and Westfall (eds), *Foundations of Scientific Method: The Nineteenth Century*, 1973. For an interesting short review from a realist perspective, see also McMullin, 'The goals of natural science', 1984, pp. 37–64.

[43] Halfpenny, *Positivism and Sociology*, 1982, p. 141; Walsh, 'Varieties of positivism', Stockman, *Antipositivist Theories of Science*, 1983, pp. 3–15.

program, is a positivist or not. Popper clearly supports the unity of science thesis, the covering-law model of explanation, the central role of deductive logic in the analysis of science and the concept of a 'logic of science', but he also rejects any extreme form of empiricism, holding instead that scientific propositions cannot be verified or given probability values. In fact Popper himself claims to have refuted the logical positivism of the Vienna Circle at an early date.[44]

It is apparent, then, that those calling themselves positivist, or who have been called positivist by others, are united more by tendencies and interests than by a definite set of shared principles such as those identified here as composing the LP/E research programme. As with words like democracy and Marxism, positivism lacks a single precise definition when closely examined − a circumstance which promotes irrelevant attacks and misunderstandings. Still, the definition of positivism chosen here seems to capture the form of positivism that most strongly influenced New Archaeology and the social sciences in the 1960s.

Implications of Logical Empiricism for Social Research

What are the implications for social research of the dominating philosophy of science that developed in the 1950s and 1960s from the LP/E research programme? This view, called the 'standard view' by Scheffler,[45] strongly influenced the New Archaeology and remains widely held among the social sciences today. Although overly simple and brief, the 'standard view' can be summarized in the following manner.[46]

1 *Science is an objective rational practice.* Science is to be regarded as an utterly rational, logical and impersonal activity that results, in principle, in true knowledge, i.e. in knowledge that is true at all times and in all places. Individual genius may be important in conjuring up hypotheses and in articulating theories, but the 'logic of science', if employed properly, ensures the objective validation of knowledge claims; good science is not tainted with the ideological predilections or personal quirks of individual scientists. Although a caricature, the idea of the

[44] Popper, *Unended Quest*, p. 87, and *Conjectures and Refutations, 1965*. Brown regards Popper's philosophy of science as transitional between logical empiricism and the new image of science, and discusses the similarities and differences between the two research programme; see Brown, *Perception, Theory and Commitment*, pp. 67−77.

[45] Scheffler, *Science and Subjectivity*, 1967.

[46] See, for example, the description of the 'standard view' in Manicas and Secord, 'Implications for psychology of the new philosophy of science', 1983, pp. 399−413.

white-coated objective scientist pursuing laws and unlocking the secrets of the Universe is not far from the ideal image of a positivist scientist.

2 *The attainment of scientific results involves generalization.* Social scientists should search for general laws independent of any particular kind of cultural system. This goal has its roots, as we have seen, in Hume's claim that events can be brought into an intelligible connection only by being shown to be causally related to one another. Causal relations are understood to be regular contingent relations between events. In the early stages of the development of a discipline, it may not be possible to attain strict universality, and social scientists may have to be satisfied with probabilistic relationships or even something looser (say, the greater the A, the greater the B).

This goal and the conception of causality and of lawfulness on which it is based imply that the object of study of the logical empiricist social scientist is *relations* between material objects or events, not just objects themselves. In actual practice this usually means that social scientists should adopt methods that produce data amenable to statistical analysis. The goal of generalization also means that the explanation of events should be encouraged and historical narrative discouraged (an admonition that can be traced at least to Comte). This is predicated on the view that narration is limited to the arrangement of events on the basis of temporal sequence alone. In practice this admonition usually results in a view of historical narrative as 'mere chronicle', and fosters an attitude that any attempt to make sense of history through narration is an illusion. Historians and social scientists can become rigorous scientists, but to do so they must adopt methods that result in the universal generalizations that make explanation (rather than mere chronicle) possible.

3 *Scientific theories and hypotheses are to be evaluated by empirical evidence.* Theories and hypotheses are to be tested against 'data'. Although the original notion of an experiential 'given' or even a theory-neutral database was eventually weakened by the analyses of logical empiricists, a privileged position is still to be given to 'unbiased observation' and to statements of 'matters of fact' that refer to the experiential world. Social scientists must also be able to demonstrate how their theories and concepts can be reduced − if only partially − to statements about directly perceived sense data or, more loosely, to the 'facts'. In other words, the final arbiter of scientific statements remains objective observation of the material stuff of the world around us. This means, for example, that social scientists should not seek the facts or causes of social phenomena in the subjective states of individuals. A well-known attempt to satisfy this dictum of positivism was Durkheim's tactic of regarding social facts, or social phenomena, as 'things' like all others that exist in their own right 'out there'. As real entities outside the

realm of human experience, they are capable of having an external influence on people.[47]

4 *Theories are to be understood as interpreted calculi or hypothetico-deductive systems.* A goal of science is the construction of theories that describe and explain phenomena. A scientific theory is an HD system that captures the regular (either general or statistical) relations between theoretical terms or hypothetical constructs. Theoretical terms gain empirical meaning either explicitly by being converted (at least partially) to observations through 'correspondence rules' or 'interpretation sentences' in a 'dictionary', or implicitly through their systematic relations to other terms in the theory. The acid test of a theory is accurate prediction, i.e. the successful correspondence between predicted and observed outcomes. The theoretical terms of a theory can be understood 'realistically' as representing real mechanisms (e.g. a magnetic field, although unobservable, can be considered as real as sticks and stones); however, a strict positivist is agnostic on the question, preferring an 'instrumentalist' or 'operationalist' position (in which the term 'magnetic field' is regarded as only a handy fiction that describes a seemingly regular occurrence of events in phenomenal reality).

In actual research practice few social scientists attempt to develop full-blown theories, preferring instead to test isolated hypotheses whose variables can be closely tied to observations. Despite the spate of books on formal theory building that appeared in the social sciences in the late 1960s and early 1970s, formal theories themselves remained rare. In practice, then, research by logical empiricists in the social sciences has tended to be more or less atheoretical in this sense.

5 *All scientific explanation involves, explicitly or by implication, a subsumption of its subject matter under general regularities or laws.* Following Hempel, the standard view is committed to the claim that 'all scientific explanation involves explicitly or by implication, a subsumption of its subject matter under general regularities' or laws; explanation in this interpretation provides a 'systemic understanding of empirical phenomena by showing that they fit into a nomic nexus'.[48] This means, for example, that a scientific explanation of a historical event − in contrast with traditional historical narration − must show how the event is causally or statistically connected to previous events. In the Hempel model the explanation and prediction of an event are normally symmetrical.

An ideal explanation is deductive − nomological, involving universal laws which together with required initial conditions guarantee the logical

[47] Durkheim, *The Rules of Sociological Method*, 1938, p. 14.
[48] Hempel, *Aspects of Scientific Explanation*, p. 488.

necessity of the event to be explained or predicted. In actual research however, explanations are generally inductive – statistical, so that 'the conclusion is not logically implied by the premises.[49] Even though most explanations in the social sciences remain incomplete 'explanation sketches', covering-law models remain an ideal goal of logical empiricist social science.

6 *Research design in science is based on the idea of hypothesis testing and the covering-law model of explanation and prediction.* The HD approach should be used as a model in research designs in the formulation and evaluation of theories and isolated hypotheses. This process will nearly always involve the definition and use of measurable variables. Research designs intended to explain or predict an event should be constructed around covering-law models. Other research strategies formulated around qualitative and non-experimental designs and based on teleological, reason-giving or descriptive explanatory models are to be rejected. Since they do not meet the standard criteria for acceptable scientific research, they are to be regarded, at best, as 'soft' research.

7 *Scientists must be prepared to demonstrate the relevance to society of their research projects and theories.* As mentioned earlier, this dictum has played an important role in the origin and history of the positivist tradition.

8 *Scientific writing should be clear and precise.* The rationale of this dictum is that the careful and systematic statement of an argument will more readily reveal serious problems and difficulties with its formulation than will a statement that is diffuse and imprecise.

It is instructive to note that the standard view has implications for how we should understand and approach the study of social science disciplines. Four that are relevant to later chapters will be mentioned here.

First, the assumption that there is a common 'logic of science' shared by all sciences suggests that individual disciplines should sooner or later pass through a series of growth phases that ever more closely approach mathematical physics. The scale formed by this reconstruction (traceable to Comte) can be used as a standard against which the relative maturity of disciplines can be judged. Thus the relative lack of success of archaeology in imitating the results of mature physical sciences could, according to this view, be attributed to its relative youth.

Second, the examination of the history of disciplines is of interest in identifying 'pioneers' and growth phases. However, the laggardly developement of the social sciences suggests that our time would be better spent looking outside our disciplines at the 'logic of science' in the

---

[49] Hempel, 'Theoretician's dilemma' p. 40.

process of reconstruction by philosophers of science. The notion that the subject matter of social science disciplines might require a separate methodology should also be rejected, for all disciplines share a common methodological as well as substantive unity. There is only one logic of science, and if the social sciences aspire to the title of science, they must conform to this logic.

Third, the 'logic of science' should be regarded as a largely autonomous conceptual framework which is not significantly affected by the social context of its formation and use. That is, the methods of social science are independent of the social world of the social scientist and of that segment of social reality studied. Science as a process is based on the rules of logic and grounded in objective observation; true knowledge is above all a question of method and of its systematic application.

Finally, the tasks of the philosophy of science and the social sciences are to be considered clearly separate: the task of the social scientist is to unlock the laws of social reality; the task of the philosopher of science is that of the 'underlabourer' who works to expose more clearly the universal 'logic of science' that underlies the process of science. It is also worth noting that belief in the unity of science thesis renders a philosophy of social science redundant, for, if there is only one science, there can be only one philosophy of science.

Conclusion

The LP/E research programme provides firm authoritative answers to questions central to any social science research endeavour. Among these are: What should be the object of study and the goal of research? What should an adequate understanding of human behaviour consist of? Should we be concerned with understanding present and past events or with predicting future ones? Can we safely ignore human consciousness or human behaviour and concentrate on one or the other? Is description adequate research?

The struggles of logical positivists and empiricists with these and similar questions resulted in the formulation of a series of presuppositions or commitments for practising science. Although the interpretation of these principles — just what an observation or the scientific method is, for example — were debated and considerably modified over time, their general commitments — to the primacy of observation and a 'logic of science', for example — remained relatively stable. In fact leading logical empiricists like Carnap and Hempel remained remarkably faithful to these principles. An attempt to provide a brief reconstruction and review of this programme has been made in this chapter.

Positivism was and remains today a system of thought in process. As we have seen, it has meant and continues to mean different things to different people. Logical empiricism, which so strongly influenced American social science in the 1950s and 1960s, was only one expression of a long and varied tradition in philosophy — a tradition that dominated the philosophy of science throughout most of the first half of the twentieth century. Indeed, many philosophers regard LP/E as the leading movement in western philosophy during this period.

This brief introduction with its emphasis on the underlying presuppositions of LP/E has not adequately portrayed the spirit of the movement. Positivism has been more than a series of principles and research programmes. It has been a movement surrounded from its inception by a crusading evangelical aura.[50] The positivists whom we have mentioned were, for the most part, questing intellectuals, often as harshly critical of their own assumptions and procedures as they were of those of others. They intended to make a difference, to help to build a better more secure world by exposing the illusions of metaphysics and by clarifying the 'logic of science'. As a result, they tended to adopt a prescriptive attitude, to advocate normative standards, rather than to be content with the explication of an idealized conception of science. In the process they tended to be sceptical, nearly always lively, sometimes dogmatic and often sarcastic individuals.

Although philosophers generally ignore the style of a debate, it will be argued in chapter 6 that, from an anthropological perspective, this neglected aspect of scholarly debate may well provide clues to at least part of its (underlying) purpose and message.

---

[50] Ayer, for example, refers to the 'missionary spirit' of the Vienna Circle (*Logical Positivism*, p. 6), and Kolakowski compares Comte's positivism to 'a Messianic vision' (*Alienation of Reason*, p. 70).

3

Problems with Logical Positivism/Empiricism

Since the 1950s, the mood of Anglo-American philosophy of science has been definitely antipositivist or at least anti-logical positivist/empiricist. Logical positivism/empiricism (LP/E) has progressed from a remarkably influential philosophy of science to one that has few adherents today. A typical epitaph is Suppe's claim that 'Positivism today truly belongs to the history of the philosophy of science . . . .'[1]

There were several reasons for this sudden collapse.[2] First, the research programme itself was increasingly criticized from many angles. In the end it failed to hold up under continued self-examination and a storm of criticism from Stephen Toulmin, Thomas Kuhn, Paul Feyerabend, Imre Lakatos, N. R. Hanson and other philosophers and historians of science. Second, the arguments of other research programmes, while not necessarily raised in opposition to positivism, were effective in drawing attention away from positivist philosophies.

In the first section of this chapter a few of the criticisms raised against interpretations of the presuppositions of the programme are reviewed, and in the second challenges raised against the presuppositions themselves are discussed. In this book criticisms of interpretations of the presuppositions of a programme are regarded as internal criticism, while challenges raised against the presuppositions themselves are

---

[1] Suppe (ed.), 'Afterword − 1977', in Suppe (ed.), 1977, p. 632. The following statements are representative of this mood: 'The dominant tendency in contemporary philosophy of natural and social science is antipositivist' (Giedymin, 'Antipositivism in contemporary philosophy of social science and humanities', 1975, p. 275); 'My subsidiary aim is thus to show once-and-for-all why no return to positivism is possible' (Bhaskar, *A Realist Theory of Science*, 1978, p. 8).

[2] Certainly the weakening of the claims of the programme contributed to its loss of attractiveness. However, rational argument alone is usually not sufficient to overthrow a research programme. A few of the undoubtedly complex reasons for the demise of the programme are discussed in chapters 6 and 8.

considered external criticism. Internal criticism is usually an attempt to clarify a point within the framework of a programme or, less benignly, an attempt to demonstrate that a programme is faulty because it cannot meet its own criteria of adequacy. External criticism, in contrast, is most often an attempt to overturn a programme by challenging the validity or fruitfulness of its most basic assumptions. Although the distinction between internal and external criticism is not always an easy one to maintain, it is a useful one to make in a brief review.[3] Some of the currents of thought swirling around the social sciences since the fall from favour of the LP/E research programme are introduced in the third section.

Internal Criticism

At the height of confidence in LP/E it was assumed that the programme would eventually provide, at least in principle, a secure foundation for certain and indubitable knowledge. The programme has proved vulnerable, however, in many areas. The inability of positivists to demonstrate the validity of the analytical–synthetic distinction between theoretical and observational statements, the lack of attention to the context of discovery and the failure to discover a procedure for verifying hypotheses through inductive methods are examples. It is probably fair to claim that not a single standard interpretation of a core assumption of the programme has escaped severe criticism.[4]

[3] The distinction between the 'external' and 'internal' criticism of a research programme is useful for several reasons. Most criticisms of positivism today are based on a preference for alternative epistemological and methodological systems. Critiques reject positivism by simply showing that it does not satisfy the assumptions of the alternative programme. However, as Caldwell argues, 'a methodological critique of one system (no matter how perverse that system's tenets may seem) based wholly on the precepts of its rival (no matter how familiar those precepts may be) establishes nothing' (Caldwell, *Beyond Positivism: Economic Methodology in the Twentieth Century*, 1982, p. 124). The stronger attack is criticism from within the framework of the programme itself. Popper has the interesting habit of trying to strengthen alternative programmes or theories as much as possible before showing that even in this strengthened position they remain inadequate on their own grounds.

[4] See Suppe, 'Critical introduction', in Suppe (ed.), 1977, p. 116, for a listing of criticism. Excellent sourcebooks for the philosophical debates of the 1940s and 1950s include: *Philosophy of Science: The Delaware Seminar*, vols 1, 2, New York: Wiley, 1962, 1963; *Minnesota Studies in Philosophy of Science*, vols 1–8, Minneapolis, MN: University of Minnesota Press, 1956, 1958, 1962, 1970, 1975, 1976, 1977; Feigl and Brodbeck (eds), *Readings in the Philosophy of Science*, 1953; Feigl and Maxwell (eds), *Current Issues in the Philosophy of Science*, 1961; Brodbeck (ed.), *Readings in the Philosophy of Social Science*, 1968; Brody (ed.), *Readings in the Philosophy of Science*, 1970.

Antipositivists such as Toulmin, Feyerabend, Popper, Kuhn, Hanson and Michael Scriven were not united in opposition to a commonly conceived philosophical position. Their interests, motives and backgrounds varied considerably. Although all opposed the research programme, some supported particular interpretations and presuppositions. Their debates were complex, and the undermining of one interpretation of a presupposition (for instance, the hypothetico-deductive model of science) did not necessarily invalidate the presupposition itself (the unity of science thesis for example). However, the cumulative effect of their criticism was sufficient to render LP/E an unattractive if not untenable research programme.

Some idea of the direction taken by these critiques can be illustrated by a brief review of attacks on standard interpretations of one of its most basic assumptions, the epistemologically and ontologically privileged position of observation, and of its concept of science. This discussion is not to be mistaken for a comprehensive review of the debate; only some of those concerns that seem in retrospect to be most relevant to our discussion of New Archaeology are stressed.

The privileged position of observation

Comte, who introduced the term, meant by 'positive' something physical, observable or given, rather than something speculative, metaphysical or fictive. It was the positive that provided the programme with its 'rock-hard' epistemological and ontological foundation. It was the ideal and promise of certainty that the logical positivists had used to banish other research programmes, such as the hermeneutic, that were considered inextricably rooted in metaphysical speculation. It was against the positive – the belief in the epistemologically and ontologically privileged position of the observation language – that the critics of logical positivism directed their most caustic criticism. Logical empiricism developed primarily through attempts to defend the logical positivist programme against these criticisms, but positivists were still unable to defend the ontologically privileged status of the observation language successfully.

As logical empiricists became increasingly aware of the complexity and indirect nature of the connection between observations and high-level theoretical terms, they responded by retreating from their commitment to extreme positivism, i.e. the empiricist programme formulated by Russell and the logical positivists. Hempel's concept of 'open meaning', and in particular his article on the standard conception of scientific theories and the importance of an antecedently understood scientific language, indicate the extent of this retreat, which clearly amounts to a rejection of the sharp distinction between observation and theory.[5] These relaxed interpretations were far removed, of course, from Hume's original trenchant empiricism. Indeed, it is fair to say that the privileged position of observation was undercut and with it the assumption that the only kind of sound knowledge available to human-kind is that of science grounded in observation. Since many fundamental features of the programme were predicated upon this foundation, the programme itself eventually approached internal collapse.[6]

The assumption of a theory-neutral independent observational language was also challenged from outside the programme. For instance, Feyerabend,[7] Kuhn,[8] Hanson[9] and other conventionalists attacked the assumption of the theory neutrality of observation. Each argued from a somewhat different perspective that interpretations of sensory percep-tions are theory laden — that observations are dependent in some important sense upon world views and theories.[10]

These severe external challenges to what Sellars has called the 'myth of the given' raised additional difficult issues for positivist epistemology and called into question the very possibility of an objective neutral observationally controlled science.[11] For example, if the language of science is laden with anthropomorphisms and metaphors, what are facts? If the dichotomy between facts and theories can no longer be maintained and if knowledge is conceptualized — and in this sense subjective — in what sense are tests meaningfully objective? If obser-vational tests are theory laden and therefore ambiguous in their im-plications, what should count as evidence? If expectations direct sensory receptors to some sensations more frequently than others, how can the

[5] Hempel, 'Studies in the logic of confirmation, in Brody (ed.), 1970, pp. 384–409, and 'On the "standard conception" of scientific theories', in Radner and Winokur (eds), *Minnesota Studies in the Philosophy of Science*, vol. 4, pp. 142–63, 1970. Nagel concludes that all perception, even 'immediate experience', involves interpretation and ordering; there is no 'autonomous language of bare sense con-tents' (Nagel, *The Structure of Science*, 1961, p. 121), See also the introduction to Shapere (ed.), *Philosophical Problems of Natural Science*, 1965, and Taylor, *The Explanation of Behaviour*, 1964, ch. 4.

[6] Positivism is often referred to as a 'foundational' philosophy, because it has grounded itself onto a foundation, in this case 'observations' or 'sense data'.

[7] Feyerabend, 'Explanation, reduction, and empiricism', in Feigl and Maxwell (eds), 1962, pp. 28–97, 'How to be a good empiricist — a plea for tolerance in matters epistemological', in Baumrin (ed.), 1963, pp. 3–40, 'Problems of empiri-cism', in Colodny (ed.), 1965, pp. 145–260, and *Against Method*, 1975.

[8] Kuhn, *The Structure of Scientific Revolutions*, 1970.

[9] Hanson, *Patterns of Discovery*, 1958.

[10] As Hanson notes, 'there is more to seeing than meets the eye' (Hanson, *Perception and Discovery*, 1969, p. 61). See also Hooker, 'Empiricism, perception and conceptual change', 1973, pp. 59–75; Dretske, *Seeing and Knowing*, 1969.

[11] Sellars, *Science, Perception and Reality*, 1963, p. 164.

claim be maintained that scientists are passive observers of an external reality? Finally, if reality is unknowable, what role does the concept 'empirical test' play in contemporary science?

If the existence of a fixed observational given, i.e. an uninterpreted realm of basic facts, is an untenable assumption, then many positivist conceptions must be called into question and possibly rejected. Among these are the empirical criterion of meaning, the objectivity and rationality of science, the distinction between facts and values, the synthetic – analytical distinction, the sharp distinction between observation and theory, the existence of independent and impartial tests, the orthodox conception of theories and concepts, the context of discovery and the context of justification (predicated upon the assumption that the interpretative and evaluational bases are separate), the conception of progress as the amassing of factual knowledge in a cumulative manner, the unity of method and even what science and non-science are.[12] This conclusion even led some philosophers and historians of science to challenge the conception of science as a systematic, objective and even rational enterprise.[13]

The standard view of science

Criticism of the 'given' and of so many of the principles based upon it naturally led to criticism of the conception of science advocated by leading positivists such as Hempel. The positivist conception of explanation is an example. According to its critics, the deductive model fails for a number of reasons: while it may provide necessary conditions for an explanation, it does not provide sufficient conditions (i.e. it does not always tell us *why* something happened or will occur); the actual logic of scientific explanation does not follow this form; the covering-law models ignore the substantive (conceptual) context in which explanations are offered; it assumes that laws are necessary for an explanation as premises in a deductive argument when they are not; and so on.

The inability of positivists to isolate clearly an objective observational realm also undermined the distinction between theoretical and non-theoretical terms, a distinction which is basic to the interpretation of

---

[12] These and other implications of the loss of the observational given are discussed by: Ashby, 'Verifiability principle', in Edwards (ed.), 1967, pp. 240–7; Austin, *Sense and Sensibilia*, 1962; Ayer, *Language, Truth and Logic*, 1946; Feyerabend, *Against Method*; Kuhn, *Structure of Scientific Revolutions*; Popper, *Conjectures and Refutations*, 1972; Quine, *From a Logical Point of View*, 1953; Scheffler, *The Anatomy of Inquiry*, 1963, pp. 127–62.

[13] See Feyerabend, *Against Method*, and Kuhn, *Structure of Scientific Revolutions*. There is some debate as to whether Kuhn ever viewed science as 'irrational' in the same sense as Feyerabend.

scientific theories as hypothetico-deductive systems. For example, if a theory is nothing more than an abstract hypothetico-deductive calculus which gains empirical content when certain of its terms are given an observational interpretation, the status of theoretical terms and the theory itself become ambiguous when the observational realm is also claimed to be theoretical.

The viability of the hypothetico-deductive account of theories was also questioned for other reasons. For instance, despite repeated attempts, positivists remained unable to demonstrate logically how it was possible to prove a theory to be generally true. The stumbling block remained Hume's problem of induction, according to which it is impossible to guarantee the truth of a law or any other statement which has to be empirically secure for all possible empirical observations — past, present and future. The reason, as expressed by Giddens, is that 'no matter how many tests are carried out, the laws cannot be said to be certainly verified since there always remains the possibility that the $(n + 1)$th observation following a finite series will be inconsistent with it'.[14] Furthermore, since it is possible to construct different theories which generate the same empirically consistent conclusions (the deductive paradox), it is possible that conflicting propositions could be promoted to the status of laws (certainly an untenable situation for positivist science) unless a means was found to identify true theories. In this case it does not help to appeal to criteria like elegance, simplicity or fruitfulness as substitutes for truthfulness, for such terms are subjective and should have no place in a rigorously positive science.[15] If we cannot tell whether theories are founded on real laws or not, it becomes impossible to separate legitimate from illegitimate theories.

Still others, in particular historians, have argued that positivists made a mistake in choosing mathematical physics as their model of science. The result, according to this view, has been both the disparagement of the results of the historical sciences and ill-conceived attempts to make them conform to an inappropriate model. This is nowhere better illustrated than in the debate over the most appropriate model of explanation for the historical sciences. Comte had dreamed of a science of history — a method of historical analysis which would eliminate narrative exegesis in favour of scientific explanation. According to the standard view, as mentioned earlier, narration is either an affair of tracing causal relationships, and thus must be a kind of causal explanation, or else it provides no explanatory insight at all. The alleged contrast between history and

[14] Giddens, *New Rules of Sociological Method: A Positive Critique of Interpretative Sociologies*, 1976, p. 140.
[15] Guelke, 'Problems of scientific explanation in geography', 1971, p. 47.

science has been reinforced by the entire positivist tradition, and there is a voluminous literature attacking or defending the positivist conception of explanation as it bears on historical explanation. If the standard view is accepted, narrative exegesis is entirely different from scientific explanation; by insisting on reconstructing history in narrative form, historians have cut themselves off from science.

One response to this argument, as we shall see in the next section, is to question the very image of explanation − the covering-law model − that positivists accepted as an ideal in their programme. Another reply, however, while not challenging the unity of science thesis or other core assumptions of the LP/E programme, has been that positivists have misleadingly identified the word 'science' with mathematical physics and the word 'history' with the mere enumeration of dates and successions of kingdoms. If this is in fact a correct contrast, then the narration − explanation polarity might be a good way of characterizing the difference between history and science. However, suppose, it has been argued, that by science we mean geology, and that by history we also mean geology? Geology is a historical science, and one of the tasks of the geologist is to produce a narrative history of the Earth. Similarly, an evolutionary biologist produces a narrative history of the origin of species as well as other results. From this perspective history and the social sciences are complementary and have a relationship not unlike that between historical geology and earth sciences such as geophysics and petrology. The Comtean tradition has been in error in its attempt to eradicate narrative exegesis, for, according to many historians, narrative exegesis and causal explanation are different but not competitive tasks of science. A costly misunderstanding exists because positivists have insisted that physics is the best model for science.

Other arguments against the standard view of science have stressed its lack of agreement with actual scientific practice. Rudner, for instance has argued that the accumulation of separate generalizations is more characteristic of science, especially the human sciences, than the positivist ideal of constructing large theoretical systems.[16] Still others have argued that, even though LP/E is based on a deductive model of scientific reasoning, an inductive mode of reasoning has continued to play a significant role in actual scientific practice since the time of Bacon. These inconsistencies were a product of the belief among logical empiricists and logical positivists that the logic of science could be better reconstructed a priori than by looking at the actual history of

[16] Rudner, *Philosophy of Social Science*, 1966, pp. 47−53. See also Harré, *The Philosophies of Science*, 1972, p. 170.

science. The result, according to critics, was the elaboration of a conception of science that strayed ever further from what any practising scientist would recognize as science.

These and a barrage of other criticisms challenged the LP/E conception of science on the grounds of its own criteria of adequacy, i.e. from the 'inside'. Undoubtedly the most severe disruption of the programme was caused by the undermining of the privileged position of observation. The early heady optimism that science could be founded on a secure 'given' base of experience, and that this foundation would clearly demarcate it from unsound metaphysical speculation, faded under the uncompromising analysis to which the LP/E programme was subjected, not least of all from within the empiricist camp itself. As we have seen, logical empiricists responded to these problems by stepping back from their commitment to the more extreme but pivotable positions of the logical positivists. Although positivists like Hempel argued that these were forward steps towards a more sophisticated conception of science, they did amount to a drastic retreat from the idea of a 'rock-hard' irrefutable database and generally true theory. In the end it was a retreat that opened once again that Pandora's box of metaphysical oddities that positivists had worked so hard to close once and for all.

External Criticism

While internal criticism of interpretations of the basic assumptions of the LP/E research programme drastically weakened the original claims of the logical positivists, there were other external challenges that called into question the very assumptions themselves. At least some of these arguments are as old as the roots of positivism and only received renewed attention with the internal weakening of the LP/E programme. The sample of arguments presented below provides some indication of the diversity of these alternative views. Whether one agrees or not that these arguments are decisive, they did provide sufficient fuel to divert many young scholars from the positivist programme. In this way they contributed to its demise, or at least to its fall from favour.

1 *Truth cannot be the proper objective of theories in the human sciences.* According to the standard view of science, the point of theorizing is to discover the true, or approximately true, structure of reality (core assumption (1)). Indeed, truth is considered by many theories to be the overarching goal of scientific research. It is held that this purely theoretical goal can be pursued independently of any practical application which a theory may have. For this reason allegations that truth is not attainable in the human sciences, or that it should play

a secondary role in theory selection, threaten to upset standard methodological preconceptions.

There are at least two philosophical arguments to show that truth cannot be the proper objective of theories in the human sciences. The first derives from Quine's thesis of the 'indeterminancy of translation', and the second from the conviction that research into the nature of social reality changes social reality. Quine's thesis applies to any social or psychological theory which relies upon the interpretation of verbal behaviour as data. The thesis questions the generally accepted idea that there is a true way to interpret a sentence: the way which best reflects the structure and meaning of the thought which the speaker intended to communicate. If the latter notion is granted — that theories of interpretation can be true — then the interpreted data that they generate become good scientific data, on equal footing with observational or measured data, and social theories supported by interpreted data can be literally true, just as theories in the natural sciences can be true. Consequently, disputes between social scientists over the proper interpretation of certain sentences are not different in principle from disputes between natural scientists over the proper description of observations which are highly theory laden. The general view, then, is that there is a fact to the matter of interpreting sentences, even though there may always remain conflicts of interpretation between actors, observers, psychoanalysts, functionalists and so on.

Now in Quine's opinion this account cannot be correct, for a linguist can never provide a theory which defines for every utterance the precise meaning and structure of the thought which allegedly gave rise to it. This is so because the best description of the meaning and structure of a thought is given by the best description of the meaning of the sentence that expresses it — and there is always more than one way of describing that. The demand that truth be the goal of theories in the human sciences is based, then, on a deep misunderstanding of the relation of thought to language: theories of language structure and language meaning do not describe determinate features of the world. While linguistic theories purport to describe an objective linguistic reality, there are no genuine facts concerning meaning or synthetic structure to constitute such a reality. Agreement in linguistic judgement, therefore, can only give the illusion that there is an objective subject matter being judged; in fact, according to Quine, there is no determinate structure underpinning such judgements.[17]

---

[17] Quine, 'Ontological relativity', 1968, pp. 185–212, and *Word and Object*, 1960, p. 26. See also Hookway, 'Indeterminacy and interpretation', in Hookway and Petit (eds), 1978, pp. 17–41.

A correct understanding of linguistic phenomena, then, would re-cognize that sentences can be understood in different ways for different purposes, with no one way being absolutely true or right. If Quine is right, it follows that any theory that is tested by interpreting verbal behaviour cannot be strictly true. Thus, since many theories in the human sciences are tested by assessing the replies subjects make to questionnaires, for example, they cannot be said to be true. Further-more, if there is any indeterminancy in translation between different languages at the public level, it reappears at the private level between the sentences in the inner language and the public sentences into which they are translated.

How, then, can thoughts, which from a hearer's perspective are doubly indeterminate, be used to lessen the indeterminacy of public translation? The fact that it is not possible to determine cognitive structures and processes uniquely poses a clear limitation on our ability to understand the nature of human intelligence. As a result, if we accept Quine's argument, truth as a theoretical virtue must be displaced in many instances in the human sciences by other virtues, such as practical application. Quine's thesis raises many problems for the social sciences. For example: If truth is impossible, what sort of objectivity can we hope to obtain? How can non-true theories be rationally preferred?

The second argument maintains that if a social theory cannot be tested without affecting the society it pertains to, then no social theory can ever be confirmed as an accurate characterization of that society as it would have been had it not been observed.[18] Furthermore, because the availability of social theories may radically alter social conditions, additional complications enter into the assessment of social theories that do not confound theories in the natural sciences. For instance, an observer may actually affect what an agent will decide to do in the future. A classic example is a change in stock-market behaviour brought about by the predictions of an eminent stock-market analyst. How, then, can truth be the goal of social theories when self-fulfilling prophecies are a real possibility? How can we decide whether an anthropologist's questioning changed the way in which a people perceived the rules of a ritual and, consequently, their responses to directed questions? Is there a fact of the matter? Here a pre-reflective under-standing has been exchanged for an explicit self-awareness, and this added awareness has affected the way decisions are made. In social theories, then, interaction can actually bias the probability that a theory will be shown to be predictively adequate. In fact the distinct possibility

[18] See, for example, Devereux, *From Anxiety to Method in the Behavioral Sciences*, 1967.

exists in our example that an alternative theory might well have won support if some other anthropologist had visited the society instead. What is the place of truth in such theories? There is no easy answer.

It can be argued, then, that a good interpretation of social behaviour is not the same as a true interpretation. More strongly stated, it can be argued that truth cannot be the right objective of the human sciences. This claim obviously raises issues that have broad methodological consequences for anthropology. It must not be presumed, however, that I am arguing for the truth of this claim. My aim is only to demonstrate that its acceptance (or even an inability to refute it conclusively) opens the way to challenges of the conception of the task of social theory that follows from the presuppositions of the LP/E programme.

2 *All sciences do not share the same methodological and substantive base.* Perhaps the most persistent charge against the LP/E research programme has been that it is an insufficient methodology for tackling just those problems of greatest interest to scholars who study human beings. Because humans possess traits like consciousness, volition and reflectivity, they cannot be treated like rocks and rabbits. A special methodology is required. Only two of these arguments are considered here.

i) *Can we assume cultural invariance in rationality?* A familiar research strategy in the social sciences is to assume that human beings are rational agents. For instance, where understanding the nature of group interaction in a specific context is the goal of a research project, it has been found useful in fields like economics and sociology to assume that members of the group are rational beings with goals and beliefs who strive in the most rational way possible to achieve those goals, given the constraints of their situation. Research is carried on as if rational beings form an autonomous level of a hierarchy.[19]

By taking a human to be a rational being, human scientists believe that they can find meaningful generalizations about human behaviour without attending to details at cognitive or subrational levels and without concern for regularities that hold at higher levels in the group or society as a whole. The idea is that if people are well adapted to their environment they will tend to respond to that environment rationally. Similarly, it does not matter how one's actions contribute to group regularities, for it is assumed that individual actions can be studied in abstraction from the society to which they belong. All that is required is a specification of the context in which a person is acting.

[19] Feyerabend, *Against Method*, pp. 17–22.

The type of rational-agent approach being described is one which fits the methodological assumption of universal hierarchy. But can it be made to work? Is there really no interaction between the rational level and higher levels? Since an agent's actions are rational only relative to some context E, it must be possible to provide (1) a precise definition of each E the agent might be in and (2) a method for deciding whether any possible action A in E is rational. Unless these two requirements are met there will be cases where there is no well-defined rational action for the agent to perform. Requirement (1) assumes that the agent's world can be objectively partitioned into a system of task or problem contexts. Requirement (2) assumes that there is an objective method of deciding the rational action in every possible context that the agent might be in. Together they set down the conditions for approaching humans as rational beings.

Both these assumptions are highly questionable. Most of the more important tasks or problems that we confront are not undertaken in well-structured contexts. There is continued scope for innovating means to achieve our ends, and the rules constricting our alternatives are much freer than (1) demands. However, let us assume for argument's sake that (1) can be achieved, i.e. let us assume that an agent can be treated as a being who moves from one type of chess game to another. Is it plausible to suppose that there could be a culturally invariant conception of rationality as demanded by (2)? Is there always an objectively best course of action which all societies would recognize?

Cultural invariance in rationality is required by the hierarchy model because, if we were to allow rational agents in different societies to hold different conceptions of how to act rationally, we would lose whatever chance we had of studying their conduct without considering their psychological processes or their sociocultural conventions. We would cease to treat the rational level as an autonomous level. Of course alien cultures may have different norms of thought, but, in so far as these are conventional, their maintenance is explained in terms of the rational expectations that agents hold about each other's conduct. Hence, since rationality explains cultural norms, it must be independent of culture. Yet should this not be an empirical discovery? Are the a priori arguments for defending the cultural invariance of rationality sound? There is a substantial philosophical debate surrounding these issues, but the fact that they are not settled opens the gate to other perspectives quite at variance with the positivist programme and calls into question the methodological unity of the natural and human sciences.

ii) *Understanding social phenomena from the actor's own perspective is legitimate, even necessary, social theory.* There has been a second major but more subdued perspective in the history of the human sciences that has constantly challenged positivism. With the fall from favour of the positivist programme, this perspective — which might be called 'phenomenological' — has risen to prominence once again in the last few decades.[20] The phenomenologist is committed to *understanding* social phenomena from the actor's perspective. He or she examines how the world is experienced; the assumption is that reality (or the reality which is most worth knowing about in the human sciences) is what people perceive it to be. The phenomenologist seeks understanding through qualitative methods such as participant observation, in-depth interviewing and other methods which yield descriptive data. In contrast with a natural science approach, they strive for what Max Weber called *verstehen* — understanding on a personal level the motives and beliefs behind people's actions.[21] Since phenomenologists study social life 'phenomenologically', the search for social causes in the positivist sense of correlations between observable events is not where their research interests lie.

The phenomenological perspective challenges the positivist research programme from several angles. In its more radical form it attacks the enlightenment conception of rationality itself. For example, in an extreme version — held, for instance, by Nietzsche and his followers — the claim is that the enlightenment ideal of science is itself a myth which, the philosophers of the Frankfurt School add, legitimates a technocratically ordered society.[22]

Peter Winch's application of Ludwig Wittgenstein's later work on language games to the social sciences is another strong statement within this tradition. For Winch, 'beliefs and actions must always be understood in the context of the language game or the form of life in which they are located. In other words, one must adopt the rules of the game in order to understand the plays. They cannot be understood from outside, because the boundaries between systems are not permeable, will not

---

[20] See Polkinghorne, *Methodology for the Human Sciences*, 1983, pp. 15–57, 201–40, for a brief review and references.

[21] Weber, *The Theory of Social and Economic Organization*, 1964, pp. 88–115. See also Keat and Urry, *Social Theory as Science*, 1975, pp. 145–75; Huff, *Max Weber and the Methodology of the Social Sciences*, 1984.

[22] For a brief review of the Frankfurt School relevant to the concerns of this chapter, see Stockman, *Antipositivist Theories of the Sciences*, 1983, pp. 28–71, 139–65, 240–6. From another angle, they also claim that positivist philosophy includes in its subject matter material which cannot be treated as the object of a scientific theory, i.e. that it is itself inherently metaphysical.

allow understanding to pass through'.[23] For Winch, understanding social action amounts to understanding the meaning embedded in that action, and this involves understanding the language games that are being played. Human behaviour is not merely bodily movements to which people attach subjective meanings, for behaviour is situated within a system of rules, norms, standards and so on, and has a purpose or a reason within this system of ideas. Thus, an 'action' is only meaningful within a language game; it has no meaning in and of itself. Indeed, it could have different meanings within other language games and even within subgroups of the same society. Social science research does not focus on bodily movements as such to isolate patterns of movement; it focuses on actors' ways of viewing their world. This kind of understanding is more akin to 'tracing the internal relations' of a system of ideas than to 'the application of generalizations and theories to particular instances'.[24] The 'social relations between men and the ideas which men's action embody are really the same thing considered from different points of view'.[25]

3 *Theoretical terms have ontological status.*   A central goal of the positivist research programme was to rid science of its metaphysical content, to ground it in the 'rock-hard' observational base. The argument was not that metaphysical forces like the Universal Spirit or theoretical entities like protons and magnetic fields do not exist, but that the claim that they do is an unnecessary speculation. While some logical empiricists, such as Nagel, argued that whether one viewed theoretical terms as making real references was immaterial, strict

---

[23] Winch, *The Idea of a Social Science and Its Relation to Philosophy*, 1958, and 'Understanding a primitive society', 1964, pp. 307−24. Winch's position was part of a broader sceptical response to logical empiricism in the 1950s and 1960s called *Weltanschauungen* (world view) analysis. The principal assumption of this sceptical response is a familiar one to anthropologists: 'All knowledge is relative to one's perspective; there is no absolute point of view outside of one's historical and cultural situation' (Polkinghorne, *Methodology for the Human Sciences*, p. 103). Whorf's hypothesis that people's language systems mould their perception of reality and, as a result, the world we think we inhabit is primarily a linguistic construct was influential in the formulation of this movement (Whorf, *Language, Thought and Reality: Selected Writings of Benjamin Lee Whorf*, 1965). See also Sampson, *Schools of Linguistics*, 1980; Suppe 'Critical introduction', pp. 125−221, and Afterward − 1977, pp. 633−49. Others stimulated by Wittgenstein's work on language games who have written from a *Weltanschauungen* perspective include Stephen Toulmin and N. R. Hanson. See Toulmin, *The Philosophy of Science*, 1953, *Foresight and Understanding*, 1961, and *Human Understanding*, 1972; Hanson, *Patterns of Discovery*.
[24] Winch, *Idea of a Social Science*, p. 133.
[25] Winch, *Idea of a Social Science*, p. 121.

positivists would deny ontological status to theoretical entities and adopt some brand of instrumentalism in their analyses of the status of theories and theoretical terms. Theories are not true or false but are merely computational devices. All that we can meaningfully say exists is what we can observe, i.e. sense data. The goal of theory construction is to seek higher and more extensive correlations among these data.

However, instrumentalism has been opposed for a number of reasons. Perhaps the primary objection is that it allows scientists to abandon the search for truth.[26] Although the search for correlations is an important goal of science, a still more basic and important goal is the search for ever fuller explanations. One way of accomplishing this goal in a realist conception of science is to assume that theoretical terms do refer to real entities and therefore that theories are true or false. This assumption is in line with scientific practice, for scientists generally believe that their theories are more than just computational devices, that they make true statements about reality. From a realist perspective, then, theoretical entities have ontological status. Again, whether the arguments of realists are found convincing or not, realist philosophy of science has provided an appealing alternative to the ontological position of the positivist programme.[27]

4 *Science is a social process.* As we have seen, concepts like valid theory, acceptable observations and appropriate methodology are enmeshed in relations of mutual interdependence in the positivist research programme. In addition to the theory dependence of observations that arises from the nature of human communication, it has also been proposed that there is a theory dependence of observations which is mediated by methodological rules.[28] If theoretical preconceptions are an unavoidable component of methodological rules, and if such rules mean that only certain kinds of observations will ever be made, then a certain predetermination of observation by theory must follow. We have here the possibility of a methodological circle where methods based on assumptions about the nature of the subject matter only

[26] For arguments against instrumentalism, see Popper, *Conjectures and Refutations*, pp. 107–14; Lakatos, 'History of science and its rational reconstruction', in Buck and Cohen (eds), 1971, p. 95. But see also Giedymin, 'Instrumentalism and its critiques', in Cohen et al., (eds), 1976, pp. 179–207.
[27] See chapter 7 for one account of a realist philosophy of science. See also Suppe (ed.), *The Structure of Scientific Theories*, 1977, pp. 716–28; Keat and Urry, *Social Theory as Science*, particularly pp. 27–45. Realism, like many other 'postpositivist' perspectives in the human sciences, reemerged in importance in response to the presumed demise of the positivist programme.
[28] Böhme, 'Die bedeutung von experimentalregeln für die wissenschaft', 1974, pp. 5–117.

produce observations which must confirm these assumptions.[29] Within such a circle theoretical change would be limited to the set of theories which share the assumptions incorporated in the methodological rules. Any theoretical change beyond this would have to involve a methodological (paradigm) change. The point is that the methods used to test a theory may presuppose the truth (or falsity) of the theory to be tested. As a result, not all kinds of outcomes have an equal chance of appearing in research situations.

There have been several currents of thought that have emphasized the constitutively social character of knowledge. For example, Kuhn's contribution to the sociology of knowledge provided, at a time when it was most needed in the 1960s, a clear indication of how forms of natural knowledge could be understood sociologically.[30] This encouraged the empirical studies of scientific culture which were then beginning in the social sciences, and it inspired awareness of the constitutively social character of knowledge generally – an awareness which had faded away in the postwar period in part because of positivist denials that the social context of knowledge was of constitutive importance.

The phenomenological critique also sought to expose the connections between the conduct of a scientific discourse and the social conditions which made its particular processes and forms both possible and acceptable. An example is Habermas's critical theory, which rejected the possibility of an autonomous science altogether and insisted that conceptions of science are given in determinate social practice.[31] Arguments by Bachelard, Althusser, Habermas and others also stressed the urgent need for the exposure of connections between forms of knowledge and forms of existence concealed in and ultimately by social practice.[32] As one example, we should not placidly accept the theoretical entities we encounter in the human sciences as given. In speaking of residential differentiation, we need to clarify the status of concepts like class and rent and to recognize their essentially and intrinsically political connotations. Terms like these cannot be used innocently, for interests are submerged and are made to surface through time. By denying the social component of science and hiding behind the facade of objectivity, positivists were avoiding the political and ethical implications of their views.

5 *Principia logic is an inadequate tool for the analysis of science.* As we saw in chapter 2, severe problems were generated by the structure

[29] Danziger, 'The methodological imperative in psychology', 1985, pp. 1–13.
[30] Kuhn, *Structure of Scientific Revolutions*.
[31] See, for example, Habermas, *Knowledge and Human Interests*, 1971.
[32] See, for example, Althusser, *Lenin and Philosophy and Other Essays*, 1971.

of the new logic adopted by logical positivists as their primary tool for the analysis of science. While positivists strove to resolve these problems, others were intent on showing how they led in some instances to absurd reconstructions of the logic of science. Just what these conclusions implied, however, remained a focus of contention. Some critics concluded that they demonstrated that principia logic was an inappropriate model for the analysis of science, although they remained committed to the presupposition that there was a discernible logic to science. Others argued that they only supported what a close examination of the history of science seemed to show, i.e. that the notion of a logic of science was a myth. Since these arguments are long and involved, only a brief and partial review is presented here. It should be sufficient, however, to indicate the tack that these arguments have taken.

The sort of absurdities generated by the logical part of LP/E is well illustrated by the paradoxes of confirmation. For instance, if the equivalence condition which states that whatever confirms one of two logically equivalent sentences also confirms the other is accepted, then, for the hypothesis 'All ravens are black', the discovery of any instance of an object which is neither black nor a raven would seem to confirm the hypothesis. In fact Nelson Goodman argued that the discovery of anything that is either not a raven, such as a pencil, or is black, such as a lump of coal, would confirm the hypothesis 'All ravens are black'.[33] Of course, conclusions like this seemed absurd to scientists as interpretations of actual scientific practice.

As absurdities generated by the extensional nature of principia logic accumulated, some critics began to look seriously at alternative approaches to the philosophy of science. For some this involved a search for a more appropriate model of logic, while for others it meant a reexamination of the role of logic in the analysis of science. One suggestion was to abandon the syntactical analysis of confirmation generated by the LP/E presuppositional framework for a close examination of the historical record of previous observations.[34] It was this set of observations, it was argued, that should determine whether a given hypothesis has been confirmed or not. Of course, this alternative approach to confirmation reintroduced questions that logical empiricists were trying to avoid, such as just how much of this set of prior observations must

---

[33] Goodman, *Fact, Fiction and Forecast*, 1965, pp. 70–1. On the equivalence condition, see Hempel, *Aspects of Scientific Explanation*, p. 13. For a review of logical difficulties generated by principia logic, see Swinburne, 'The paradoxes of confirmation – a survey', 1971, pp. 318–30, and Brown, *Perception, Theory and Commitment*, 1977, pp. 25–36.

[34] Goodman, *Fact, Fiction and Forecast*, pp. 84–5.

be considered in any one case. None the less, the approach did at least take into consideration the meaning or context of the propositions involved in an argument, a consideration that the demand for a completely truth-functional propositional logic with its ps and qs ignored. Other contexts rather than formal logics were proposed as well. For instance, some critics pushed for the use of a dialectical logic, such as Aristotle's 'man of practical wisdom' model, which, while 'looser' than principia logic, did seem to mirror the thought processes of scientists better.[35]

Yet other critics, most notably Feyerabend, vigorously attacked the basic assumption that there is a logic to science. Feyerabend argued that the world and history in general are much too complicated, varied and subtle to be explored adequately by rigid adherence to a set of simple methodological rules 'which have been set up in advance and without regard to the ever-changing conditions of history'.[36] In his *Against Method*, he uses examples from the history of science to support his contention that many significant advances have occurred only after prevailing rules were cast aside. In fact, according to Feyerabend, adherence to well-specified rules not only does not guarantee progress in science, it may even hinder its advance. In his words:

> given any rule, however 'fundamental' or 'necessary' for science, there are always circumstances when it is advisable not only to ignore the rule, but to adopt its opposite. For example, there are circumstances when it is advisable to introduce, elaborate and defend *ad hoc* hypotheses, or hypotheses which contradict well-established and generally accepted experimental results, or hypotheses whose content is smaller than the content of the existing and empirically adequate alternative or selfconsistent hypotheses, and so on.[37]

Feyerabend's thesis that methodological anarchism is a precondition of progress in science stands in stark opposition to the positivists' commitment to discovering the method or logic of science. In a frequently quoted comment, he even claimed that 'there is only *one* principle that can be defended under *all* circumstances and in *all* stages of human development. It is the principle "anything goes"'.[38] Again:

> . . . the principles of logical empiricism (be precise; base your theories on measurements; avoid vague and unstable ideas; and so on) give an inadequate account of the past development of science and are liable to hinder

[35] See, for example, Brown, *Perception, Theory and Commitment*, pp. 146–51.
[36] Feyerabend, *Against Method*, p. 17.
[37] Feyerabend, *Against Method*, pp. 23–4.
[38] Feyerabend, *Against Method*, p. 28.

science in the future. They give an inadequate account of science because science is much more 'sloppy' and 'irrational' than its methodological image. And, they are liable to hinder it, because the attempt to make science more 'rational' and more precise is bound to wipe it out . . . . What appears as 'sloppiness,' 'chaos' or 'opportunism' when compared with such laws has an important function in the development of those very theories which we today regard as essential parts of our knowledge of nature. *These 'deviations,' these 'errors,' are preconditions of progress.*[39]

Feyerabend's ideas carry a fairly straightforward message: the world is a very complicated place; all methodologies have their limits; adherence to a single set of methodological rules may prevent us from obtaining certain kinds of knowledge; methodological anarchism is a precondition of progress in science; science and the scientific world view have been given too much prestige in modern society. Regardless of whether one is convinced or not by Feyerabend's arguments, he did raise fundamental questions concerning the viability as well as the desirability of viewing scientific method as a single set of discoverable rules at a time when the attractiveness of positivism was fading.

These and other arguments amounted to a call for the abandonment of principia logic as a tool for the analysis of the structure of science or, at the very least, for a severe constriction of its scope of application. In proposing alternative logics or that 'anything goes', philosophers of science were, of course, well on their way to formulating new philosophies of science.

6 *Positivists are mistaken in denying ontological status to theoretical terms.* The goal of the LP/E research programme to rid science of its metaphysical content was also subjected to severe criticism from a variety of positions. Here our interest will be restricted to the argument that all philosophies of science, like all scientific theories, must have a metaphysical base. As an example, consider the problem of the ontological status of theoretical terms. Positivists, as we have seen, conceived of the world for purposes of scientific investigation, at least, as constituted of given atomistic facts. The purpose of this restriction was not to deny that theoretical entities, like protons and magnetic fields, did 'in fact' exist, but to rid science of unnecessary speculation. Since whatever is given-in-experience is certain (or so it was assumed), it can be said to be known or knowable in a manner in which protons and magnetic fields are not. While Nagel attempted to liberalize this view by arguing that it is immaterial or a matter of personal choice whether theoretical terms make real reference or not, strict positivists continued to deny ontological status to theoretical terms and to support some brand of

---

[39] Feyerabend, *Against Method*, p. 179.

instrumentalism in their analysis of the status of theories and theoretical terms. According to instrumentalism, theories are not true or false but merely computational devices, for all that can be meaningfully said to exist are sense data. On this view the goal of theory construction is confined to seeking more inclusive correlations among these data.

This argument has been opposed for a number of reasons. For instance, the view that all that can be said to exist is determined by what can be positivistically seen with the human eye has been labelled anthropocentric and an expression of an outmoded spectator theory of knowledge.[40] Why should what exists be limited to what people can see? Others have argued that it is not possible, even in principle, to eliminate theoretical terms from science. Consider, for example, the problem of partial interpretation. If the list of correspondence rules for specifying the meaning of a theoretical term is not finite in number for all possible situations, then only a partial replacement of the term by observational terms has been provided. Since it seems unlikely that complete lists of correspondence rules can be provided for particular theoretical terms, it may not be possible to avoid an ontological commitment to theoretical terms. If this argument is correct, then the ontologically privileged status of the observation language must be called into question. Furthermore, the subsequent observation of 'unobservables', such as 'virus' and 'electrical charge', through the development of special instruments like electron microscopes and scanning devices call into question the 'rock-hard' objective base that positivists have argued must be used in assessing the relative merit of competing scientific theories. Should a 'rock-hard' foundation be able to change?

7 *The systems of the world are for the most part open, not closed.* A condition for the possibility of positivism is the existence of spontaneously occurring closed systems. Remember that a Humean causal law is an empirical invariance or constant conjunction of an epistemically non-vacuous kind among observable objects or 'atoms' of one kind or another. It is this ontology of atomistic events and view of laws which requires an ontology of closed systems, for patterned conjunctions of 'atoms' would hardly be constant if, for instance, 'atoms' could disrupt patterns of relationships by entering and leaving a system in an irregular manner. Critics have contended that disruptions like this must normally occur in nature, for a strong case can be made that no Humean laws are known at present.[41] That this is so, they argue, is also evident in the

[40] Hacking, 'Experimentation and scientific realism', in Leplin (ed.), *Scientific Realism*, 1984, pp. 154–72; Bhaskar, *Realist Theory of Science*, p. 58.

[41] See, for instance, Donagan, 'The Popper–Hempel model reconsidered', in Dray (ed.), 1966, pp. 127–59. See also the discussion of closed and open systems in Bhaskar, *Realist Theory of Science*, particularly pp. 259–60, and *The Possibility of Naturalism*, 1979.

rapid backsliding of positivist criteria for the adequacy of laws. This is particularly evident, it is maintained, in the loosening of criteria of adequacy for laws in scientific explanations 'so as to accommodate deductive–statistical, inductive–probabilistic, partial, incomplete and elliptical explanations, and so-called explanation sketches until in the end their position reduces to (the refuted) doctrine of regularity determinism'.[42] A philosophy of science that does accommodate open systems is examined in some detail in chapter 7.

8 *Science and all philosophies of science have a metaphysical base.* A central claim of LP/E is that science has no presuppositions. Since the programme itself was regarded as a 'scientific' philosophy, it should also be presuppositionless. Science escapes the distorting grip of metaphysical speculation because it rests on the bedrock of observation; LP/E is presuppositionless because it is soundly based on scientific empiricism and principia logic (and thus is rational). It would be a severe blow to LP/E, then, if it could be demonstrated that both science and philosophies of science are controlled by a body of presuppositions. Claims of just this type have been made from a variety of perspectives.

The difficulty of convincingly defending the sort of absolute presuppositions being referred to here should be apparent. As examples, take the claim that 'society is law governed' and 'every event has a cause'. As they are neither formal tautologies nor refutable by straightforward empirical tests, they are neither analytical not ordinary empirical propositions. Therefore their defence cannot be logical or empirical in the usual sense. While often taken to be eternal self-evident truths, the fact that they have been revised and even abandoned in practice argues against this line of defence. For all these reasons, they are probably best thought of as paradigmatic propositions accepted as a result of research and cultural experiences. It is no wonder, then, that their defence rapidly collapses into dogma or slides off into an infinite regression of justification. Also, since they are neither logical tautologies nor empirical propositions – and therefore metaphysical – it should be clear why positivists have tried to exorcise them from both science and philosophy. But how successful have they been in this endeavour?

Take the LP/E identification of the logical with the rational, and the logical with deductive logic, as an example. What grounds are there for maintaining that these identifications are presuppositionless? What grounds are there for rejecting a dialectical logic, such as an Aristotelian logic which is a context rather than a formal logic, as a viable tool for the analysis of science? Is the very existence of logical calculi of any kind sufficient reason for assuming that they are appropriate tools for

[42] Bhaskar, *The Possibility of Naturalism*, p. 160.

the analysis of science? Similar questions can be raised about other basic assumptions of the programme. For instance, to assume that we cannot validly derive normative statements about how science should function from descriptions of how it does function is a presupposition; to assume that the construction of logical calculi and the use of simple empirical generalizations like 'All ravens are black' to illustrate their implications will somehow elucidate the structure of science is a presupposition; to assume that scientific knowledge must have a practical use for people in their day-to-day lives is a presupposition. While assumptions like these may seem reasonable in a particular sociocultural context, there seem to be no 'logical' or straightforward empirical grounds to accept them as truths about the world rather than as statements of faith or preference.

Quite a different picture emerges if we view presuppositions like these as possible components of science and philosophies of science, as components that provide points of view or guiding principles that summarize the accumulated wisdom of research and cultural experiences.[43] From this perspective, both overriding concerns of LP/E, such as logical questions, and neglected topics, like the process of discovery and the dismissal of the actual history of science as relevant to the analysis of the structure of science, become understandable (with hindsight) results of the working out of the implications of the programme. However, if this is so, then we can ask (1) how adequate these assumptions are as an account of science, and (2) what the social and political consequences are of adopting this set of presuppositions rather than another. Positivists, with their commitment to a presuppositionless scientific philosophy, avoid questions like these. However, Comte, for instance, saw science as an instrument of control over physical and social conditions; once the laws of social physics were discovered, people would have to accept the inevitable. Critics have charged that positivists, in refusing to examine the social roots and implications of their presuppositions, have made themselves the (unwitting?) dupes of capitalism.[44]

---

[43] For one view of the role of metaphysics in science, see Watkins, 'Confirmable and influential metaphysics', 1958, pp 344−65, and 'Metaphysics and the advancement of science', 1975, pp. 91−121. For a brief review, see Brown, *Perception, Theory and Commitment*, pp. 95−109. See also Grene, 'Empiricism and the philosophy of science, or *n* dogmas of empiricism', Cohen and Wartofsky (eds), 1983, pp. 89−106.

[44] Boeselager, *The Soviet Critique of Neopositivism*, 1975. The critical theory of Habermas and others also contains arguments along these lines. For a discussion of the image of the person generated by a positivist philosophy, see Hollis, *Models of Man: Philosophical Thoughts on Social Action*, 1977.

Whether the presuppositions of LP/E are adequate tools for the analysis of science is not the question of interest here. What is important is the nature of the metaphysical commitment of the programme. What were these commitments? Why did philosophers and scientists alike find them attractive? What are the social, political and moral consequences of adopting these particular presuppositions? Regardless of the answers to these and similar questions, critics, by exposing the metaphysical base of LP/E, eased the way for the re-emergence of alternative conceptions of science banished earlier because of their own explicit metaphysical commitments.

Whether or not we find any of these arguments decisive, they clearly challenged the basic assumptions of the LP/E research programme. Given the programme's weakened and vulnerable state from severe internal criticism, they were sufficiently attractive to draw young scholars away from it – a movement which contributed to its further collapse. It is probably fair to conclude that at present LP/E is a degenerating research programme.[45]

Postpositivist Philosophy of Science

Postpositivist conceptions of the task of the social sciences have been diverse and more often than not based upon incompatible competing presuppositions. Many still remain tentative and impressionistic, and all certainly lack the illusion of concreteness once enjoyed by positivism. A useful way of considering the dilemma of the postpositivist or post-empiricist methodological debate in the philosophy of science and in the social sciences in general is to consider the distinction between *doxa* (opinion or belief) and *episteme* (certainty and knowledge).[46] There is a difference between what we believe to be true (*doxa*) and what we know with absolute certainty to be true (*episteme*). The standard of absolute indubitable certainty (*apodictic* knowledge) has been accepted in general by western epistemologists. LP/E sought to reconstruct science from a foundation of indubitable facts – the facts of sense experience plus statements connected by logical necessity. As we have seen, this epistemological framework has provided the grounding for

---

[45] This does not mean that there are no longer philosophers and scientists who refer to themselves as positivists or even empiricists. See Lakatos, 'History of science', for the characteristics of a degenerating research programme.

[46] Polkinghorne, *Methodology for the Human Sciences*, pp. 9–13.

the hypothetico-deductive approach. The standard of absolute indubitable knowledge is understandably attractive. We know from experience that believing is not enough to ensure certainty, and that acting on what we believe to be true can lead to amusing if not calamitous results.

Postpositivist philosophy of science has questioned whether the certainty required by the concept of *episteme* is possible. As we have argued in this chapter, attempts by LP/E philosophers of science to find a strictly apodictic base for knowledge have not been successful. At best these attempts provide a framework for developing *assertoric* knowledge, i.e. knowledge claims that we have good but not indubitable reasons for believing are true. In recent decades this admission has brought about a shift to a 'postempiricist' understanding of science, the re-emergence of alternative conceptions of the human sciences and a general re-assessment of the methodology appropriate for the human sciences. It has also focused attention on the adjustments made by the human sciences to conform to the demands of positivist philosophy of science.

Some of the main components of this 'new image' of the philosophy of science can be briefly summarized: (1) a rejection of formal logic as the primary tool for the analysis of science; (2) its replacement by a reliance on detailed study of the history of science; (3) an awareness that conceptual frameworks and their presuppositions are at base difficult to justify without relapsing into dogma or an infinite regress of justification; (4) an awareness of the fundamental role that conceptual frameworks play in determining what problems must be solved, what counts as a solution, what is observed and so forth; (5) a realization that observation is in some sense theory laden; (6) an awareness that the significance of observational data and the meaning of concepts change in the context of different theoretical frameworks; (7) an emphasis on continuing research and the context of discovery, rather than accepted results, as the core of science; (8) an interest in the nature of theory or paradigmatic change.

Despite these common themes, postpositivist philosophy of science does not, like positivism, propose a unified view of science. Its point is not that the positivist conception of what constitutes proper methods for obtaining certain knowledge should be replaced by another conception of how apodictic knowledge should be produced. Rather, it challenges the tradition that knowledge actually is apodictic truth and asserts that we do not have access to indubitable truths. The knowledge claims that a community of scholars accept are those that withstand the test of practical argument and use. Knowledge is understood to be the best understanding that we have been able to produce thus far, and not a statement of what is ultimately real. Postpositivism is not then a method of thought with an agreed set of presuppositions; it is an attitude about knowledge.

This attitude — fuelled in part by the experiences of a faltering positivism — was brought to expression by diverse, though overlapping, movements often based upon incompatible assumptions. A few of these are (1) the 'linguistic turn' in the philosopy of science as elaborated by Quine, Kuhn, Toulmin, Hesse and others, who call into question the truth status of the statements of science and the kind of link such statements have as an extra-linguistic reality, (2) the continued development and increased sophistication of systems theory and its application to the study of the workings of complexly organized wholes such as human beings and societies, (3) the concerted effort to develop a theory of human action that includes the notions of purpose and deliberate activity, (4) the challenge of Heidegger and Gadamer in philosophical hermeneutics to the idea of a foundational epistemology that yields apodictic truths, and (5) the re-emergence of realist forms of science that give an ontological commitment to theoretical terms quite foreign to positivism.[47]

Conclusion

It is too easy today to assume from the widespread rejection of positivism that positivists were an overly naive group of individuals fascinated with the spectacular accomplishments of the 'hard' sciences. However, most positivists believed themselves to have good reasons — methodological, epistemological and ontological — for rejecting alternative approaches to knowledge of the human realm. As I have attempted to emphasize, it was often the careful and systematic analysis of their own views that revealed serious problems and difficulties with the programme. Although their attempt to establish a 'rock-bottom' base of

---

[47] Among the founding works of postpositivist philosophy of science are: Polanyi, *Personal Knowledge*, 1964; Hanson, *Patterns of Discovery*; Toulmin, *Foresight and Understanding*; Kuhn, *The Structure of Scientific Revolutions*; Feyerabend, 'Explanation, reduction, and empiricism'. Examples of more recent general works on postpositivist philosophy of science include: Brown, *Perception, Theory and Commitment*; Bhaskar, *Realist Theory of Science*; Pratt, *The Philosophy of the Social Sciences*, 1978; Polkinghorne, *Methodology for the Human Sciences*; Achinstein, *Concepts of Science*, 1968; Hanson, *Observation and Explanation*, 1971; Suppe (ed.), *Structure of Scientific Theories*; Chalmers, *What is This Thing Called Science?*, 1976; Krimerman (ed.), *The Nature and Scope of Social Science: A Critical Anthology*, 1969; Thomas, *Naturalism and Social Science: A Post-empiricist Philosophy of Social Science*, 1979. The literature is vast.

certain knowledge failed, their reasoned arguments against alternative approaches makes it clear why overhasty rejection of the positivist tradition itself and the embracing of alternative positions may be premature. Positivism has historically managed to re-emerge in a new form from more than one supposedly catastrophic defeat.

None the less, the cumulative effect of their own arguments was a thicket of logical problems. Many of their key ideas, such as that science has a certain base and a deductive structure, their mechanistic conception of action and model of human beings, and their assumption of naturally occurring closure have been subjected to damaging attack. The cumulative weight of these arguments was sufficient to open the gate to a diversity of new (or renewed) research programmes for the human sciences. Today, while some scholars are in the process of attempting a reformulation of positivism and the maintenance of the naturalist stance, others are attempting to develop strategies unique to the human realm.

4

The New Archaeology

The professionalization of North American archaeology has an unusual early history that significantly affected the development of the field throughout the twentieth century. Although professional archaeologists existed before the mid-nineteenth century, it was at this time that archaeology as a field of employment received a major stimulus. This stimulus was a growing concern that the lifeways, languages and material culture of the North American Indian would be irretrievably lost unless quickly and systematically recorded. Pioneer archaeologists, cultural anthropologists, linguists and physical anthropologists were hired with government funds to implement this programme. Since these individuals were employed through common agencies, they tended to be concentrated together, especially in major eastern museums such as the Smithsonian and the Peabody. When anthropology emerged as an academic discipline at the turn of the century, this combination of specializations was maintained in order to continue the original programme and as a reasonable division of labour for studying any society. As a result of this association, the majority of North American archaeologists eventually came to regard themselves as anthropologists, and to identify their ideal goals with the ideal social science goals of anthropology rather than with the particularizing goals of history.[1]

Since its merger into anthropology, the most outspoken and trenchant criticism of North American archaeology has been directed at its perceived failure to pursue these ideal goals vigorously. Although several attempts to reorient archaeology took place before 1960, especially in

[1] For a review of the early history of North American archaeology, see Willey and Sabloff, *A History of American Archaeology*, 1980, and Fitting (ed.), *The Development of North American Archaeology*, 1973.

the late 1930s, few ever moved beyond the admonition phase.[2] The New Archaeology of the 1960s and 1970s has been the most vigorous of these reform movements. In this chapter we shall focus on two standard questions asked of any reform movement: What was the nature of the dissatisfaction that initiated the movement? What alternative was proposed? Criticism and an assessment of the proposed alternative programme are reserved for the following chapter.

The history of New Archaeology is divided here into an early phase (1962−70) and a late phase (1970−8). Some archaeologists might quibble over these dates and others might prefer a more complex scheme.[3] However, this simple division seems to capture the main trends of the movement and is sufficient for our purposes. The early phase is reviewed in the first section and the late phase in the second section of the chapter. In the third section New Archaeology is reformulated as a research programme, and some of its implications for archaeological practice are drawn out. As we shall see, this programme is firmly based on logical empiricist principles.

The Early Phase

The label New Archaeology was first used by Joseph Caldwell in 1959 to signal the approach of a new era of revitalization in North American archaeology.[4] This new era was soon launched through a series of 'fighting' articles and critical reviews by Lewis R. Binford, beginning in 1962 with the publication of 'Archaeology as anthropology'.[5] As well as publishing frequently and forcefully, Binford was highly visible at

[2] Steward and Setzler, 'Function and configuration in archaeology', 1938, pp. 4−10; Kluckhohn, 'The place of theory in anthropological studies', 1936, pp. 328−44, and 'The conceptual structure in Middle American studies', in Hay et al. (eds), 1940, pp. 41−51; Strong, 'Anthropological theory and archaeological fact', in Lowie (ed.), 1936, pp. 359−70; Bennett, 'Recent developments in the functional interpretation of archaeological data', 1943, pp. 208−19, and 'Empiricist and experimental trends in eastern archaeology', 1946, pp. 198−200. Although Walter Taylor's trenchant criticism of archaeology was not published until 1948, it was essentially completed as a Ph.D. dissertation under Kluckhohn's guidance in the early 1940s; completion and publication were delayed by the Second World War. See Taylor, *A Study of Archaeology*, 1948.
[3] Watson, 'Archaeological interpretation', in Meltzer et al. (eds). 1986, pp. 439−57.
[4] Caldwell, 'The new American archeology', 1959, pp. 303−7.
[5] Binford, 'Archaeology as anthropology', 1962, pp. 217−25, 'A consideration of archaeological research design', 1964, pp. 425−41, and 'Archaeological systematics and the study of culture process', 1965, pp. 203−10. These and other early writings are included in Binford, *An Archaeological Perspective*, 1972.

national conferences and surrounded himself with an active group of students, who quickly became known as the 'young turks'.[6] The first key symposium to attempt to implement Binford's developing programme was held in Denver in 1965 at the national meeting of The Society for American Archaeology. The procedures were published in 1968 as *New Perspectives in Archeology*.[7] Additional exemplars of the 'new perspective' by William Longacre and James Hill appeared at about the same time, as well as an influential review by Kent Flannery of the debate that had erupted in North American archaeology.[8]

The early phase of the New Archaeology movement was characterized by trenchant criticism of 'traditional' archaeological practice, a heady optimism that archaeology could contribute to anthropology as an active rather than a passive partner and the formulation of a new research programme – the 'new perspective' – to carry out this goal. As in the implementation of any research programme, this process in archaeology was accompanied by a shuffling of the importance and meaning of disciplinary terms. Key terms like culture, archaeological data, science and analogical interpretation were given new definitions; others like process, system, model and explanation were promoted to a new importance and also redefined; still others, especially diffusion, taxonomy and history, were demoted in importance. In the following review we shall concentrate on (1) the nature of the dissatisfaction with 'traditional' archaeology and the new positive attitude, (2) the redefinition

[6] For Binford's reflections on the early history of New Archaeology, see Binford, *An Archaeological Perspective*, pp. 1–14, 450–6. The 'young turks' included Stuart Struever, William A. Longacre, Robert Whallon, James Hill, Leslie Brown and James Brown (Binford, *An Archaeological Perspective*, p. 10). Some of the most forceful programmatic statements in early-phase New Archaeology were comments and papers delivered at major conferences, especially the annual meetings of the Society for American Archaeology (SAA). Although these are a valuable source of information for a more complete and thorough treatment of the rise of New Archaeology, especially for the tone and style of debate, attention here is confined to published materials.

[7] Binford and Binford (eds), *New Perspectives in Archeology*, 1968.

[8] Hill; 'A prehistoric community in eastern Arizona, 1966, pp. 9–30, 'Broken K Pueblo: patterns of form and function', in Binford and Binford (eds), 1968, pp. 103–42, and *Broken K Pueblo: Prehistoric Social Organization in the American Southwest*, 1970; Longacre, 'Archaeology as anthropology: a case study', 1964, pp. 1454–5, and 'Changing patterns of social integration: a prehistoric example from the American Southwest', 1966, pp. 94–102; Flannery, 'Culture history v. cultural process: a debate in American archaeology', 1967, pp. 119–22. Criticism by New Archaeologists of archaeological practice was not limited, however, to the archaeology of the Americas. See, for example, Binford and Binford, 'A preliminary analysis of functional variability in the Mousterian of Levallois facies', in Clark and Howell (eds), 1966, pp. 238–95.

of culture and archaeological data and (3) the testing programme vision of science proposed by Binford. Since Binford was the major proponent of the New Archaeology in its early phase and provided its foundational statements, we shall concentrate on his views here.

The spirit of new archaeology: a critical stance and a positive attitude

A definite sequence seems involved in the emergence of new research programmes, paradigms or, more generally, approaches. In the beginning a fundamental issue is squarely faced. The issue may be a problem, a new method or technique, a perceived failure or a dissatisfaction, and so on. As pioneers move confidently to solve the problem, and if they meet with enough initial success, great expectations are raised about the triumph of the emerging approach. This process is normally accompanied by promotional rhetoric in which the apparent virtues of the approach are lavishly praised and the real or fabricated failings of contending approaches exposed. As the approach proves increasingly successful or is more widely accepted, the intensity of the promotional rhetoric becomes more subdued.

Although this scenario is a considerable oversimplification of complex processes, it does seem to capture many of the main features of emerging perspectives. Certainly, the early phase of the new perspective in archaeology seems an example. For instance, Binford's early position is marked by a very critical stance and a positive attitude toward the promise of this programme as the foundational structure of New Archaeology was being worked out and gradually accepted by increasing numbers of archaeologists as a rallying point for reform. Here we are interested in the promotional rhetoric, in what was being derided and what promoted. Whether the accusations were fair or the positive goals worthwhile or attainable is not at issue at the moment.

New Archaeology is commonly regarded as a response to a growing and widespread internal dissatisfaction with traditional archaeological practice. Although the perceived failures of traditional archaeology were considered numerous and diverse, the main accusations against traditional archaeological practice (which are not always consistent with one another) can be summarized as follows:

(1) it failed to treat archaeological data as cultural material and therefore as a source of evidence that could contribute to broader, specifically anthropological, problems;

(2) it failed to realize any substantial understanding of the cultural past;

(3) it treated the recovery, description and systematization of archaeological data as an end in itself;

(4) it lost much valuable information because research was not conducted with specific problems in mind;

(5) it failed to establish an understanding of archaeological, let alone cultural, phenomena because of the lack of an adequate conceptual framework;

(6) it assumed that an understanding of the past would simply emerge as knowledge of the archaeological record became more complete;

(7) as a result of (6) it minimized the importance and difficulty of theory construction;

(8) it assumed that archaeological interpretation became more speculative and suspect as it focused on what were seen as increasingly less concrete cultural phenomena, such as social, religious and ideological systems;

(9) it assumed that the empirically given 'facts' exhaust the legitimate content of archaeological knowledge and therefore that the proper task of archaeology is to ascertain the 'facts' (and, as a corollary, that any interpretative extension beyond description of the contents of the archaeological record is speculative and empirically uncontrollable);

(10) it assumed that a comprehensive database had to be established as a first priority before historical or broader anthropological questions could be effectively addressed;

(11) as a result of (10) it effectively displaced social scientific and historical objectives into some unspecified time in the future (though still paying them 'lip service');

(12) it missed the point of historical enquiry by restricting historical research to chronicle and narration of either change in the composition of the archaeological record through time or change in the reconstructed past;

(13) it largely confined itself to 'historical' modes of enquiry, thereby neglecting the ultimate and unifying goal of anthropology, which is the explanatory understanding of general cultural processes;

(14) it did not test the empirical adequacy of interpretations, which consisted for the most part of ethnographic knowledge imposed on archaeological data (i.e. analogical interpretation);

(15) as a result of (14) it relied on purely conventionalist modes of interpretation, which were speculative and controlled only by the current standards of the archaeological community;

(16) it treated interpretation as something carried out on established 'facts' after and independent of their collection;

(17) as a result of (16) it assumed that there was a radical separation between the empirical and theoretical aspects of research;

(18) it conceived of culture as a system of norms or ideas;

(19) it assumed that similarities and differences between archaeological assemblages could be simply and primarily explained by the diffusion or transmission (through migration, for example) of ideas or norms through space and time;

(20) it treated the 'cultures' identified as entirely archaeological phenomena that could be defined by lists of traits.

The statements that express these failings are frequently qualified by adding terms like 'tended', 'usually' and 'seemed to', or made more intense with 'always', 'never', 'impossible' and similar words. Perhaps it is fitting at the end of this long but still only partial list to recall that Binford, in a review of the accomplishments of traditional archaeological practice, concluded that it had failed to achieve effectively any of the traditional objectives of archaeology, i.e. to use the archaeological record as a potential source of information about (1) cultural history, (2) past lifeways and (3) general cultural processes.[9]

According to New Archaeologists, the root causes of most of these problems were the empiricist and inductivist presuppositions that pervaded traditional archaeology. These presuppositions severely constrained the nature and limits of archaeology by limiting legitimate knowledge to what was directly observable or, at most, to low-level statements about technology and subsistence. Since the subject matter of archaeology was the archaeological record, the option seemed either to remain at the level of data description or to engage in suspect speculative thinking in pursuing reconstructions of past cultural systems

---

[9] Binford, 'Archaeological perspectives', in Binford and Binford (eds), 1968, pp. 5–32. Wylie has called this critical attitude or thesis, 'perhaps, the defining feature of the New Archaeology ...'; see Wylie, 'Positivism and the New Archaeology', 1981, p. 63. A relatively extensive list has been provided here, since the critical thesis is so central to New Archaeology and much of the New Archaeology programme was formulated in opposition to these perceived faults.

and processes. It was no surprise, then, that in their view archaeology had become mired in uncertainty and remained a sophisticated form of antiquarianism.

Having exposed the counterproductive empiricist and inductivist pre-suppositions of traditional archaeological practice, New Archaeology began to explore new options which could achieve an understanding of the cultural past. An important feature of this process of exploration was the statement of a number of directives which helped to define the new perspective and guide the search for a new methodology. In the language of research programmes, directives like these function as positive heuristics which provide direction to developing programmes.[10] In turn, it is the failure to satisfy these directives or a growing pessimism that they can be satisfied with the methodology employed that defines a degenerating programme.

Among the directives of New Archaeology were the following:

(1) archaeology must make use of archaeological data as evidence of the past;

(2) it must serve broader more legitimate objectives than the antiquarian concerns of traditional archaeology;

(3) it must make historical and anthropological questions the focus of research at all levels;

(4) it must give the generalizing explanatory goals of anthropology priority over the particularizing and reconstructive goals of history (i.e. treat archaeology as a social science rather than a branch of history);

[10] See Lakatos, 'Falsification and the methodology of scientific research pro-grammes', in Lakatos and Musgrave (eds), 1970, pp. 91–196, and 'History of science and its rational reconstruction', in Buck and Cohen (eds), 1971, pp. 91–136, for the function of positive heuristics in research programmes. Research pro-grammes are also accompanied by negative heuristics, i.e. statements concerning what should be avoided, what is to be considered inadequate and so on. In New Archaeology sentiments like, 'Data collection and classification for their own sake are not sufficient or justifiable research goals' and 'Empiricist and inductivist presuppositions provide a completely inadequate basis for anthropological arc-haeology' seem to have functioned in this capacity. Although nearly always expressed as accusations against traditional archaeological practice, the fact that they were for the most part distortions of actual practice suggests that they were fulfilling some role other than that of objective descriptions of that practice. See Kuhn, *The Structure of Scientific Revolutions*, 1970, for a description of the nature of clashes between 'paradigms'.

(5) it must make the explanatory understanding of past cultural systems and processes its primary concern;

(6) it must treat archaeological data as evidence that can test hypotheses about the past and confirm universal laws of human behaviour;

(7) it must adopt a methodology by which the generalizing explanatory goals of anthropology can be achieved;

(8) it must define specific research objectives to guide the selection of relevant facts (since there is a potentially limitless pool of (sense) data);

(9) it must realize that broader anthropological or theoretical concerns cannot be detached from empirical research but must suffuse every step of a scientific investigation;

(10) it must make its theoretical presuppositions explicit and subject them to examination;

(11) it must contribute knowledge of social value.

Perhaps the single most defining feature of the positive heuristic was the assumption that the explanatory social science goals of the New Archaeology could only be reached through the identification, confirmation and use of universal laws as defined in the logical empiricist (specifically Hempelian) research programme. The new perspective was a startling contrast to that of traditional archaeology. In fact the logic of science upon which it was based seemed so promising to some New Archaeologists that they proclaimed a paradigm revolution in the discipline.

Key elements of the New Archaeology research programme

If New Archaeologists were to make knowledge claims that extended beyond the archaeological record, they needed procedures that would be immune to the charges of uncontrolled community-governed speculation that they themselves had levelled against traditional archaeological practice. The answer was a theory and problem-sensitive testing methodology which would impose stringent empirical constraints on interpretative claims about past cultural systems and processes. According to Binford, this was the 'final link in scientific procedure' which traditional archaeology had failed to develop.[11] The procedures adopted

[11] Binford, 'Archeological perspectives', p. 14. Binford characterized his own position as a 'shift to a consciously deductive philosophy (Binford, 'Archeological perspectives', p. 18; he also found 'from a practical science point of view, the arguments of Karl Hempel (sic) were the most useful', (Binford, An Archaeological Perspective, p. 18).

were the hypothetico deductive approach and the covering-law model of explanation.

However, before we can fully appreciate how these procedures were to function in archaeology, it is necessary to understand how the concepts culture and archaeological data were redefined.

Redefinition of culture and archaeological data

According to Binford, traditional archaeology had adopted an inadequate 'normative' view of culture that was dominated by internal mental factors. For the traditionalist — it was claimed — a culture is composed of and defined by a specific aggregation of internalized ideas or norms. As a mentalistic phenomenon, it is localized in individuals and transmitted by diffusion and socialization. A cultural tradition is a patterned and integrated whole formed by a set of covarying ideas or norms which 'flows' across space and time.[12] Since a culture is a univariate phenomenon, i.e. a set of ideas, it can be understood in terms of this single variable — the spatial — temporal transmission of ideas.[13] For example, culture change or variability can be assumed to be the result of the invention and differential communication of ideas. Change is expected to be gradual and continuous. By analogy with historic people, we are justified in assuming that prehistoric people were also partitioned into 'culturally maintained distinctive populations, ethnic groups'[14]

This normative view as reconstructed by Binford was rejected for a variety of reasons: it is too simple and does not capture the complexity that must be present to account for the sort of variability encountered in the archaeological record (and therefore it is wrong); it is mentalistic (and therefore presumably metaphysical); by specifying ideas as the only variable responsible for change, it neglects other possible variables and assumes that human behaviour is controlled solely by an internalized cultural system; it cannot account (on its own terms) for anomalies such as discontinuities or reversed trends in the archaeological record or for variability within artefact types; it is not able to explain adequately why norms themselves vary; it assumes that past and present cultures are alike and therefore precludes the possibility that present and palaeolithic cultures are fundamentally different.[15]

[12] Binford, 'A consideration of archaeological research design', p. 205, labelled this an 'aquatic view of culture', because, in his view, it invoked an image of culture as 'flowing' across space and time. See Deetz, *Invitation to Archaeology*, 1967, for a contemporary version of the normative view.

[13] Binford, 'Archaeological systematics', p. 205.

[14] Binford, *An Archaeological Perspective*, p. 290.

[15] The 'normative' view of culture was rejected for a variety of reasons. Perhaps most basically, however, it was because 'our current knowledge of the structure and functional characteristics of cultural systems' shows the normative model to be inadequate (Binford, 'Archaeology as anthropology', p. 218).

The materialist ecosystem conception of culture that Binford chose to replace the normative view was regarded as just one of many choices which were better than the old view. Called the systemic view of culture, it proposed that a culture is a complex, systemic, integrated, adaptive, extrasomatic and material-based organization of behaviour, and not a mental phenomenon.[16] As a cultural system, it was presumed to be composed of a number of closely interrelated operational subsystems and functional contexts, in particular functional—technological, social and ideological. Material culture was or could be articulated with or function in any number of these contexts. As a result, all subsystems of a culture are reflected (manifested or instantiated) to some degree in the material culture of the system; in turn, the cultural significance of the material culture is potentially multidimensional. Since subsystems mutually condition each other, knowledge of the functional whole is necessary to understand a subsystem and material culture fully. According to this perspective, ideas or norms can be selectively drawn on in adaptive situations, but their presence alone, as knowledge, is not sufficient to cause human behaviour.[17] Culture, then, is the 'extrasomatic means of adaptation for the human organism',[18] and 'changes in the ecological setting of any given system are the prime causative situations activating processes of cultural change'.[19]

Not only has the mentalistic normative conception of culture been replaced by a materially based systemic conception, but internal ideational conditions of change or cause have been replaced by external material conditions. Although ideas remain somewhat of a puzzle (e.g. their ontological status), culture seems to have taken on a behavioural and thing-like definition. As should be apparent from chapter 2, the materialization of the culture concept is necessary if the empiricist research programme is to make sense in this context.[20]

---

[16] Binford, *An Archaeological Perspective*, p. 8, states that 'Culture ... (is) a material system of interrelated parts ... and in, 'Archaeological systematics', p. 209, he says that a culture system 'involves a complex sets (*sic*) of relationships among people, places, and things ....' Also within the realm of this natural system are psychology and philosophy; they can be made accessible, none the less, through operational definitions and empirically testable hypotheses; see, for example, Binford, 'Archeological perspectives', pp. 22–3. See also Watson et al., *Explanation in Archeology: An Explicitly Scientific Approach*, 1971, for another version of a materially based ecosystem model of culture.

[17] Binford, *An Archaeological Perspective*, pp. 244–94: 'transmitted knowledge and belief are ... a reservoir of accumulated knowledge *to be used differentially when appropriate*' (quote on p. 259).

[18] Binford, 'Archaeology as anthropology', p. 218.

[19] Binford, 'A consideration of archaeological research design', p. 440.

The concepts culture, cultural material and archaeological data (more properly archaeological material) are intimately related, but what culture is thought to be affects our conception of the nature of the other two concepts. From the normative view, archaeological data are considered to be the surviving fragments of cultural material. Tools, ornaments, houses and similar material items are regarded as cultural material because they were manufactured in accordance with and therefore embody or manifest a mental template, i.e. a set of ideas concerning the proper form for and way of manufacturing a house, a type of knife and so on. A group of people are said to be members of the same culture because they share the same norms or mental template. The patterning observable in the archaeological record is therefore due to and explainable by reference to one causal factor: shared but distinct ideas integrated into a template.

Since archaeological data embody distinct ideas, all cultural traits can be regarded as similar in kind and therefore as equal and comparable. Furthermore, the degree to which two assemblages of artefacts share traits in common can be used as a direct measure of their cultural affinity.[21] In traditional archaeology this resulted in the construction of present–absent trait lists in order to facilitate the quick and easy comparison of numbers of shared norms. In a more sophisticated version, the frequency of individual traits (e.g. numbers of scrapers of a particular type) is quantified and frequency profiles (histograms) are compared.[22] Although different levels of trait list similarity were assigned purely archaeological terms, like aspect and focus, they were assumed to correspond to familiar anthropological concepts, such as culture,

[20] If 'culture' is to 'cause' behaviour in a Humean sense, then something pheno-menal must be constantly conjoined with something else phenomenal, i.e. constantly conjoined elements or 'atoms' cannot be from different ontological realms. Culture must be patterned behaviour or, perhaps, ideas given an operational definition (see note 16). If it is some form of rule-based non-empirical system, then it is inconsistent with strict logical empiricist presuppositions. As is pointed out in chapter 5, positivist social scientists have always had problems with ideas and consciousness. For a relevant discussion of concepts of culture in anthropology during early-phase New Archaeology, see Keesing, 'Theories of culture', in Siegel (ed.), 1974, pp. 73–97; Keesing's comments on the culture concept in New Archaeology suggest that it was intended to be a materially based set of socially transmitted *behaviour* patterns (pp. 74–7, 82–3).
[21] Binford, *An Archaeological Perspective*, pp. 330–1, and 'Archeological perspectives', p. 8.
[22] An example of a sophisticated version is Bordes' typological procedure for comparing Mousterian artefact assemblages. See Binford, *An Archaeological Perspective*, p. 260.

tribe, family and tradition.[23] Because change was due to a shift in ideas, it followed that change in the past as embodied in the archaeological record should normally be gradual and continuous. Anomalous situations, such as discontinuities in the spatial distribution of similar traits through time or the sudden discontinuity or appearance of traits through time, would have to be explained by 'idea-related' processes such as parallel invention or invasion.

Perhaps most important for our discussion here is that in the normative view both archaeological data and cultural material are a different kind of phenomenon from culture. They are things and empirical, while culture consists of ideas and is mentalistic. This ontological break has meant that many aspects of culture, especially social relationships and religious or philosophical views, are only poorly manifest, if at all, in the archaeological record. In addition the ontological break severely entangled 'empiricist' traditional archaeology within a web of methodological problems that enervated the discipline.

This conception of the nature of archaeological data was, of course, rejected by Binford. According to the systemic view, cultural phenomena are no different in kind from cultural material. Material objects result from the various sorts of activities and functional contexts which make up a cultural system. Therefore there is a direct empirical link between cultural systems and cultural material, with the former being the antecedent cause of the latter. In fact there are good reasons for considering cultural material to be part of the materially based cultural system itself and therefore as material culture — a dimension of cultural systems — rather than simply as cultural material. Given the integrated nature of cultural systems and the additional assumption that the material dimensions is articulated with and conditioned by all the other various interrelated dimensions and subsystems which comprise these systems, it follows that 'data relevant to most, if not all, the components of past sociocultural systems are preserved in the archaeological record'.[24] If we accept these assumptions, then virtually all aspects of past cultural systems are potentially accessible to archaeological investigation.

Since material culture was once an integral part of functioning cultural systems and is 'mirrored' in the archaeological record, archaeological materials have in principle the capacity to inform on all aspects of past cultural systems. Given their multidimensional origins, the information

---

[23] On trait list similarity and its traditional uses see: McKern, 'The midwestern taxonomic method as an aid to archaeological study', 1939, pp. 301−13, and Willey and Sabloff, A History of American Archaeology, pp. 104−8.
[24] Binford, 'Archaeology as anthropology', pp. 218−19.

content of artefacts and assemblages is not exhausted by the reconstruction of norms. Although the archaeological record may be patterned, its contents have no single meaning and are therefore a source of information about many features of past cultural systems and processes. Furthermore, the variability in the archaeological record now becomes an important source of information about the past. For example, artefact variability between sites may be evidence of seasonally specific tasks in a diversified environment.

We can begin to see how the systemic view of culture and its linked image of the archaeological record are consistent with a logical empiricist philosophy of science and, in theory, make a logical empiricist archaeology possible. Although culture retains a normative or mentalistic dimension, it is materially based, thing-like and extrasomatic; it is the same kind of phenomenon as the empirical archaeological record. Unlike the normative model in which behavioural activity and material objects are simply objectifications of norms, all three dimensions in the systemic model — the normative, the behavioural and the material — are assumed to interact with and mutually condition one another. The cultural system is the causal antecedent of the archaeological record which retains a complex, though still empirical, imprint of the cultural system. Most important for archaeology, the record is an empirical reality, i.e. objective, knowable in itself and independent of anyone's ideas about it. Since there is no ontological break, archaeologists are able to work back from empirical effect to empirical cause. However, past cultural systems are not inherent in the record or readily obvious from informed observation or statistical measures as traditional archaeology supposes. Hypotheses must be proposed and their adequacy tested in a manner consistent with scientific practice — and that requires imagination and effort.[25]

The essential link between scientific explanation and a testing methodology

As mentioned earlier, according to Binford the traditional objectives of archaeology are to use the archaeological record as a source of information about cultural history, past lifeways and general cultural processes. In this interpretation history proper refers to the sequence of

---

[25] Empirical data remain meaningless unless approached from a particular problem context. It is not, for example, 'self evident [that there is] a single context of relevance for facts as they relate to scientific method' (Binford, 'Some comments on historical versus processual archaeology', 1968, p. 271). See also Hill and Evans, 'A model of classification and typology', in Clarke (ed.) 1972, p. 250.

events that occurred in the past from which the archaeological record is derived, while a past lifeway refers to how particular people once lived. While the factual reconstruction of prehistory and past lifeways is a necessary task of the archaeologist, it is not sufficient or adequate alone for an anthropologist or social scientist. What is needed, according to Binford, is an understanding of the cultural–ecological processes operative in the past which were responsible for these sequences or lifeways. This involves an understanding not only of the causal connections between past events and the archaeological record, but also of the causal connections among the components of the cultural ecosystem responsible for these events. It is just this sort of explanatory understanding that is the proper task of archaeology: to answer the question 'why' in addition to the traditional 'what', 'where', 'when' and 'how'.

The model of explanation found most satisfying was the Hempelian logical empiricist covering-law model. For example, Binford characterizes scientific explanation as 'simply the demonstration of a constant articulation of variables within the system' whereby 'processual change in one variable can be shown to relate in a predictable and quantifiable way to change in other variables'[26]; a sequential relationship between events does not provide an explanation unless a causal connection is established between them such that 'if we know that the earlier events have taken place, we would be able to predict the event we wish to explain'.[27] Frequent explicit references are also made to the covering-law model, and Hempel is quoted as in the last extract above. As indicated in chapter 2, an observed event is explained by showing it to be an instance of a regular contingent relationship in nature, i.e. a natural law. The event is said to be explained in the logical empiricist sense that it was predictable or expected. A law is no more than a statement of a constant or known statistical rate of conjunction among phenomenal events. Although these are causal connections, they do not imply in Hume's regularity thesis of causality any notion of a metaphysical natural necessity or production by an idea, spirit or other purely non-empirical entity.

It was accepted, then, that if archaeologists were to explain in a fully scientific manner, they must appeal to a body of general laws which

---

[26] Binford, 'Archaeology as anthropology', p. 217.
[27] Binford, 'Some comments on historical versus processual archaeology', p. 268. He also cites Hempel to the effect, for example, that 'the assertion that a set of events ... have caused the event to be explained, amounts to the statement that, according to certain general laws, a set of events of the kinds mentioned is regularly accompanied by an event of the kind [for which an explanation is sought]' (pp. 267–8). The covering-law model is frequently cited by Binford.

connect causes and effects. It was also accepted that the formulation of general laws was the ultimate goal of the sciences, i.e. that the sciences were most concerned with what is general in nature and society rather than with what is spatially and temporally unique. Since New Archaeology aspired to be a social science and laws were required for scientific explanation, the stress in Binford's foundational statements was on the necessity of developing a deductivist strategy of confirmation in archaeology.[28]

Hypothetico-deductive confirmation procedures are specifically designed to test general statements that connect two or more variables. In archaeological research the test of a hypothesis (a possible law) would proceed by deductively drawing out test implications which are then confronted with archaeological data. If the test implications are empirically verified by the data, the hypothesis receives a degree of confirmation (or corroboration in Popper's view), and if not, it is proved false. A hypothesis that continues to gather in confirming instances and to resist attempts at falsification is said to be a law candidate or, when generally accepted, a law that can be appealed to in an explanation of other events.

This simple description of the hypothetico-deductive approach points to several tasks for archaeologists. Among the most important are the formulation of relevant hypotheses, the specification of the (initial or limiting) conditions within which the potential laws hold and the design of empirical research which can adequately and convincingly test the hypotheses. The sources of hypotheses are diverse. Ethnographic analogy is one important source, but others such as animal behaviour should not be neglected, for the possibility cannot be ruled out that cultural systems may have functioned somewhat differently in the past.[29] The archaeological record itself cannot be discounted as a source of hypotheses either. Since the empirical attributes of archaeological material

[28] 'The procedure discussed here is appropriate in the context of a positivistic philosophy of anthropology and archaeology. It denies categorically the assertion of antipositivists that the final judgment of archaeological reconstruction must be based on an appraisal of the professional competence of the archaeologists (Thompson, 1956, p. 331). The final judgment of the archaeological reconstruction presented here must rest with testing through subsidiary hypotheses drawn deductively' (Binford, 'Smudge pits and hide smoking: the use of analogy in archaeological reasoning', 1967, p. 10). See also Binford, 'On covering laws and theories in archaeology', 1978, pp. 631−2.

[29] See, for example, Binford 'Smudge pits and hide smoking', and 'Methodological considerations of the archaeological use of ethnographic data', in Lee and DeVore (eds), 1968, pp. 268−73.

manifest a discontinuous variability, statistical techniques can be effectively applied as an objective means of discovering 'the cultural significance inherent in archaeological remains'.[30] What is important, however, is that these speculative hypotheses refer to cultural processes which can provide an understanding of historical events or their material records, i.e. to potential 'laws of cultural or behavioral functioning'.[31] Preferably, they should link variables within cultural systems or link variables of cultural systems and the external environment or the archaeological record. Since it is possible to formulate a large number of often conflicting hypotheses, it is helpful to propose hypotheses within a context of relevance which indicates why a particular hypothesis is plausible and warrants testing.[32]

As anthropologists whose empirical base is the archaeological record, it is useful to distinguish between hypotheses that account for the archaeological record and those that account for past cultural systems and their change. On the first or archaeological level we are interested in formulating and testing hypotheses that link variables of past cultural systems with variables of the archaeological record. Since virtually all aspects of these past systems have left empirical traces in the archaeological record, given our general knowledge about how cultural systems operate, it should be possible to make a tentative reconstruction of a functional model of the 'entire extinct cultural system' causally responsible for the record. This process generally has to be initiated by some archaeological excavation, but it quickly becomes a dialectic between the formulation of interpretative propositions about the cultural significance of the data and the testing of these propositions through additional excavation and/or artefact analysis. Because cultural systems are complex integrated wholes, a functional model of the entire system must be the goal of excavation. This means that regional approaches to excavation and a sampling procedure must be adopted to ensure that a representative

[30] As recommended, for example, by Binford's mentor Spaulding in 'Statistical techniques for the discovery of artefact types', 1953, p. 313.

[31] Binford, 'Some comments on historical versus processual archaeology', p. 270. Hypotheses, in addition, which refer to the 'conditions and mechanisms by which cultural changes are brought about' (Binford, 'A consideration of archaeological research design', p. 425).

[32] On arguments of relevance, see Binford, 'Some comments on historical versus processual archaeology, pp. 271, 273, and 'Archeological perspectives', p. 25. See also Fritz, 'Archaeological systems for indirect observation of the past', in Leone (ed.), 1972, pp. 135–57. Arguments of relevance are also used to justify the treatment of hypothesis as law like in an explanation before it has been adequately confirmed. There is obvious room for abuse here, but it remains a common practice in positivist social science.

sample of the material remains of the entire past system is recovered.[33]

Even though the hypotheses tested at this level can be formulated within the context of a single cultural system and its material remains, according to New Archaeologists they are intended to be potential general laws which specify kinds of behaviour within specific kinds of contexts. Therefore they are open to test in any archaeological or, more importantly, ethnographic context where such behaviour occurs. We can also see why New Archaeologists claim that the archaeological record remains meaningless unless approached with a particular hypothesis in mind. The hypothesis articulates some aspect of the record back into a past system along a link that another hypothesis might not. It is the multifaceted nature of culture, then, that assures that the meaning of even single artefacts is not exhausted by one hypothesis, especially a hypothesis which only connects it with a single function or, in traditional archaeology, a single set of norms.

Even though archaeologists may spend the bulk of their time excavating, processing and interpreting archaeological materials, their first priority as anthropologists and social scientists is to contribute to an understanding of the second or anthropological level. Therefore, first-level hypotheses should be formulated with the aim of reconstructing or 'bringing into view' features of past cultural systems which would provide a source of evidence relevant to the testing of second-level hypotheses, i.e. hypotheses that account for the cultural system itself. This is the main reason why New Archaeologists claimed that the focus of research in archaeology at all levels must be anthropological questions.

The systemic model of culture is particularly fruitful in this regard, for it assumes that a cultural system serves a pragmatic adaptive function and responds most directly to changing variables of the natural environment. In fact the cultural system as a highly integrated materially based functional system whose purpose is to adapt human beings to their natural environment is a (largely) closed system that remains in a state of stability unless disrupted or impinged upon by changes in the natural environment.[34] Second-level hypotheses (anthropological hypotheses)

---

[33] See, for example, Binford, 'A consideration of archaeological research design'. Other statements of interest here include: 'Explanation begins for the archaeologist when observations made on the archaeological record are linked through laws of cultural or behavioral functioning to past conditions or events ... [thus] ... Hypotheses about cause and effect must be explicitly formulated and tested' (Binford, 'Some comments on historical versus processual archaeology', p. 270), and 'The archaeologist must be continuously engaged in the development of "models" of the past, specifying the conditions which, if true, would accommodate our observations in the present' (Binford, An Archaeological Perspective, p. 334).

[34] See note 42 in chapter 5.

would primarily be propositions linking environmental and cultural variables, as well as variables of the dimensions and subsystems of the culture itself as they covary with each other in adjustment to the externally motivated change. Since first and second-level hypotheses are intimately related, archaeologists must 'continually work back and forth between the contexts of explaining the archaeological record and explaining the past'.[35] Still, for Binford, the primary objective of scientific archaeological investigation remains the formulation and testing of general causal connections in cultural systems, for it is only by pursuing this objective that archaeologists can contribute to the general anthropological understanding of the causal processes and dynamics operative in cultural systems.

According to this account, traditional archaeology had worked itself into an impasse by adopting the normative conception of culture. If norms or ideas are the sole source of variability in cultural systems and the archaeological record, then the very possibility of investigating non-ideational causes is precluded. Furthermore, it implies that in principle no further explanatory account of culture beyond tracing the origin and flow of ideas need nor can be given. That is, it 'ignores the possibility that there are processes selectively operating on a body of ideas or knowledge' itself.[36] Because it does not allow for the possibility that non-ideational factors might account for cultural systems, it does not and cannot approach a truly anthropological second level of investigation. It must remain a sophisticated antiquarianism at best. The systemic model or theory of culture opens up at least the possibility of investigating these non-ideational dimensions and of explaining past cultural systems as well as norms themselves.

Proposing or locating plausible hypotheses which explain relevant empirical facts of the archaeological record or a past cultural system, however, is only an initial step in the testing methodology. As tentative laws, hypotheses are propositional statements which connect two or more theoretical variables.[37] They are universal in the sense that they do not contain proper names, but hold in any situation − past, present or future − where certain conditions prevail. Because they are theoretical statements, they are also empirically empty and must be given an

---

[35] Binford, 'Some Comments on historical versus processual archaeology', p. 271.

[36] Binford, 'Mortuary practices: their study and their potential, in Brown (ed.), 1971, p. 29.

[37] In the technical literature terms like hypothesis, proposition and theorem are differentiated and given specific tasks in theory construction. See, for example, Gibbs, *Sociological Theory Construction*, 1972, pp. 111−225. These differences are ignored here.

empirical interpretation through correspondence or bridging rules if they are to be tested or applied in an explanation. For these reasons, empirical generalizations which summarize the associations of attributes in specific archaeological assemblages are not hypotheses or laws. They might suggest a hypothesis or be an empirical instance of a test, but they are not universal or theoretical.

Ideally, hypotheses are also a part of a theoretical system — a theory — which links them with other law-like statements, provides them with theoretical meaning, places them within a deductive structure, states the nature of the relationships between their variables and so forth. An isolated hypothesis which merely states that 'Wherever and whenever X, then A follows B' lacks this supportive structure and, as a result, tends to remain fuzzy and *ad hoc*. Whether a hypothesis is isolated or not, it must still be linked to facts by correspondence rules if it is to gain empirical content.

Let us now see how this conceptual framework was put to work in several exemplars of early phase New Archaeology. As a challenge, archaeologists attempting to develop and implement the new perspective chose the social dimension of past cultural systems as a test case.[38] This was an area of research, it was claimed, either where traditional archaeological practice feared to tread or, more damaging, with which it was incapable of grappling because of its stultifying conception of science. In addition to demonstrating that virtually all aspects of past cultural systems were accessible to archaeological research, the test was intended to demonstrate why all levels of research must be problem oriented, why the significance of archaeological material is theory dependent and how archaeology can contribute to an understanding of general cultural phenomena.

Two important early studies were provided by Hill and Longacre, students of Binford. Both attempted to use archaeological data to test explanatory hypotheses concerning the descent system and residence pattern of prehistoric pueblo towns in the American Southwest. In each case it was suggested that these dimensions of the social system were responsible for the distinctive patterning of artefacts in pueblo settlements. Using information from ethnographic studies of historic pueblos, they argued for test purposes that the prehistoric pueblos were also matrilineal, had a similar division of labour and allocated space for specific functions in a similar manner. Hypotheses linking these elements

---

[38] Nearly all Binford's early examples are of this sort, as are the exemplars by Longacre, Hill and Deetz. In addition the seminal 1965 Denver Symposium was organized around the problem of investigating social systems through archaeological materials.

of the social system with attributes of material culture were proposed and tested. For example, design elements or material items manufactured by women should be less diverse than male-related items because of continuity in learning context. Both studies also attempted to demonstrate how analogical inferences could be tested to provide operational definitions of terms like storage room and dwelling unit.[39]

Most of Binford's substantive examples during the early phase appear in the context of position papers and therefore remain only sketches of what an explanation or hypothesis within the new perspective should look like. For instance, it was proposed in 'Archaeology as anthropology' (1962) that the decline in production of sophisticated copper tools in the Old Copper complex of the upper Midwest could be explained by shifting causal relationships between variables of the social and material dimensions of the cultural systems involved as adaptations were made to a changing external environment. The general idea is that in hunter−gatherer societies of a certain sort growing populations and decreasing face-to-face interactions necessitate the use of visible markers to designate individuals who have achieved high status. When the environment in the area changed, adaptive changes in social organization made these types of status symbol obsolete. A plausibility argument was made to support the suggestion that the cultural systems involved were of this sort, that the copper tools were produced and used primarily as status markers, and that the suggested changes in the natural environment and social organization actually occurred. Although only a sketch, this example was intended as an illustration of the explanatory richness of the new programme in comparison with the (assumed) sterility of traditional archaeology. It suggested why a wider range of causative factors than just norms must be taken into consideration when explaining archaeological materials, how environmental change might be responsible for cultural change, how a case of technological devolution might be explained and what a regular link between variables of the social and material dimension might look like.[40]

Binford's most extensive early-phase substantive example involved variability among Mousterian artefact assemblages in France.[41] Bordes had applied a stringent normative model in interpreting this variability: artefact assemblages displaying a similar frequency of types were said to have been produced by members of the same tribe; different types of assemblages in the same region indicated the presence of more than one

---

[39] See the references in note 8.
[40] Binford concludes that 'only within a systemic frame of reference could such inclusive explanations be offered' (Binford, 'Archaeology as anthropology', p. 224).
[41] Binford and Binford, 'A preliminary analysis of functional variability'.

tribe. The suggestion made from the perspective of New Archaeology was that this variability could be more fruitfully explained as the debris of members of one cultural system carrying out different tasks in a seasonal schedule. A functional model of the extinct cultural system was constructed and the relationships between specific tasks and fre-quencies of tool use were drawn out within the context of this model.

Some of these and additional examples of early-phase New Ar-chaeology will be considered in more detail in chapter 5.

The foundation arguments and examples of New Archaeology did not escape criticism. For example, historical research was defended as a necessary first step along the way to tackling anthropological goals or as valuable in and of itself, New Archaeologists' conceptions of descent and other features of social systems were shown to be too simple and the scientism of New Archaeology was denounced. However, the new perspective also met with increasing support, and conversions were made from among the ranks of traditional archaeologists. By the end of the early phase, New Archaeology had become a popular and influential research programme in the mainstream of anthropological archaeology.[42]

The Late Phase

In retrospect Binford saw his role in the foundation of New Archaeology as that of a 'Huxley', a 'mouthpiece' who realized a synthesis of the tentative steps taken by the two 'Darwins' of the field – his teachers White and Spaulding at the University of Michigan – towards providing 'some meaning for the endless taxonomies of the archaeologists'.[43] Although he was the founder of the movement, he would, for the most part, leave the actual construction of the programme to others.

A second wave of New Archaeologists accepted the challenge. A New Archaeology 'primer' was published by Patty Jo Watson, Stephen

---

[42] For a defence of historical research, see Sabloff and Willey, 'The collapse of Maya civilization in the Southern Lowlands', 1967, pp. 313–14. Criticisms of a New Archaeology view of descent (as essentially too simple) are contained in the comments section of Binford and Binford, *New Perspectives*, pp. 343–61. See also Allen and Richardson, 'The reconstruction of kinship from archaeological data: the concepts, the methods and the feasibility', 1971, pp. 41–53; although not published until the late phase, this paper had been widely circulated for a number of years. For criticism of New Archaeology as scientistic, see Bayard, 'Science, theory and reality in the "New Archaeology"', 1969, pp. 376–84; for a conversion, Martin, 'The revolution in archaeology', 1971, pp. 1–8; and for not untypical praise, Renfrew, 'Review of David L. Clarke: *Analytical Archaeology* and, Sally R. Binford and Lewis R. Binford (eds.): *New Perspectives in Archeology*', 1969, pp. 241–4.
[43] Binford, *An Archaeological Perspective*, p. 9.

LeBlanc and Charles Redman in 1971, and a series of studies developed central concepts of New Archaeology such as culture, system, model, law, explanation and artefact type in more detail.[44] Perhaps the main trends of the late phase were toward the following:

(1) a more systematic and programmatic expression of earlier intuitions;

(2) increasingly more explicit statements of the underlying logical empiricist presuppositions of the programme;

(3) increasing emphasis on and use of statistical techniques, mathematical modelling, sampling and quantitative approaches in general;

(4) increasing use of the positivist conception of science as a guide for developing an 'explicitly scientific' archaeology;

(5) a shift in emphasis from second-level anthropological explanations to first-level archaeological explanations;

(6) a broadening of the subject matter of archaeology to include the material aspects of all cultural systems;

(7) a greater emphasis on formal research design, prediction and logic;

(8) an increasing diversity in the interpretation of the basic tenets of New Archaeology (as the base of the New Archaeologists itself expanded and became less tightly integrated);

(9) an escalation of 'positivist' rhetoric and values.

Not all these trends pleased Binford, who became quite critical of later developments in 'so-called' New Archaeology.[45] Since late-phase trends are, for the most part, elaborations of earlier presuppositions and will be discussed in some detail in chapter 5, only a few examples are provided here in order to give the flavour of the period.

While the logical empiricist presuppositions in Binford's foundation

---

[44] Watson et al., *Explanation in Archaeology*. The following articles are representative of the mood of the phase: Fritz, 'Archaeological systems', pp. 135−57; Fritz and Plog, 'The nature of archaeological explanation', 1970, pp. 405−12; Hill and Evans, 'A model for classification and typology' LeBlanc, 'Two points of logic concerning data, hypotheses, general laws, and systems', in Redman (ed.), 1973, pp. 199−214; Leone, 'Issues in anthropological archaeology', in Leone (ed.), 1972, pp. 14−27; Schiffer, 'Cultural laws and the reconstruction of past lifeways', pp. 148−57, and 'Archaeology as behavioral science', 1975, pp. 836−48.

[45] Binford, 'General introduction', in Binford (ed.), 1978, p. 9.

statements are obvious, explicit references to positivism and the identification of the stultifying approach adopted by traditional archaeologists as empiricist are rare in the early phase. By the early years of the late phase, however, New Archaeologists had come to regard their programme as 'explicitly scientific', 'positivist' and 'anti-empiricist'. Other archaeologists were urged to adopt a 'positivistic' approach and attitude to meet the challenge of the goals of the new perspective.

Examples of explicit reference to logical empiricist presuppositions appear in a variety of contexts. For instance, Watson, LeBlanc and Redman argue for the 'strongly positivistic (view that) ... the information is there, it is the investigator's task to devise a means to extract it'; that is an objective database exists external to and independent of the investigator.[46] A 'context of discovery' and 'context of confirmation' are sharply distinguished,[47] supporting the view that objective empirical facts exist which can be used to test hypotheses. It is argued that research should be designed to further the factual scientific understanding of cultural phenomena so as to contribute to contemporary society.[48] References to these and other presuppositions of logical empiricism are numerous and explicit. The main point is that New Archaeologists clearly saw themselves as implementing and developing a positivist research programme.

It is worth noting here for later discussion, that as mentioned earlier, some late-phase New Archaeologists even declared themselves to be part of a Kuhnian revolution, insisting that their programme represented a sharp discontinuity with traditional archaeology. New Archaeology was not only a new research programme, it was a revolutionary new paradigm.[49]

---

[46] Watson et al., *Explanation in Archeology*, p. 113.

[47] 'No matter how any given proposition is generated (i.e., whatever its source), it can only be *tested* by deducing test implications and checking them against the data'; 'The two procedures should be kept separate. While their are no particular "rules" with regard to the source of inspiration for a hypothesis, there are commonly accepted rules for testing once a hypothesis has been generated (Hempel 1966)' (Hill, 'The methodological debate in contemporary archaeology: a model', in Clarke (ed.), 1972, p. 95).

[48] The following comment by Fritz and Plog is typical: 'We suspect that unless archaeologists find ways to make their research increasingly relevant to the modern world, the modern world will find itself increasingly capable of getting along without archaeologists' (Fritz and Plog, 'Nature of archaeological explanation', p. 412).

[49] See Meltzer, 'Paradigms and the nature of change in American archaeology', 1979, pp. 644–57, for a review and a strong continuity thesis. For a criticism of Meltzer's continuity thesis, see Wylie, 'Positivism and the New Archaeology', p. 9.

The flavour of late-phase New Archaeology can be savoured in part by reviewing a few of the trends mentioned above.

Understanding the processes of site formation

An explicit goal of New Archaeology was an understanding of those processes that produced the archaeological record. One of the main accomplishments of the late phase was a significant increase in the sophistication of this understanding. Even the casual observer can see that an archaeological site is not really a mirror image of the material system of a society, for a large proportion of the organic remains have decayed and tools are broken and scattered. None the less, archaeologists had still regarded the connections between the two material systems as relatively straightforward.

Michael Schiffer and other late-phase New Archaeologists demonstrated just how complicated these connections might be.[50] Consider these two simple examples. Ceramic vessels in everyday use tend to be broken more frequently and therefore to be over-represented in the archaeological record compared with vessels used only for special occasions; natural processes such as frost upheaval or rodent burrowing may severely disturb the context of artefacts in the ground. Schiffer called the processes responsible for site formation 'formation processes', and initiated a behavioural archaeology whose objective was the formulation and testing of covering laws. Laws were understood to be general statements of the regular relationships that occur between discrete variables. The emphasis upon behaviour, covering laws, the discreteness of variables, the 'givenness' of the database and other core features of this programme was explicitly positivist in conception and consistent with the development of the New Archaeology research programme.

Expanding the subject matter of archaeology

The first wave of New Archaeologists had argued that the universality of laws meant that hypotheses formulated by archaeologists could and should be tested in ethnographic contexts. Deetz later expanded this argument by proposing that the study of 'the material aspects of culture in their behavioral context, regardless of provenence' should be the object of study of archaeologists.[51] This proposal was also consistent with an elaboration of the programme, for, if archaeologists are to contribute to an understanding of general cultural phenomena, their contributions will primarily concern the dimension of material

[50] Schiffer, *Behavioral Archeology*, 1976.
[51] Deetz, 'Archaeology as a social science', 1970, pp. 115–25, quote on p. 122.

culture — a dimension largely ignored by contemporary sociocultural anthropologists.

Gould's call for 'a new kind of anthropology — the anthropology of human residues', — was clearly intended to be an extension of the New Archaeologists' positivist research programme.[52] The objective of the new science of refuse was to 'discover consistent relationships that exist between different kinds of material remains and human behavior', and 'following suggestions by Schiffer ... and others, positing them as ... potential "lawlike propositions".[53] According to Schiffer, such 'lawlike propositions' were 'atemporal, aspatial statement(s) relating two or more operationally defined variables'.[54] Gould argued in addition, however, that the laws in his proposed science should also be regarded as cognitive principles similar to the rules which govern language use. In this late-phase perspective, then, laws are both atemporal aspatial statements of constant conjunction and '"rules" that govern the patterns of human residue behaviour in particular societies'.[55]

Diverging programme objectives

Binford had insisted that the first priority of archaeology must be the testing of first-level anthropological hypotheses, if the discipline was to contribute to the broader understanding of cultural phenomena. Watson, LeBlanc and Redman draw back from this objective in their primer by interpreting testing in archaeology to mean the test of the appropriateness of an explanatory argument itself; that is, it is 'the explanation that is tested and confirmed or not' and not the law or laws contained as premises in the deductive argument.[56] In this view a test only determines whether or not a law (really the set of premises involved in the argument) applies to a specific set of archaeological phenomena. The purpose of testing is not to evaluate the validity of the (proposed) law itself. If accepted, this means that testing only determines whether the initial conditions which define the scope of application of the law include this set of phenomena or not. Archaeology is concerned with the scope of laws, and not with their generation or testing.

The reason given for this shift in disciplinary objectives was that 'the form of the deductive method (must be) preserved'.[57] Hypothesis

---

[52] Gould, 'The anthropology of human residues', 1978, p. 816.
[53] Gould, 'Anthropology of human residues', p. 816.
[54] Schiffer, 'Cultural laws and the reconstruction of past lifeways', p. 148.
[55] Gould, 'Anthropology of human residues', p. 816.
[56] Watson et al., *Explanation in Archeology*, p. 27. For a more extended discussion of this shift, see Wylie, Positivism and the New Archaeology, pp. 250–3.
[57] Watson et al., *Explanation in Archeology*, p. 15.

formulation involved a form of ampliative inductive inference from archaeological materials which should in their view be eliminated from a 'strictly scientific', deductive approach. However, this was not a consistently held position, for they also argued that 'archaeologists are uniquely situated to formulate and test evolutionary laws about human behavior'.[58]

The nature of laws and the form of explanations

The late phase is also characterized by an increasing awareness of the nature of a scientific law and of disputes over the most appropriate form of an explanation. Laws remain statements of constant conjunction between classes of phenomena. However, this statement itself is not a sufficient definition of a law as reconstructed by logical empiricists. A causal law also contains an element of necessity (in the Humean sense) in that 'whenever A, then B'. This criterion is meant to exclude regular but accidental associations and cases where B may also be caused by C and D. For example, every test ever made except the last may have demonstrated a constant conjunction between A and B. The conjunction was accidental, then, and causal. As a result, the discovery of an instance of B in an archaeological site does not necessarily mean that it was caused by A, for it could have been caused by C or D. To establish a law, therefore, a constant conjunction between A and B must be demonstrated. Both Fritz and Plog (1970) and Read and LeBlanc (1978) suggested solutions to this problem.[59]

Hempel and Oppenheim, in their 1948 paper, solved the problem by simply requiring that laws must be true causal connections (see chapter 2). How this is to be established remains a problem. Fritz and Plog suggest that arguments can be made that show why a conjunction should be regarded as causal and not accidental. As an example, they consider the problem of establishing a lawful connection between a type of artefact called a chopper and a type of tool with a chopping function once thought to exist in some palaeolithic societies. To secure this connection archaeologists must demonstrate that the artefact is the residue of and only of past chopping tools. They suggest that replication studies which reproduce the tool, assess its chopping capability, compare use marks with those on the artefacts and so on can provide good if not certain reasons for believing in the reality of such a connection.

---

[58] Watson et al., *Explanation in Archeology*, p. 26.

[59] Fritz and Plog, 'Nature of archaeological explanation', p. 407; Read and LeBlanc, 'Descriptive statements, covering laws, and theories in archaeology, 1978, pp. 307–35. The point is made more explicit in the latter paper.

In the same paper they also present Hempel's covering-law model of explanation more formally than in previous references in New Archaeology and suggest how it might be applied in archaeology. They suggest that there are two interlocking levels of argument ('arguments of relevance') of particular concern to the discipline. The first attempts to establish linkages between attributes of the archaelogical record and attributes of past events, and the second between attributes of these past events and attributes of the antecedent events which 'produced' them. They also suggest that archaeologists will have to rely on 'proto-laws' ('a set of ideas or beliefs which function as laws') until causal laws can be established.[60]

This Hempelian model was rejected by Tuggle, Townsend and Riley, who proposed a paradigm model for a system in which explanation was achieved by creating an abstract calculus which identifies all relevant variables in the system and specifies how they are related. An explanation was a demonstration that the result to be explained was to be expected. Although they claimed that this model does 'not deal with general laws of any sort', it remained, as several commentators have pointed out, a 'positivist' model.[61] A more sophisticated multilayered covering-law model was developed later by Read and LeBlanc.[62]

Practising Archaeology on Logical Empiricist Assumptions

New Archaeologists never produced a systematic statement of the presuppositions of their research programme.[63] None the less, they have

---

[60] Fritz and Plog, 'Nature of archaeological explanation', p. 408. See also Fritz, 'Archaeological systems', and Watson et al., *Explanation in Archeology*, pp. 3–19.

[61] For the arguments involved see Tuggle et al., 'Laws, systems and research designs: a discussion of explanation in archaeology', 1972, pp. 3–12; Tuggle, 'Review of Patty Jo Watson, Steven A. LeBlanc and Charles L. Redman, *Explanation in Archeology: An Explicitly Scientific Approach*', 1972, pp. 564–6; LeBlanc, 'Two Points of logic', and Flannery, 'Archeology with a capital S', in Redman (ed.), 1973, pp. 47–53.

[62] Read and LeBlanc, 'Descriptive statements'.

[63] This should not be construed as a criticism, for few practitioners of any research programme list their presuppositions. In a sense Lakatos's methodology of scientific research programmes is a procedure for exposing the presuppositions of a movement or school of thought in order to assess its implications, consistency, progress and so forth. Watson et al., *Explanation in Archeology*, provide the most programmatic statement, although they diverge in certain important respects from Binford and other New Archaeologists. Wylie, 'Positivism and the New Archaeology', provides the first attempt to state the presuppositions of New Archaeology in a search programme format.

been expressed, if often only by implication, many times. Most succinctly stated the programme is governed by two presuppositions: (1) the primary goal of archaeology is to contribute to the boarder concerns of anthropology as a social science; (2) positivist (logical empiricist) philosophy of science is to serve as a standard and a guide in pursuing this goal. Both presuppositions are equally important in that they serve different but necessary functions in the research programme: the first delimits the area of interest (anthropological concerns) and the sort of research to be undertaken (social scientific); the second indicates the conceptual framework (logical empiricism) to be used in tackling research of this nature in the area of interest delimited, i.e. it provides an ontology and epistemology which define what can be said to exist in an area of interest, what (scientific) knowledge about this area of interest consists of and how this knowledge is to be obtained.

These two presuppositions define the task of New Archaeology. The subject matter of anthropology must be identified, logical empiricist epistemological tools understood and applied, and knowledge claims secured. There are many corollaries to the main presuppositions which guide this process. Among the more important are the following: the goal of science is the establishment of regular law-like connections between empirically observable phenomena; all phenomena belong to a single natural world; the natural world is uniform, lawful and causally interrelated, and therefore the language used to describe it is causal; scientific laws are statements of constant conjunction between classes of empirically observable phenomena that apply to all times and places; theories are networks of universal statements about regular contingent relationships in nature; a statement can only be properly regarded as scientific if it is possible to ascertain its truth or falsity by means of empirical observation; theoretical terms are genuinely scientific only if they can be defined by reference to observables; empirical facts, which are known independently of any theory, guarantee the objectivity of science; there is a distinction between the context of discovery and the context of justification; the basic pattern of scientific explanation is the deductive pattern; the primary function of scientific knowledge is the explanation and prediction of observables; statements are only properly scientific if they have predictive consequences that can be tested; science can provide true descriptions and explanations of an external reality; scientific research must be relevant to broader social concerns; no adequate inductive logic can be constructed; the domain of anthropology is all peoples and their cultures at all times and places. If archaeologists accept these assumptions, then it is clear what their task is: they must search for general laws, operationalize theoretical terms, conduct relevant research and so forth. It is not difficult to provide a more complete and formal definition of the New Archaeology research programme. As an exercise the interested reader might try constructing such a definition using chapter 2 and this chapter as a guide.

Conclusion

Even though the presuppositions and corollaries of New Archaeology were never formalized, it was a surprisingly consistent logical empiricist research programme. The culture concept was given a behavioural interpretation, and terms like archaeological data, model, system, law, process, hypothesis, explanation and cause were redefined in a manner consistent with logical empiricist philosophy of science. There were inconsistencies and a rather loose use of terms at times. However, this is to be expected, especially in the early phase of the development of a programme. There were also disagreements among New Archaeologists over the best or most appropriate interpretation of some features of the programme, such as deductive explanation or hypothetico-deductive testing. Again, however, this is consistent with the development of a programme, as we saw in chapter 2.[64]

New Archaeology was an energetic attempt to transcend the limitations of traditional practice. It promoted a new conception of science that stressed, among other things, the testing of general laws, covering-law explanation and prediction, the construction of mathematico-logical models, quantitative techniques of data manipulation, a behavioural perspective and formal analysis. It even distinguished itself from other approaches by a new name, processual archaeology, or, more grandly, New Archaeology, and by an unusual spelling of archaeology (archeology). In broader perspective it was a mid twentieth-century answer to the old question of the purpose of archaeological research. Although

---

[64] Wylie, 'Positivism and the New Archaeology', p. 12, refers to New Archaeology as a 'coherent research programe'. Although it is relatively easy to construct a formal definition of New Archaeology, a comparison of attempts to complete the exercise in the last paragraph of the text will demonstrate how personal understandings and preferences can result in discrepancies and differences of opinion in such an exercise. Increases in the numbers of New Archaeologists by the late phase, attempts to resolve problems intrinsic to the programme and the absence of a tightly knit school of thought (as existed around Binford in the early phase) make the late-phase loosening of the parameters of New Archaeology understandable. As noted in chapter 2, roughly parallel processes distinguish logical positivism from logical empiricism.

New Archaeologists were never a numerically dominant group in North American archaeology, they did introduce a new conceptual, especially epistemological, research programme. Like positivist philosophy of science itself, it was not without its problems.

5

Problems with New Archaeology

The 'good times are here' message of New Archaeology began to be heard less stridently in the early 1970s. By the middle of the decade, New Archaeology had become a severely degenerating research programme, and by the end of the decade it had fizzled away as a popular reform movement. The revolution had been launched but never consummated, the castle stormed but never taken. No non-trivial general laws of cultural process were ever systematically tested and formally confirmed or falsified; no formal covering-law model explanations were ever presented except in 'they would look like this' illustrative examples; no deductive theory nets were ever formally proposed. In 1978 Binford himself was led to conclude:

> The term 'new archaeology' has been much used. In the absence of progress toward usable theory, there is no new archaeology, only an antitraditional archaeology at best. I look forward to a 'new archaeology,' but what has thus far been presented under the term is an anarchy of uncertainty, optimism, and products of extremely variable quality.[1]

[1] Binford, 'General introduction?' in Binford (ed.), 1977, p. 9. The following paragraph continues:

> In my opinion, the new archaeology was something of a rebellion against what was considered sterile and nonproductive endeavors by archaeologists. Rebellion cannot continue simply for rebellion's sake. The 'stir' created in the 1960's has not resulted in many substantial gains. If we are to benefit from the freedom of nonparadigmatic thought that has perhaps resulted from our little rebellion, such benefits must be in the form of substantial new theory and knowledge of both the archaeological record and the relationship between statics and dynamics — archaeological formation processes (pp. 9–10).

Binford's reference to 'the freedom of non-paradigmatic thought' is a typical positivist assumption, i.e. that the positivist conception of science is objective and not mired in the metaphysical commitments that plague other approaches.

What went wrong? Why did New Archaeology fail to make progress towards 'usable theory'? A large part of the answer is, of course, the fatally flawed nature of its philosophical base. However, there were other problems also, such as a very hazy understanding of logical positivism/empiricism (LP/E) itself and its history. In the first two sections of the chapter we follow the pattern of chapter 3, and review internal and external criticisms. Since the New Archaeology research programme, as an extension of logical empiricism, is also fatally flawed, the greater effort is devoted to the second section. In the third section the legacy of New Archaeology is briefly considered.

Internal Criticism

Internal criticism identifies problems that arise from the presuppositions or from particular interpretations of the presuppositions of a research programme. Both proponents and opponents of a programme may engage in internal criticism, with the former attempting to strengthen it by resolving its problems and the latter determined to show that it fails on its own standards. Whatever their source, the accumulation of internal problems that resist solution is one mark of a degenerating programme. The inability of logical empiricists to defend the ontologically privileged status of the observation language is an example. Another was their failure to provide a procedure for verifying hypotheses through inductive methods. Both these failures contributed to the demise of their programme. New Archaeologists, by adopting logical empiricism as the philosophical base of their programme, inherited these unresolved problems. As a consequence, their programme was already degenerating at its inception in the mid-1960s.

However, the problems of New Archaeology were even more basic than these philosophical disputes. For instance, there seems to have been a genuine lack of familiarity with logical empiricism itself and its history, in practice there was slippage into other programmes such as realism, there was a lack of rigorous pursuit of the full implications of the programme and there were problems in transferring LP/E to archaeology. For whatever reason, logical empiricism remained primarily a conceptual club used to batter traditional archaeology and a methodology to be applied fully some time 'in the future'. Again, for whatever reason, its theoretical and substantive implications were never developed in archaeology to the extent that they were in other disciplines.[2] Indeed, the New Archaeology research programme seems never to have been given much of a chance to grapple with the deep-seated problems of its philosophical base. Since many of the latter problems have already been reviewed in chapter 3, we will concentrate here on the failure of New Archaeologists to develop their programme fully in an internally consistent manner.

Fundamental weaknesses and ambiguities

It may seem boorish to point out that many New Archaeologists lacked an adequate grasp of the implications and criticisms of logical empiricism and of its history, but this failure helps us to understand many features of New Archaeology such as its enthusiastic support of LP/E years after its demise in philosophy and in some other social sciences.

Some inconsistency, of course, should be expected in early-phase New Archaeology when the programme was being shaped and its philosophical base explored. Binford, for example, characterized his own position as involving a 'shift to a consciously deductive philosophy'.[3] Adjustment to the shift may account for his attack on traditional archaeology as 'empiricist' or his mention of processes producing or generating in some sense the archaeological record.[4] Although he seems consistently to equate process with the notion of Humean causality, the use of these terms has non-positivist overtones which open his position to conflicting interpretation.[5] References to culture as 'extrasomatic'

[2] Although uneven, the logical empiricist literature in the other social sciences is prodigious. On the construction of formal theories alone in sociology, see Gibbs, *Sociological Theory Construction*, 1972; Hage, *Techniques and Problems of Theory Construction in Sociology*, 1972; Stinchcombe, *Constructing Social Theories*, 1968; Reynolds, *A Primer in Theory Construction*, 1971; and Mullins, *The Art of Theory: Construction and Use*, 1971.

[3] Binford, 'Archeological perspectives', in Binford and Binford (eds), 1968, p. 18. See also Binford, *An Archaeological Perspective*, 1972, p. 17: 'At the time I wrote "Archaeology as Anthropology," (1962) I had not explored the implication of the epistemological problems associated with the task of explanation. At that time, explanation was intuitively conceived as building models for the functioning of material items of past systems.'

[4] For instance: '. . . archaeologist must proceed by sound scientific method. We begin with observations on the archaeological record, then move to explain the differences and similarities we observe. This means setting forth processual hypotheses that permit us to link archaeological remains to events or conditions in the past which produced them' (Binford, 'Some comments on historical versus processual archaeology', 1969, p. 270), and 'a growing interest in questions dealing with the isolation of . . . mechanisms by which cultural changes are brought about' (Binford, 'A consideration of archaeological research design', 1964, p. 425). In *An Archaeological Perspective*, p. 245, for example, Binford disparagingly refers to traditional archaeology as 'empiricist'. Similar references are made by Hill and Evans, 'A model of classification and typology', in Clarke (ed.), 1972, pp. 231–73. New Archaeology was, of course, empiricist also.

[5] Wylie, 'Positivism and the New Archaeology', 1981, argues that many of Binford's substantive proposals are realist. See also chapter 6 of this book.

and a system as 'more than the sum of its parts' are also poorly explicated and therefore potentially confusing. 'Extrasomatic' seems to be tacked on to the definition of a cultural system to counter the view that culture is internalized inside people in the form of ideas. It was not intended to refer, I assume, to some 'superorganic' metaphysical entity, but rather to stress the sociocultural nature of culture as defined in chapter 4. Similarly, to say that a system is greater than the sum of its parts may simply mean that the pile of parts does not capture the causally integrated nature of a system. The point is that the use of these terms is open to interpretation — that there is room for ambiguity. As a last early-phase example, at times both Hill and Longacre confuse an attempt to explain with the test of a hypothesis.[6]

While this sort of slippage in the use of terms is normal early in the formulation of a programme, inconsistencies of all kinds actually reach their peak in the late phase. For instance, Kuhn's concepts of paradigm and revolution are clearly incompatible with logical empiricism, reference to suggestions by Hanson to vindicate a 'problem-oriented' hypothetico-deductive approach on the Hempelian model is puzzling at best, inclusion of Deetz among New Archaeologists shows a misunderstanding of New Archaeology or of Deetz or of both, references to Hill's work at Broken K Pueblo as an example of hypothesis testing confuse hypotheses and operational definitions, and the suggestion that reasons may be causes and that functional explanations explain are problematic at best in terms of the programme.[7] We should not linger too long over examples like these, but they do make the point that even in the late phase logical empiricism and its context within the philosophy of science were not well understood by many New Archaeologists.

More interesting is the nature of the products of New Archaeology. For instance, few formal law-like statements or theories were ever produced. Instead, explanations and even tests of hypotheses were nearly always presented as hypothetical sketches or incomplete constructions which required systematic restatement and testing. As a result, severe issues of confirmation were never explicitly grappled with, and the task of the New Archaeologist was never clearly laid out.

---

[6] See Hill, *Broken K Pueblo: Prehistoric Social Organization in the American Southwest*, 1970, and Longacre, *Archaeology as Anthropology: A Case Study*, 1970. Although Binford's foundation programme was in my opinion logical empiricist, I do not think that he always adequately grasped the implications of its presuppositions. For Leslie White's brand of techno-economic determinism (and in particular his emphasis on cultural materialism and nomothetic explanation — and his disparagement of 'historical particularism'), see Leslie White, *The Evolution of Culture*, New York: McGraw-Hill 1959.

In addition, the reader was left with the impression that, for example, an explanation sketch, while incomplete, was an adequate form of explanation. Binford's early examples are particularly notorious for an absence of systematic expression. In his 1962 Old Copper example, for instance, it is simply suggested that the distinctive copper tools of the industry can be explained as status symbols in a certain type of society. When this type of society changes, items of this sort lose their symbolic function. A formal restatement might read as follows: in societies of type X, if A (a high status individual), then B (a visible portable status indicator); at level of technological capability M (hunter – gatherer), if environmental features O (features 1, ..., n), then societies of type Z. It would follow deductively that at level of technological capability M, if environmental features O in time t_1 are succeeded by environmental features P in time t_2, then societies of type Z in t_2 will succeed societies of type X in t_1; as a consequence, visible portable high-status indicators will not be present in t_2. By formulating acceptable operational definitions of the predicates ('high-status individual', 'society of type X', and so on) appropriate to the Old Copper case, an archaeologist could determine in principle whether the definitions were satisfied and therefore whether the case was an instance subsumed by these (proposed) laws.

Of course, even if operational definitions are realized in this particular case, the proposed laws in the explanans must be true (or, in everyday science, highly confirmed or corroborated) before the covering-law model can be applied. If the phenomena covered by the laws are only statistically associated or, more loosely, if they only tend to be associated, then something weaker than a sure explanation of this particular case

[7] See Meltzer, 'Paradigms and the nature of change in American archaeology', 1979, pp. 644–57, for a review of references in New Archaeology to Kuhn's concepts. Morgan, in reference to Watson et al.'s mention of 'Kuhn and Hempel in the same breath', remarks that 'it is difficult to imagine two more incompatible views on the nature of science' (Morgan, 'Archaeology and explanation', 1973, pp. 259–76). In this regard Wylie refers to an 'inconsistent and almost indiscriminate use of elements of incompatible philosophical positions' in the same New Archaeology primer (Wylie, 'Positivism and the New Archaeology, p. 224). Binford also labels older views as Kuhnian paradigms (Binford, *An Archaeological Perspective*, pp. 244–5). Deetz, as is clear in *Invitation to Archaeology*, 1967, and *In Small Things Forgotten*, 1977, and in Binford's reaction to his position (see Fitting, 'The structure of historical archaeology and the importance of material things', in Ferguson (ed.), 1977, pp. 64–6), was and remains a realist. It is perhaps not inappropriate to mention that Binford even misspells Hempel's name, when he says that he found 'from a practical science point of view, the arguments of Karl Hempel (*sic*) were the most useful' (Binford, *An Archaeological Perspective*, p. 18).

has been provided.[8] Although rather formal in appearance when stated this way, the task of the archaeologist becomes clearer. By loosely stating his alternative explanation, Binford leaves the reader with the impression that it is fairly straightforward and unproblematic.

As another early-phase example, consider how a theory constructed within the framework of the programme might relate the variables of residence pattern, sex and material culture. Its central and most abstract proposition might simply state that residence patterns in kin-based societies are directly connected to the degree of attribute clustering on sex-related manufactured material items. The rationale of the theory is as follows: in kin-based societies most household items are manufactured by the residence group or family; in some residence systems the members of one sex are exchanged as marriage partners among resident units while those of the other remain within the unit; since the learning context is the resident unit, items manufactured by the spatially stable sex will display less diversity and more intergenerational consistency than those manufactured by the other sex in the unit.

Subsidiary propositions deductively draw out the more specific implications of the general proposition. For instance, in kin-based societies with a matrilocal residence pattern, the same types of female-related manufactured items will be less diverse than types of male-related items. For testing purposes, a still more specific proposition can be derived: in kin-based societies with a matrilocal residence pattern where women manufacture all pottery vessels, the decorative attributes on particular types of vessels in any one residence unit will be tightly clustered and similar. The terms of the proposition remain general, and initial or limiting conditions have been specified. The dictionary of the theory will provide definitions of terms such as kin-based society, matrilocal residence pattern, residence unit and highly clustered.

Testing therefore becomes a matter of providing operational definitions for those terms specific to an archaeological or ethnographic situation, and of specifying what empirical conditions would confirm or falsify the proposition being tested. If the conditions of the operational definitions are fulfilled and the anticipated empirical relationships are demonstrated, the proposition and the theory as a whole gain a degree of

---

[8] On statistical explanations, see Hempel, 'Deductive−nomological vs. statistical explanation', in Feigl and Maxwell (eds), 1962, pp. 98−169, and Salmon and Salmon, 'Alternative models of scientific explanation', 1979, pp. 61−74. In Binford's defence he was merely making the point that social factors may be important in the explanation of the archaeological record. The point remains, however, that he will not be able to prove that he is right on the terms of his own programme on the basis of a loose plausibility argument alone; he eventually has to show that it is an adequate well-supported explanation as well.

confirmation. The theory can gain additional confirmation by testing the same proposition in other situations or by formulating additional low-level propositions that make reference to other female-related items, male-related items, patrilocal residence groups and so forth. In fact a wide range of types of evidence and situations can be brought to bear on the test of the theory. As confirming instances accumulate, confidence in the theory and its propositions as adequate explanations of other archaeological materials will grow. As a social science research goal, researchers would eventually consider integrating the theory with other theories in the never-ending process of building ever more comprehensive social theories.[9]

As a last example of this type consider the problem of interpreting the function of an artefact. As we have seen, some New Archaeologists have argued that this can be accomplished by establishing law-like connections between a specific type of item in a past cultural context and a specific type of artefact in a present-day archaeological context. The explanation of an artefact type as a chopper was an early example. However, several problems immediately arise. For example, it must be demonstrated that only the type of tool called a chopper is causally associated with the type of artefact called a 'chopper'.

One solution to this problem is to argue that the association between the two types of items is not causal but in a sense definitional. That is, the theoretical term 'chopper' refers to a type of stone tool with certain functional and physical attributes which can exist at any time or in any place. The attributes provide a theoretical definition of the tool type as well as a basis for constructing empirical or operational definitions with which to measure their presence among actual pieces of stone. For instance, 'chopping motion' could be operationally defined by a series of measures (an index) such as the presence of vertical striations along the working edge and a certain use-chippage pattern. The research task now becomes one of refining our empirical measures (e.g. through experiment) so that they capture more fully the theoretical meaning of the tool type. Processes which distort the tool through time after discard (deterioration of organic attachments, breakage etc.) would have to be taken into consideration in constructing these measures. But from this perspective, the archaeological record now becomes a pool of empirical data which can be used to determine the presence or absence of certain things or events in past cultural systems. The task has been shifted from one of establishing causal relations to one of providing

---

[9] For one criticism of the adequacy of the underlying assumptions of the theory, see Stanislawski, 'Review of archaeology as anthropology: a case study', 1973, pp. 117–21.

convincing empirical measures.[10] The point of this simple example is that problems within the programme can be identified and solutions proposed that are consistent with its presuppositions. It is not to suggest that these solutions will ultimately be satisfactory.

A more disguised problem occurs in New Archaeology in cases where the relevant variables of a cultural system are reconstructed and an item of the material dimension (or a subsystem itself) is explained by reference to its function within the system. Function simply means its position within a network of Humean causal relations. No sense of 'purpose' or 'activity' is (or can be) intended other than that of constant conjunction (or a statistically known rate of conjunction). Functional explanations of this sort are present even in relatively sophisticated New Archaeology theories (or models as they are generally called).[11] Hempel has argued, however, that this form of explanation is incomplete (from a logical empiricist standpoint) unless the association can be shown to be that of an instance of a universal law; if it is not, then it may just be a fortuitous association.[12] This does not mean that the models are wrong, but just that they remain incomplete – that the "final step" has not been taken. To fulfil the dictates of their programme, archaeologists must show that they can be subsumed under a comprehensive universal theory.

These examples are not intended to imply that relatively sophisticated theories were never formulated in New Archaeology, for they were.[13] They do suggest, however, that the programme itself was not pursued vigorously enough to impinge consistently on the deep-seated problems of logical empiricism. When it was, the flaws in the programme became

[10] In this regard, see Merilee Salmon's review of Levin's, 'On the ascription of function to objects, with special reference to inference in archaeology', 1976, pp. 227–34 (Salmon, 'Ascribing functions to archaeological objects', 1981, pp. 19–26).

[11] Binford, for example, refers to this sort of model of explanation as one he intuitively held at an early stage (Binford, An Archaeological Perspective, p. 17). Although incomplete from a Hempelian position, they are consistent with a realist perspective. This is one reason why Wylie feels justified in referring to a realist undercurrent in New Archaeology.

[12] See, for example, Hempel, 'The logic of functional analysis', in Gross (ed.), 1959, pp. 271–307. Also of interest here is his discussion of explanatory incompleteness in Hempel, Aspects of Scientific Explanation and Other Essays in the Philosophy of Science, 1965, pp. 415–25.

[13] Some of the best recent examples are, perhaps not unsurprisingly, Binford's own studies of archaeological site formation processes, especially natural processes such as the attrition of bone. See, for instance, Binford and Bertram, 'Bone frequencies – and attritional processes', in Binford (ed.), 1977, pp. 77–153, and Binford, 'Willow smoke and dog's tails: hunter – gatherer settlement systems and archaeological site formation', 1980, pp. 1–17.

obvious – at least from the perspective of an external critic. Some of these examples will be considered in the next section.

Perhaps the criticism presented here can be softened by mentioning that these problems have been common to positivist social science in all disciplines. Positivist social science has rarely adhered to a consistent positivist position, which would be, in the study of human beings, both methodologically individualist and behaviourist. Few have been able to avoid treating the cultural or social as *sui generis* in character or referring in some way or other to the subjective states of individuals. Durkheim, for example, although an avowed positivist, insisted on the *sui generis* nature of social facts.[14] In a strict positivist programme these references ought to be ruled out on grounds of non-observability. The result has been a certain tension between an official positivist methodology and the partial adoption of non-behaviourist explanations.

External Criticism

External criticism, as indicated in chapter 3, is criticism of a research programme from the point of view of the presuppositions of other programmes. As such, defenders of the programme may believe that they have adequate reasons for rejecting or refuting this form of criticism. Still, external criticism must be carefully examined, for it may provide sufficient reasons for abandoning a programme. That is, even if the goals of a programme could be achieved, counterarguments may convince large numbers of scholars that these goals are insufficient and that potentially more rewarding alternatives should be explored. Arguments that positivist conceptions of culture, the individual, a system or model, and explanation are inadequate are of this nature.

Still other arguments claim that the proponents of a programme have misconstrued the nature or relevance of other approaches or of a set of procedures. It can be argued that the general conception in New Archaeology of traditional archaeology, historical research, anthropology and measurement are of this nature. While not properly external or internal criticisms in that they are not based on the presuppositions of the programme in question, they still influence the manner in which it is carried out and its justification. Therefore they should also be considered in evaluating a programme.

[14] For a review of this tension in Durkheim's position, see Keat and Urry, *Social Theory as Science*, 1975, pp. 80–7.

Traditional archaeology has been misrepresented

New Archaeologists identified traditional archaeology as empiricist, inductivist and antipositivist. They claimed that this philosophical stance provided no objective empirical grounds for accepting or rejecting interpretative claims, and that it condemned traditional archaeology either to purely descriptive analysis of the archaeological record or to speculative interpretation uncontrolled except by conventional community standards. Limited by its methodology, by its normative view of culture and by its 'univariate' conception of archaeological data, traditional archaeology as a research programme – a disciplinary-wide 'paradigm' – had failed, and had failed badly. Instead of a science, it was merely a sophisticated antiquarianism.

These claims have a certain appeal, for who among modern archaeologists would prefer to be on the side of a curio-collecting antiquarian rather than on the side of a law-forming Newton? When carefully examined, however, they embody a host of contradictions. If traditional archaeologists were strict empiricists, how could they possibly have referred to norms or ideas as causes? How could they possibly have embraced conventionalism? What were 'mental templates' doing in their conceptual repertoire? The answer seems to be that they were not only empiricists but very confused empiricists indeed – or that they were practising some other form of science or scholarship than that attributed to them by New Archaeologists.

Programmatic distortion is a common feature of 'paradigm' disputes, and therefore is understandable in the context of an emerging New Archaeology. Whether this is a correct interpretation of many New Archaeology claims or not, the fact remains that they were, for the most part, distortions, exaggerations or just plain false. More to the point, their simplistic nature glosses over the real problems and accomplishments of an earlier generation of archaeologists.[15] Many traditional archaeologists prided themselves on being tough-minded scientists: they advanced hypotheses and tested them; theories were formulated. Even though the dominant received philosophy of science was inductive and some theoreticians in archaeology or anthropology referred to this perspective as a standard, I know of no systematic study that shows that actual practice between the 1930s and 1960s was different in principle from what it is today. Was traditional archaeology inductive and empiricist? Is contemporary archaeology deductive and positivist?

---

[15] Moberg, 'Review of Lewis R. Binford's *An Archaeological Perspective*, 1972, p. 742, for example, remarks: 'undoubtedly, the picture of archaeology before this movement as entirely dominated by one, "traditionalists" "paradigm" is an over simplification'.

These are contingent questions that must be answered by case studies of actual practice. A good argument can be made, I believe, that the answer to both questions is in the negative. This does not mean that theorists did not attempt to formulate research programmes around these philosophical positions. Binford's deductive testing programme is an example, as is Taylor's inductive contextual model. The claim is that they remained largely at the level of rhetorical polemic and were not incorporated to any significant extent in actual practice. Let us examine some of these arguments in more detail.

A common complaint against traditional archaeology is that its inductive empiricist stance in principle precluded interpretative claims that could be sustained by empirical support.[16] Without ceding that traditional archaeology had adopted this stance, does the inductive method preclude ampliative interpretative claims? On the contrary, it was formulated to secure just such claims. It was thought that, by beginning with certain facts, a conclusion whose truth was not immediately apparent could be revealed through an inductive and supposedly non-hypothetical argument. For instance, by noting that the planets do not twinkle and that objects seen to be steadily shining are near, the certain conclusion that the planets are near can be inductively drawn. Accordingly, the emphasis in research should be on getting the facts first and getting them right, and on moving with assurance from the known to the unknown. The goal of developing such a method dominated theoretical discussions of the scientific method for several hundred years. It can therefore be argued that traditional archaeologists were too timid in carrying out their inductive programme, if that was their programme, but not that ampliative interpretative claims were precluded in principle. There were no limits to knowledge — just the challenge of finding the proper links from the known to the unknown.[17]

Intent on distorting the inductive method, New Archaeologists ignored

[16] See, for example, Hill, 'The methodological debate in contemporary archaeology: a model', in Clarke (ed.), 1972, particularly pp. 67–8, and the discussion of inductive and deductive research strategies in Robert J Sharer and Wendy Ashmore, *Fundamentals of Archaeology*, (Menlo Park; CA: Benjamin/Cummings, 1979, pp. 477–535, especially 'initial inquiry based on the application of inductive reasoning allows the formulation of questions which may then be investigated deductively' (p. 509). For a general review, see Salmon, ' "Deductive" versus "inductive" archaeology', 1976, pp. 376–81.

[17] On the early importance of the inductive method, see Kockelmans (ed.), *Philosophy of Science: The Historical Background*, 1968, and Giere and Westfall (eds), *Foundations of Scientific Method: The Nineteenth Century*, 1973. For a brief review of the shifting goals of science, see McMullin, 'The goals of natural science', 1984, pp. 37–64.

two important points about it: why it failed, and its historical relationship with their own deductive method. Both the inductive and deductive conceptions of science that are being discussed here were expressions of the same stringent empiricist current of philosophical thought. Their differences were largely epistemological. They also enjoyed different periods of popularity, with the deductive method succeeding the inductive following the perceived failure of the latter. Of the two, the inductive method is in principle the more intellectually satisfying, for, in its stepped procedure, there is no recourse to speculation, hypothesis or testing. However, the inductive method was eventually abandoned. No certain procedure was ever found for moving in science from hard facts to hypotheses of a general kind within the guidelines set by empiricist philosophy.[18] The hypothetico-deductive approach also eventually failed for the same reason. The process of testing laws is not a strictly deductive one that secures its conclusions with logical certainty; its success depends upon induction.[19] If the dilemma of induction cannot be resolved, the hypothetico-deductive approach must also fall by the wayside. The New Archaeologists' appeal to deductive logic failed because they were unable to distinguish between the certainty of a valid deductive argument and the truth of the argument (which depends on the truth of the premises as well).

New Archaeology is therefore the heir of traditional archaeology in the same sense that logical empiricism is the heir of earlier inductive conceptions of science. Both archaeologies were positivist and empiricist, and therefore both failed to attain their goals for very similar reasons. There was a conceptual (epistemological) shift in how it was thought that science could best attain its goals but not a 'revolution' in what these goals were or in ontology.

All of this assumes that traditional archaeology was inductive, empiricist and positivist. Was it? There are several lines of argument that lead me to doubt that it ever was. First, the ideal reconstructions of science by philosophers of science are just that − ideal. They are intended to capture what is essential in scientific activity and sometimes, as in the case of positivism, to provide a standard for the more laggardly disciplines. The passing popularity of various forms of positivism, the bitter disputes over the unity of science thesis and the variety of

[18] On the problem of induction, see Popper, *The Logic of Scientific Discovery*, 1968, pp. 27−30. For general reviews and suggested resolutions, see Skyrms, *Choice and Chance: An Introduction to Inductive Logic*, 1966; Brody (ed.), *Readings in the Philosophy of Science*, 1970, pp. 439−510, 571−617; and Salmon, *The Foundations of Scientific Inference*, 1966.
[19] Salmon, *Foundations of Scientific Inference*, pp. 18−21, 108−11.

contending conceptions of science today should make us more than mildly cautious in accepting any of these reconstructions as correct summaries of actual practice. While the theoretical rhetoric of traditional archaeology may have been suffused with references to inductive procedures (after all an inductive positivism was the dominant philosophy of science at the time), this is not sufficient reason to believe that actual practice was any more inductive then contemporary practice is deductive; in fact, the nature of the admonitions of critics at the time (e.g. Kluckhohn and Taylor) suggests that it was not.[20]

Even if we still insist on ascribing a logic of science to traditional archaeology, there seem better choices than empiricism. For instance, while New Archaeology was forced to reject traditional archaeology, a realist conception of science (to be discussed in chapter 7) seems to be able to accommodate the central features of both. From a realist perspective there is a constant interplay in science between taxonomic and processual concerns, i.e. between identifying the significant entities of concern and their explanation. Given this dual interest, the histories of disciplines usually show a similar pattern. Early phases are dominated by data collection and systematization, and, as entities become better known, later phases shift to processual or explanatory studies. An argument can be made that North American archaeology displays this pattern, with the decisive shift in emphasis occurring some time in the late 1950s or early 1960s.

As well as offering a different reconstruction of the history of disciplines, a realist science suggests that a different form of argument characterizes science. A retroductive argument moves back and forth between evidential data and a model of a mechanism which may have produced it to assess goodness of fit. This has often meant the postulation of 'hidden mechanisms' such as genes, molecules, atoms and cultures. Traditional archaeology's use of analogical argument, reference to norms and testing procedures seem to fit this form of argument better than an inductive approach grounded in empiricism. If this view is correct, traditional archaeology becomes empirical but not empiricist, retroductive but not inductive, and scientific but not antiquarian. I hasten to add that I am not claiming that this is an adequate reconstruction, only that it makes the point that there are alternative and possibly better interpretations of traditional archaeology than that offered by New Archaeology.

---

[20] Taylor, *A Study of Archeology*, 1948 (*passim*); Kluckhohn, 'The place of theory in anthropological studies', 1939, pp. 328–44. Kluckhohn suggests, for instance, that anthropologists and archaeologists could improve their scientific procedure by paying attention to Mill's five steps of induction.

Did New Archaeology misrepresent traditional archaeology? I think so. In doing so it deflected attention from a series of questions that should be asked. For instance: How much diversity was there within traditional archaeology? What was the nature of this diversity? What was the 'normative' view of culture? Did the 'radiocarbon decade' of the 1950s hasten the shift to processual interests by establishing taxonomic charts on a firmer basis? Was scepticism and dismay over the potential of archaeology any more rampant among traditional archaeologists than it is today? What were the accomplishments of traditional archaeology? These questions and others like them deserve attention.

Is history merely chronicle?

New Archaeologists consciously adopted the generalizing goals of social science rather than the particularizing goals of history, for the former were regarded as more relevant and of greater intrinsic value.[21] A historian might reply that by putting the past in service to the present in the search for socially relevant laws, archaeologists are promoting an ahistorical point of view, denying the importance of the uniqueness of cultures and ignoring the value of understanding the past on its own terms. Whether archaeology should be a social science or a historical discipline, or whether it can be both, is not of concern here. What is important is New Archaeology's interpretation of history. For many New Archaeologists, history seems to mean the reconstruction of sequences of past events. Indeed, traditional archaeologists are taken to task for not even having achieved this low-level objective.[22] But is this a fair interpretation of the objectives of history, for historians themselves have maintained that, while concerned with the particular, their goal is the interpretation and explanation of that particular without reference to covering laws.[23]

[21] See, for example, Spaulding, 'Archeology in the active voice', in Redman (ed.), 1973, pp. 338−42; Binford, 'Archaeology as anthropology', p. 217, argues that the ultimate aims of archaeology are the explication and explanation of cultural differences and similarities, and not the reconstruction of the past (i.e. culture history), and in An Archaeological Perspective, p. 112, he argues that 'anthropology should be a science'. An early influential statement was Kluckhohn, 'The conceptual structure in Middle American studies, in Hay et al. (eds), 1940, particularly p. 49.

[22] Binford, 'Archeological perspectives', p. 26.

[23] See, for example, the arguments against the relevance of a covering-law model of explanation for historical inquiry in W. H. Dray (ed.), Philosophical Analysis and History, 1966. The literature on the subject is quite large. For recent positions and references, see Graham, Historical Explanation Reconsidered, 1983, and Dray, 'Narrative versus analysis in history', 1985, pp. 125−45. It should be emphasized, however, that Binford's conception of history is consistent with a logical empiricist position; see, for instance, Hempel, 'Reasons and covering laws in historical explanation', in Hook (ed.), 1963, pp. 143−63.

This discrepancy raises several interesting questions. Why was traditional archaeology identified with an obviously stunted and distorted view of history? Was it merely part of the attempt mentioned above to promote one research programme over another? Or, perhaps, was it an attempt to dissociate archaeology from what was perceived to be a less relevant and 'soft' discipline? One possible answer to the latter question is suggested in chapter 6.

Culture and the positivist fallacy

The New Archaeologists' definition of a culture as a materially based 'thing-like' ecosystem with the same ontological status as material reality is consistent with the presuppositions of positivism. However, even if we were able to reconstruct past human behaviour in its entirety, would positivist covering-law explanations of this behaviour be adequate? There are numerous arguments in the social sciences suggesting that the answer must be in the negative. The main charge has been that positivist conceptions of culture and society ignore what is characteristically human about them and therefore fail to explain human behaviour. According to this account human behaviour has two main dimensions: an empirical dimension (the sociocultural system of observable behaviour and its material products) and a non-empirical dimension (consisting of rules and dispositional concepts or human agency). Since the non-empirical dimension structures and gives meaning to the empirical dimension, any explanation of human behaviour which ignores it must be inadequate. The reconstruction of regularities among observables may be a necessary phase in research, but in itself it is insufficient social science.[24] Positivists have replied that their programme does accommodate the notions of both a rule and a human agency. To see why there is widespread dissatisfaction with their reply, we shall briefly examine their notion of what it means to be rule governed. We shall turn our attention to criticism of their notion of human agency in the following subsection.

Briefly stated, positivist social scientists accept the idea that human behaviour is rule governed, i.e. that there are sanctioned expectations or norms to which a person as a social actor fulfilling a set of roles within a network of social relationships is subject. These expectations suggest or even dictate appropriate behaviour, and are 'external' to the individual in that they exist prior to his or her occupancy of a position and are

[24] On the 'positivist fallacy' in definitions of culture, see David Bidney, *Theoretical Anthropology*, New York: Schocken Books, 1967, p. 32. For this criticism of social science in general, see Blumer, 'Sociological analysis and the variable', 1956, pp. 683–90. On the focus in New Archaeology on sociocultural systems, see Keesing, 'Theories of culture', in Siegel (ed.), 1974, pp. 82–3.

learned through the process of socialization.[25] Social patterning occurs because people occupying the same positions act in accordance with similar 'external' rules. What appear to be stable and recurring features of these patterns can be identified and given names, such as social structure, institution and the economic system. A culture, then, has a normative order which is nothing more than a cognitive agreement among a group of people to act in more or less the same way in certain situations.[26]

In this view the task of the social scientist is to discover the regular contingent relationships which exist between rules, behaviour, social relationships and situations (as well as motives or dispositions). Any explanation of observed behaviour must be structured in a deductive form showing that it (the explanandum) was the expected outcome of regular relations between the elements mentioned above and certain precisely stated empirical conditions (the explanans). In order for the covering-law model to apply, each of these elements must be considered to be analytically separable and only contingently related to the others. This means that they must be defined or described independently of each other as well. For example, a behavioural act must have a stable meaning independent of the circumstances of its occurrence, the rules involved or the network of social relationships of which it is a part.[27]

The reconstruction given above is simple, but I believe that it captures what is involved in attempting to make the explanation of social life scientific within the liberalized version of logical empiricism. I also believe that it is sufficient to reveal some of the severe methodological problems of positivist social science. Consider the problem of controlling inferences to rules. Rules are usually inferred from what people say or do. If we are applying the covering-law model of explanation, then we must know that the piece of 'concrete behaviour' to be explained is consistent with only one rule or set of rules. Rawls's distinction between 'action in accord with a rule' and 'action governed by a rule' is useful here.[28] Any behavioural act could be in accord with a number of rules. For instance, the raised hand of a student in a classroom would be in accord with socially established rules for showing a willingness to

---

[25] This notion of the 'externality' of social rules led Durkheim to ascribe a 'thinglike' quality to them. See Keat and Urry, *Social Theory as Science*, p. 86.

[26] See, for example, Wilson, 'Normative and interpretative paradigms in sociology', in Douglas (ed.), 1974, pp. 57–79, and Weider, *Language and Social Reality*, 1974.

[27] See Wilson, 'Normative and interpretative paradigms', and Quine, *Word and Object*, 1960.

[28] Rawls, 'The two concepts of rules', 1955, pp. 3–32. The distinction is owed to Wittgenstein, *Philosophical Investigations*, 1968, paras 199–202.

answer a question, for asking a question or for requesting permission to leave the room, but it would be governed only by the action intended, say asking a question. Even if researchers were able to determine which rule applied, however, the example suggests that there is an aspect to rules which is not entirely separable from behaviour. This is usually expressed by saying that rules are constitutive of behaviour in that they tell us how to do something, such as asking a question in a classroom. If rules like this are suspended, then the behaviour in question ceases to exist. Therefore rules cannot legitimately be seen as independent and external to the behaviour to which they apply, for we cannot claim to be doing something independent of the rule.[29]

Even if we were to grant the separation of rules and behaviour, a severe problem remains for the positivist social scientist, for rules do not have to be followed. We can intentionally break a rule, make a mistake in applying a rule or change a rule. A well-known example is the control of traffic by traffic lights. We could ignore the lights, mistake red for green, not see a red light and so on. What we have here is custom or rule-governed behaviour rather than instances of a causal law. For this reason, customs and their products cannot be the direct objects of positivist laws.[30]

Problems with the positivist view of people

What about dispositional factors, such as beliefs, attitudes, values, intentions, motives, justifications and the like? In some empiricist research programmes, behaviourism for instance, the existence of mental states is not denied, just ignored. Since the 'inner life' of humans is not accessible to observation in the normal way, it cannot be dealt with objectively. As such, it is either irrelevant to the development of an adequate science of human behaviour or possibly relevant but outside the realm of science. Whichever argument is chosen, the conclusion is the same: social science laws should be based on overt and publicly observable behaviour. In this option the language of social science is restricted in effect to an observation language that deals only with outward behaviour.

A more typical and modern approach has been to argue that, while dispositional factors are not directly observable, they can be viewed, like rules, as causal 'external' antecedents linked to social behaviour. Although this option does not preserve the epistemological principle that scientific knowledge links phenomena, it does satisfy the requirement

---

[29] On constitutive rules, see Searle, *Speech Acts*, 1969, pp. 33–42, and Taylor, 'Interpretation and the sciences of man', 1971, pp. 3–51.
[30] See, for example, Brown, *Rules and Laws in Sociology*, 1973.

of a liberalized logical empiricism that there be a 'fact about the matter', for instance, that a proposition containing these terms can be empirically tested and shown to be true or false. In some views dispositional factors are even said to be inner causal mechanisms that produce social behaviour (which is a slide into realism). This motivational aspect of behaviour seems to give it a motive, an explanation in terms of the ends it is designed to meet and so forth. Objective access to aspects of mental life is possible through interviews, questionnaires and other methods. Again like rules, however, dispositional factors must be shown to be analytically separable from behaviour itself and from rules, situations and social relationships if they are to fulfil their role in an explanation or hypothetico-deductive test.

The conception of people in New Archaeology rests uneasily somewhere between these two options. While culture is given a behavioural interpretation, reference is made to an information 'input' or subsystem of norms and reasons. However, the primary causative factors in maintaining or altering a cultural system still remain external and environmental. Just how these empirical and non-empirical dimensions interact is left unanalysed.

Given New Archaeology's suspended position, let us briefly examine some problems for social science if either view is adopted. What is left out of the study of human behaviour if we ignore dispositional factors? What difference does it make if people have reasons, wants, moods and purposes, and assign meanings to their social reality? A variety of answers have been given. For instance, it has been claimed that looking only at what in fact was done does not exhaust what the action was about and what people thought they were doing — in short just what makes it a social act; it misconceives the process of action description.[31] People explain their actions in various ways, have reasons for doing things, offer interpretations of their world and pursue goals. In the traffic light example, drivers could give reasons why they did what they did. Such reasons would involve dispositional factors as well as references to rules, rather than impersonal causal laws. Others argue that an action is only social when a meaning is attributed to it; people are able to interpret and give meaning to their own behaviour and to that of others just because meaning is attached to it.[32] Finally, dispositional factors have explanatory value in that they can be causes of behaviour.[33] People produce social behaviour and therefore have an ability to exert purposive

[31] See Blum and McHugh, 'The social ascription of motive', 1971, pp. 98–109; Wilson, 'Normative and interpretative paradigms'; and Taylor, 'Interpretation and the sciences of man'.
[32] Weber, *The Theory of Social and Economic Organization*, 1964, p. 88.

control over it; for instance, they can deliberately and self-consciously flout role expectations.

In ignoring dispositional factors in their concern to establish regular relations between external stimuli and patterns of behaviour, stringent positivist social scientists foster an implausible deterministic picture of human beings. People are assumed to conform to the given, fixed and deterministic roles that they play; they are the instantiations of the sets of laws interacting in their particular combination of roles. However, this is surely an oversocialized and overdetermined picture of human beings. Viewing people as malleable plastic figures entirely shaped by external changes in the environment is not only partial analysis but one that distorts social life in profound ways.[34] Human beings have a rich and varied mental life that cannot be ignored.

If positivists agree that behaviour cannot be described as a kind of 'brute fact' independent of dispositional factors, then they face many of the same problems involved in the analysis of rule-governed behaviour. There are highly controversial problems of operationalization, it may not be possible to prove that a particular behavioural display is linked with one and only one set of dispositional factors (the 'governed by' and 'in accord with' problem), and dispositional factors and behavioural displays may not be analytically separable, i.e. logically independent.[35]

There are also other subtle problems rooted in the view that the description and explanation of a social action is an interpretative matter for both social actors and social science observers alike. In this view there may be no one-to-one cause-and-effect relationship between a behavioural display and an action description simply because any display

[33] On the failure of positivism to detail the mechanism at the level of meaning which actually causes people to behave in certain ways, see Keat and Urry, *Social Theory as Science*, p. 94. On reasons as causes see, for example, Douglas, *The Social Meaning of Suicide*, 1967, part 2. For an argument that explanation in terms of reasons or meanings is compatible with a causal explanation, see Hart, *The Concept of Law*, 1961, and Ryan, *The Philosophy of the Social Sciences*, 1970, pp. 140–41. The question remains to what extent dispositional factors are to be part of the description of acting: see Austin, *Philosophical Papers*, 1961, pp. 148–9, and Heritage, 'Aspects of the flexibility of language use', 1978, pp. 79–103.

[34] On the positivist model of a person, see Hollis, *Models of Man: Philosophical Thoughts on Social Action*, 1977.

[35] If a description of a behavioural display is not independent of its meaning, i.e. if the display and its meaning are mutually determining in some sense, then neither the hypothetico-deductive method nor the covering-law model of explanation can be used, for they are dependent upon literal descriptions of the predicates involved: see Wilson, 'Normative and interpretative paradigms', p. 75, and Garfinkel, *Studies in Ethnomethodology*, 1967, pp. 76–103. This raises the question, of course, of whether positivist social science can be concerned at all with the causes of action.

is open to different interpretations and different descriptions as an action.[36] Legitimate disagreement over the interpretation of a social act is possible just because such interpretation is deeply sensitive to context, essentially defeasible and always selective, and any particular behavioural display may just be unintended (an accidental shooting, for instance) or ambiguous and signal several kinds of motivated actions, such as anger, desire for prestige, fear and so on.[37] As a result there may be no right interpretation of what a display might mean. Since social reality conceived this way involves possibly conflicting but equally valid interpretative schema, it cannot be studied by the methods associated with positivist social science.[38]

Explanation

If these arguments regarding rules and dispositional factors are accepted, then the covering-law model of explanation is inadequate at least for the social sciences. The strict position in ignoring those features which make social life a distinctly human product also ignores fundamental causes of human behaviour and therefore provides an inadequate explanation of that behaviour. This position has been defended by admitting that these features may indeed be important, but, since they are subjective and not open to observation in the normal way, they remain metaphysical and therefore cannot be part of social science. However, there is no reason why physical behaviour must be regarded as somehow more real than rules and dispositional factors; to insist that this is so is only a presupposition of empiricism and too simple a view of what can be said to exist in the world.[39]

The more liberal position has severe problems not only in establishing that behavioural displays, rules and dispositional factors are logically independent, but also in establishing that there is a necessary one-to-one correspondence between these elements. Positivist social scientists

[36] See, for example, Pitkin, *Wittgenstein and Justice* 1972, p. 167.

[37] Sacks, 'Sociological description', 1963, pp. 1–19; Heritage, 'Aspects of the flexibility of language use'; Garfinkel and Sacks, 'On formal structures of practical actions', in McKinney and Tiryakian (eds), 1970, pp. 337–66. In relation to rules, part of the ambiguity flows from the point that a behavioural display may not completely conform to rule expectations, perhaps because some role expectations are never fully defined, are being reworked and redefined, and so on. This again emphasizes the difference between a rule and a law.

[38] The arguments involved are much more complex than indicated by this brief review. Some of their flavour is evident in the arguments running through Krimmerman, *The Nature and Scope of Social Science: A Critical Anthology*, 1969.

[39] See Bhaskar, *A Realist Theory of Science*, 1978, p. 147, for criticism of this view of reality. Bhaskar refers to this view as a 'prejudice' which is an 'ontological legacy' of empiricism.

have defended their embarrassing inability to produce stringently tested Humean causal laws after decades of trying to the paucity of good measurements, the infancy of the social sciences or the greater complexity of the social world compared with the natural world. They have also resorted to *ceteris paribus* clauses, the idea that their explanations are only sketches to be filled out 'in the fullness of time' or to weaker forms of the deductive model such as statistical or partial formulations.[40]

All this suggests at the very least that the search for Humean causal laws in social science will be unrewarding. Where human agency is involved — when choices can be made, rules broken and so on — constant conjunctions will be, at the most, rare occurrences. The more severe claim is that the idea of a social science based on causal analysis as traditionally defined in positivism is seriously flawed; human behaviour is not a causal variable but a human one predicated on the notion of rules and dispositional factors.[41] Human social life is essentially different from that presupposed by positivist social science and requires a different form of explanation, although not necessarily one that cannot be reconciled with another view of science as we shall see in chapter 7.

Problems with the positivist view of systems

Since culture is regarded as a system in New Archaeology, a brief review of the criticism of a positivist conception of systems in social science is yet another way of showing why the conception of culture, human beings and explanation is inadequate in New Archaeology. For the positivist a system is a closed set of logically independent 'atomic' elements and the lawful or regular relations between them. On the strict view elements are physical phenomena, their attributes are sense data, and relations are empirical connections between them. These connections are only extensional and contingent, and are not necessary;

---

[40] Bhaskar, *A Realist Theory of Science*, p. 141; Hempel, *Aspects of Scientific Explanation*, pp. 376–415. As Scriven puts it, statistical explanations 'spoil the point of the deductive model, for they abandon the hold on the, individual case' (Scriven, 'Truisms as the grounds for historical explanation', in Gardiner (ed.), 1959, p. 465).

[41] The literature on the topic is quite large. See, for example, Winch, *The Idea of a Social Science and Its Relation to Philosophy*, 1958, and 'Understanding a primitive society', 1964, pp. 307–24; MacIntyre, 'The idea of a social science', in Wilson (ed.), 1977, p. 117; Gunnell, *Philosophy, Science, and Political Inquiry*, 1975, p. 193; Pitkin, *Wittgenstein and Justice*, pp. 269–72. The issue is clouded by various uses of the concept of cause. Many of these arguments concern particular actions and not whole classes of actions which are more the concern of social science. Hughes claims that it is clear that it is 'inappropriate to use a purely causal vocabulary as the only one suitable for a social science' (Hughes, *The Philosophy of Social Research*, 1980, p. 91).

in theory any element could be related to any other. A system, then, is no more than the sum of its elements and their regular relations. The only dynamic involved is one of constant or regular connection, and the only way in which a pattern of relations can be changed is in adjustment to an external stimulus which impinges upon the system. The classic example is a solar system whose planetary orbits shift slightly in adjustment to the passage of a very large meteor.

When this model is transferred to the social sciences, elements become people and perhaps other material objects, and relations become the regular empirically observable connections between them. Particular patterns of human behaviour or relationships are regarded as institutions or subsystems such as the economic, the social and the political. Their sum total constitutes the social structure of the system and provides it with a functional unity, for each institution and subsystem is taken to have a function for the system as a whole. A piece of behaviour or a subsystem is explained by showing how it fits within the functionally organized system, and by showing that they are expected or regular occurrences in a system of that type. The system remains constant unless impinged upon by exogenous factors, such as environmental change, disease, introduction of a new technology or food sources or even, paradoxically, in some views by an unusual person or by luck. This is again, although a simple reconstruction, a version of the classical structural − functional model. Its logical empiricist underpinnings should be obvious. They include an atomistic view of elements, a physical conception of action, a mechanical view of causality, the notion that change is caused only by exterior factors and the fundamental assumption that systems are closed.[42]

This behavioural model of social systems is encumbered with problems which have their origin in its logical empiricist base. For instance, the notion that social systems are closed or even properly conceived as wholes with parts which occupy space has been challenged; this is merely a lingering prejudice, it has been claimed, of the classical paradigm of celestial closure and its commitment to spatial metaphor and imagery.[43] However, even if we were to allow closure, it is again a prejudice rooted in the classical paradigm that the trigger for change

---

[42] See, for example, Hill, 'Summary of a Seminar on the Explanation of Prehistoric Organizational Change', 1971, p. 407: 'the source of change is *always* external to the system *in question*'. For other views of systems in New Archaeology, see Plog, 'Systems theory in archaeological research', in Siegel (ed.), 1975, pp. 207−24; Watson et al., *Explanation in Archeology: An Explicitly Scientific Approach*, 1971, pp. 69−87 see also Clarke, *Analytical Archaeology*, 1968; although Clarke's initial discussion of systems has a non-positivist dynamic, his subsequent discussion and treatment of systems are very much of this nature.

must always be extrinsic to the system.[44] The structural organization of an environment, a field or a society is not necessarily passive; it may contain the seeds of internal change in contradictions between and within subsystems, in the structural elaboration of some part of the structure and so on.[45]

Finally, by not moving beyond the level of behavioural modelling, we never gain an understanding of why the relations in the system hold or why they were generated in the first place: there is no mechanism which generates the pattern of the system. An example is the systems model of explanation offered as a counter by Tuggle, Townsend and Riley (1972) to the covering-law model proposed by Fritz and Plog (1970).[46] In this view, a culture is modelled as an abstract calculus of variables related by rules; an explanation is achieved by simulating interactions between variables according to the prescribed rules and showing that the explanandum is to be expected. The task of the archaeologist is to reconstruct all relevant variables and the rules that bind them. However, it still remains a sophisticated behavioural model for, as well as requiring closure, it depends upon constant conjunctions and lacks a mechanism. Although the authors claim that it makes no

---

[43] Bhaskar, *Realist Theory of Science*, 1978, p. 85: 'Societies, people and machines are not collectivities, wholes or aggregates of simpler or smaller constituents .... In the classical world view it was the function of matter to occupy space; so it was natural to assume that all "things" properly so-called were just more or less highly differential aggregates of matter, and so could be viewed either as wholes or parts (or as both).' For a review of postpositivist systems research, see Polkinghorne, *Methodology for the Human Sciences*, 1983, pp. 135–67.

[44] Bhaskar, *A Realist Theory of Science*, 1975, p. 83, refers to 'the old mechanistic prejudice crystallized in Hobbes' dictum that "nothing taketh a beginning from itself" '.

[45] See, for example, Flannery, 'Archeological systems theory and early Mesoamerica', in Meggers (ed.), 1968, pp. 67–87; Maruyama, 'The second cybernetics', 1963, pp. 164–79; Godelier, 'System structure and contradiction in capital', in Blackburn (ed.), 1972. Bhaskar, *Realist Theory of Science*, 1975, p. 85, notes that: 'There is no reason why the properties of wholes should not explain those of their component parts'. For an opposing view, see Phillips, *Holistic Thought in Social Science*, 1976.

[46] Tuggle et al., 'Laws, systems and research designs: a discussion of explanation in archaeology', 1972, pp. 3–12; Fritz and Plog, 'The nature of archaeological explanation', 1970, pp. 405–12. For a more extended criticism of this model, see Wylie, 'Positivism and the New Archaeology', pp. 263–73. Although the statistical relevance model of M. Salmon (1975) and of Salmon and Salmon (1978) avoids the more severe problems of the covering-law model, it can also be considered inadequate for the same reason (M. Salmon, 'Confirmation and explanation in archaeology', 1975, pp. 459–64; Salmon and Salmon, 'Alternative models of scientific explanation').

reference to general laws, it can be accommodated to the covering-law model.[47]

Problems with the positivist conception of measurement

Finally, consider the conception of measurement in positivist social science. Measurement procedures enter the positivist research cycle in many places, including the interpretation of concepts, the summary of data and generalization to empirical universes. An easy trap that has be devilled social science is confusion between empirical generalizations which relate observables to observables and laws which state hypothetical relationships of invariable connection irrespective of whether or not the relationship is actually exemplified.[48] While both might share the same logical form − 'When A, then B', for instance − laws are embedded in theories which show why they hold and support subjunctive and counterfactual conditional statements among other features which distinguish them from empirical generalizations. Thus the once common statistical dragnet search in social science for high correlations between variables might suggest a law, but the process itself cannot produce a law. Since this is an error of social science practice and not of a liberalized logical empiricist position, the problem need not detain us.

Even if we properly distinguish between laws and empirical generalizations, problems remain with the logical empiricist position. For instance, how are less than perfect correlations to be interpreted? In the hypothetico-deductive approach a theory dictates which concepts should be constantly conjoined. A low-level hypothesis is derived, its concepts are given an operational interpretation and statistical tests of association or correlation are applied to determine whether the predicted association is present in the test case or not. However, in nearly every case in social science the empirical associations are less than perfect and leave whether they prove or disprove the hypothesis open to question. Several strategies have been adopted to account for these discrepancies, such as attributing them to measurement error or to interference by unknown intervening variables. In order to save the programme the force of a proposed law is

---

[47] LeBlanc, 'Two points of logic concerning data, hypotheses, general laws, and systems', in Redman (ed.), 1973, pp. 199−214. Hempel would probably argue that it is inadequate precisely because it has not been accommodated to the covering-law model; see Hempel, 'The logic of functional analysis'. In this regard, see also Spaulding, 'Archaeology in the active voice', pp. 344−5.

[48] On this distinction see, for example, Willer and Willer, *Systematic Empiricism*, 1973, and Brown, *Rules and Laws in Sociology*. On the concept law, see Achinstein, *Law and Explanation*, 1971.

usually relaxed by giving it a statistical interpretation or, even looser, by redefining it in tendency terms (e.g. 'When A, then usually B'). The problem with this solution is that the certainty of a scientific prediction or explanation is lost, for nothing follows about any particular case.[49] This is an unacceptable conclusion for an archaeologist intent upon explaining the contents of particular sites, which seems to have been a goal of many New Archaeologists.

The conception of measurement in positivist social science can also be criticized from another perspective. The impression is given that measurement is an empirical matter divorced from theory, that measurement procedures provide an objective and independent test of theories, and that, by applying increasingly more sophisticated procedures, we are able to increase the precision and exactness of our measurements of variables in good scientific fashion. These claims, however, have been sharply challenged. To summarize complex arguments briefly, the main charge is that the rigid dichotomy between measurement and theory cannot be maintained, for measurement is as theory-laden as is observation. In this view, it does not make sense to ask what intensive agriculture, length or even correlation 'really is' outside the context of a theory or, more loosely, a world view.[50]

These comments are not criticisms of measurement itself, but only of the way it has been conceived and put to use in positivist social science. It seems that measurement is not the objective theory-free procedure that many positivists thought it was. Furthermore, less than perfect correlations between measured 'variables' are just one more indication that something is wrong with the positivist conception of causal laws.

Other questions could be raised about the conception in New Archaeology of the anthropology of the 1960s and early 1970s, the positivist roots of the models it borrowed from economics and geography, Binford's contention that cultures adapt and the like. However, if the views already summarized here and in chapter 3 are correct, then it should not be puzzling why New Archaeology quietly fizzled away.

---

[49] On the related problem of inferring from aggregate data to individuals, see Robinson, 'Ecological correlations and the behaviour of individuals', 1950, pp. 351−7, Alker, 'A typology of ecological fallacies', in Dogen and Rokkan (eds), 1969, pp. 69−86, and Lazarsfeld and Menzel, 'On the relation between individual and collective properties', in Etzioni (ed.), 1969 pp. 499−516.

[50] See, for example, Hindess, *Philosophy and Methodology in the Social Sciences*, 1977: Brown, *Rules and Laws in Sociology*, pp. 33−7; Douglas, *The Social Meaning of Suicide*, part 3. Bloor, *Knowledge and Social Imagery*, 1976, even questions the objective nature of deductive logic and mathematical systems.

The Legacy of New Archaeology

Legacies must always be viewed from some vantage point. As a result, what they are thought to be shifts through time. It is only necessary to look at the postpositivist rehabilitation of Vere Gordon Childe for an example. Thus an interesting question whose answer will swing with the mood of archaeology is: What is the legacy of New Archaeology? There are simple answers. At one extreme we might say that it was the first brilliant if stumbling step towards an explicitly scientific archaeology and on the other that it was a horrid example of scientism. However, shallow claims like these are surely intended more for promotional purposes than as an analysis of a legacy. Much more could and should be involved. For convenience, we shall separate what this might be into two categories, an instructive and a substantive.

The value of instructive legacies should not be underestimated. Perhaps the most fundamental of these is an understanding of why New Archaeology was unable to reach its goals. Although a seemingly straightforward undertaking, its resolution is complex, for it must take into account (1) problems with logical empiricism as a philosophy of science, (2) problems arising from transferring an abstract conception of science to the substantive discipline of archaeology[51] and (3) the failure of New Archaeologists to examine its foundations critically or to pursue its logical implications vigorously. However, there are other instructive legacies of New Archaeology, of which the following are just a few: the uses of revisionist history; the manner in which fascination with method and technique − here primarily the statistical and computer manipulation of data − can divert proponents of a programme from its goals, and the relationship of a programme to broader social issues (a topic to be discussed in chapter 7).

The identification of New Archaeology's substantive legacy is an equally complex issue. There has been a shift in emphasis during the last three decades from a concern with the systematization and dating of archaeological materials to a concern with cultural and ecological processes. But was this shift an accomplishment of New Archaeology? Would it have occurred even if the New Archaeology 'revolution' had never taken place? To assume that every substantive contribution in North American archaeology between the early 1960s and the late 1970s is to be attributed to New Archaeology is to assume that the

[51] For this reason, Giddens makes the useful distinction between positivism (the 'views of Comte and ... the leading figures of the Vienna Circle'), positivistic philosophy (views that embody important elements of positivism) and positivistic sociology (views in sociology which have adopted and adapted elements of the first two categories; (Giddens, *Studies in Social and Political Theory*, 1977, pp. 29−30).

discipline was dominated by a single paradigm, which it was not. The substantive contributions of New Archaeology can be identified by reference to a set of criteria established by its own logical empiricist underpinnings. We can ask, then: How many formal theories were proposed and tested? What were the results of hypothetico-deductive tests, covering-law explanations and predictions, and the like? It is answers to questions like these that will establish the substantive contributions of New Archaeology.

Conclusion

If the criticisms summarized here and in chapter 3 are correct, then it begins to look as if New Archaeology is an inadequate research programme for archaeology. There are many reasons why New Archaeology failed. For instance, New Archaeologists failed to examine the historical roots of their programme, to construct theories, to formulate and test laws, and so on. But the most fundamental difficulties of the programme seem to have been rooted in the flawed and misconceived interpretation of science upon which it was based. Even if New Archaeologists had vigorously developed their programme, it was flawed from the very beginning: there is no neutral observation base that provides the bedrock required by the hypothetico-deductive method; forms of knowledge are grounded in social practices, languages and meanings; archaeologists are not passive observers of constant conjunctions in nature, but active agents in the construction of the world they study; an empiricist account of science must fail to provide laws of social life equivalent in scope, certainty and predictive capacity to those offered by natural science; culture cannot effectively be viewed as behaviour alone, and so forth. In hindsight New Archaeologists launched a programme that was impossible to carry to completion.

Having said all this, we should not lose sight of the fact that both New Archaeology and logical empiricism were conceived as projects rather than as final truths. The latter was an attempt to reconstruct the scientific method and the presuppositions upon which it was based; the former was an attempt to apply that conception of science to archaeological materials. Rather than simply dismiss these attempts as flawed and misconceived, we might ask what we can learn from their failure. Are all research programmes flawed? If so, why and what does this tell us about the nature of research? What is the role of the philosophy of science in a substantive discipline like archaeology? Why do we find one conception of research more attractive than another? In the remaining chapters we explore a few possible answers to these questions.

6

Why did New Archaeologists adopt Logical Empiricism?

The early writings of Binford, Longacre and Hill were suggestive examples of the potential of a New Archaeology, but they were hardly conclusive. No laws were produced. No hypothetico-deductive theories were systematically formulated and anchored in hard facts. In the light of this the nearly complete reversal in archaeological orthodoxy that followed must have explanations more complex and subtle than Binford's 'refutations' of earlier views. Similar attempts to apply the insights of the logical empiricist philosophy of science in other disciplines both preceded and closely followed their adoption in North American archaeology. What were the reasons for these similar self-conscious attempts to make the social sciences more rigorous theoretically? Why did these events occur during the late 1950s and in the 1960s? Why has this 'explicitly scientific' approach to the study of the human realm been abandoned by the majority of social scientists for cognitive, critical and other interpretative approaches?

As we shall see, there are no firm answers to these questions at the present time. In fact the very relevance of why-questions like these is heatedly disputed today. In the first section of this chapter we review the latter dispute in order to provide a context for our subsequent suggestions. The relationship between logical empiricism and the social sciences in general is explored in the second section, and in the third section we take a closer look at this relationship as it pertains specifically to North American archaeology.

The basic questions raised in this chapter are important ones in understanding the archaeological enterprise. To be sure, it is necessary for us to become familiar with the tenets of positivist philosophies and to establish how they were adapted by North American archaeologists. But the far more fruitful and reflective task, at least from my point of view as an anthropologist, is to attempt to understand why this perspective was adopted and not another. Was it a 'logical' choice freely made from among available options? Were archaeologists somehow unwittingly manipulated into making the choice by external social trends and deep-rooted cosmologies? Or, perhaps, is the truth somewhere in between these extremes? As in the determinism—free will debate, there may be no simple answer. But becoming aware of and grappling with the problem seems a necessary part of the maturation of the discipline.

The Strong Programme in the Sociology of Knowledge

The *Concise Oxford Dictionary* defines knowledge as, among other things, certain understanding as opposed to opinion. This conception of knowledge is a fairly familiar one: knowledge is what we 'know' to be true. However, as we learned in chapter 3, what knowledge is and the question of its certainty are two separate issues. While postpositivist philosophers of science agree in general that knowledge is what we know about the world, they have challenged its claim to certainty and disagreed over its very nature.[1] What, then, is knowledge? How is it formed? How does it change? What role does it play in science? Although it may seem that these questions wander from our original why-question, it will soon become obvious that the answer to that question depends upon our image of knowledge.

For the positivist, knowledge is linked with the concept of *episteme*, i.e. with the concept of absolute indubitable certainty. Knowledge is not a matter of opinion but of truth. The special quality of science lies in this distinction: science provides statements of fact, while religion and metaphysics, for example, rest upon belief and speculation. This does not imply that scientific theories may not be false. However, it does imply that the process of testing which is at the very core of the logic of science will eventually eliminate those beliefs which are not true. Scientific knowledge itself consists of the sum total of laws or statements of constant conjunctions that form true theories. Since the logic of science eliminates or severely restricts metaphysical speculation and personal bias, 'external' factors, such as changing social values, are only trivially involved in knowledge claims. Scientists are passive recorders of constant conjunctions in nature; they do not construct knowledge or nature in any non-trivial sense. Finally, knowledge is

---

[1] For a review, see Polkinghorne, *Methodology for the Human Sciences*, 1983, pp. 11–13, 93–133.

accumulative and, because it is true, newer theories, if true, necessarily subsume older ones as special cases.[2]

It is this theory of knowledge that postpositivist philosophy of science has attacked. One effect of this attack in the social sciences has been an expansion of the context in which theoretical discourse on the nature of knowledge and its production takes place. Concentration upon the logic of science alone in understanding the production of knowledge is no longer considered sufficient. In fact to think so is to play the positivists' game. Interest has now expanded to include history, sociocultural factors and other 'external' social and psychological factors. Furthermore, ideas are no longer assumed to be passively inherited; they are adopted and adapted for some reason and purpose. Therefore any account of New Archaeology which views it simply as an internal intellectual development within North American archaeology is, from this perspective, necessarily incomplete and possibly misleading.

But what does it mean to say that disciplines are influenced non-trivially by social and even psychological factors? For convenience, we shall separate possible answers into a weak and a strong position. From the perspective of the weak position, external factors may stimulate, retard or influence the direction of research and change in a discipline. Examples of such directive factors include social, technical and economic determinants. We have only to recall how shifting political support and financing have affected archaeology in this century to appreciate the force of the weak position.[3] Many studies also document the impact of changing technology on scientific growth and change. Radiometric dating and computer technology in archaeology are forceful examples. A number of studies have also explored the influence of social factors on the organization of knowledge and its arrangement in curricula.[4] The manner in which archaeology has been parcelled out within universities in North America and Great Britain is a pertinent example. It is probably safe to conclude that the great majority of studies of science

---

[2] See, for example, Nagel, *The Structure of Science*, 1961, p. 353. The idea of theory change via theory reduction was strongly criticized by Feyerabend, 'Explanation, reduction, and empiricism', in Feigl and Maxwell (eds), 1962, pp. 28–97, and 'Problems of empiricism', in Colodny (ed.), 1965, pp. 145–260. For a criticism of Feyerabend's position, see Shapere, 'Meaning and scientific change', in Colodny (ed.), 1966, pp. 41–85. An attempt at a realist resolution of the problem is Smith, *Realism and the Progress of Science*, 1981.

[3] For a general survey of the varied causes of the political support and financing of disciplines, see Ezrahi, 'The political resources of American science', 1971, pp. 117–34.

[4] An example is Bernstein, *Class, Codes and Control*, vol. 1, 1971.

as an enterprise within the past three decades fall within this weak position.[5]

Few sociologists and historians of science today would dispute the importance of external directive influences in the development of science. The pivotal question, of course, is the extent of their importance. Supporters of the strong position contrast merely directive external factors with those which produce changes 'in modes of perception and in interpretation, or in standards of judgment'. According to this position, social and cultural factors are not only capable of causing change in direction or tempo but of constituting the very content of knowledge itself.

A prominent example of this strong position is the 'strong programme in the sociology of knowledge' centred in Edinburgh around a small group of sociologists and historians of science including David Bloor, Barry Barnes and others.[6] The strong programme defines knowledge as whatever people take to be knowledge and notes the wide variety of beliefs that have been taken for granted, invested with authority or even regarded as rather bizarre. The goal of the programme is to build theories to explain such variation. As a result, proponents of the programme characteristically ask questions which seem nonsensical or beside the point to supporters of the orthodox and weak positions. Examples include: How stable is knowledge? What processes go into its creation and maintenance? What are the connections between economic, technical and industrial developments and the content of scientific theories? How

[5] Ben-David, *The Scientist's Role in Society*, 1971; De Gré, *Science as a Social Institution*, 1967; Merton, *Social Theory and Social Structure*, 1964; Stark, *The Sociology of Knowledge*, 1958.

[6] For statements supporting a strong programme, see Barnes, *Scientific Knowledge and Sociological Theory*, 1974; 'On the conventional character of knowledge and cognition', 1981, pp. 303–33, and *T. S. Kuhn and Social Science*, 1982; Bloor, 'Polyhedra and the Abominations of Leviticus', 1978, pp. 245–72, 'The strengths of the strong programme', 1981, pp. 199–213, and 'A sociological theory of objectivity', in Brown (ed.) 1984; Barnes and Bloor, 'Relativism, rationalism and the sociology of knowledge', in Hollis and Lukes (eds), 1982, pp. 21–47; Gellatly, 'Logical necessity and the strong programme for the sociology of knowledge', 1980, pp. 325–39; Shapin, 'History of science and its sociological reconstruction', 1982, pp. 157–211; Manicas and Rosenberg, 'Naturalism, epistemological individualism and "the strong programme" in the sociology of knowledge', 1985, pp. 76–101; Forman, 'Weimar culture, causality and quantum theory, 1918–1927', 1971. Critics of the strong programme seem to include most philosophers of science and more traditional historians of ideas. For typical criticisms, see Brown, 'Bloor's strong program', 1985, pp. 199–224, Buchdahl, 'Editorial response to David Bloor', 1982, pp. 299–304, and Flew, 'A strong programme for the sociology of belief', 1982, pp. 365–85. Also of interest is Radford, 'Must knowledge – or "Knowledge" – be socially constructed?', 1985, pp. 15–33.

do features of culture influence both the creation and evaluation of scientific theories and findings?[7]

The most extensive explication of the theses of the strong programme is David Bloor's *Knowledge and Social Imagery* (1976). According to Bloor, the programme rests on four principles which guide or regulate the construction of theories which explain how knowledge is acquired.[8] These are the principles of (1) causality, (2) impartiality, (3) symmetry and (4) reflexivity.

The first principle defines the subject matter of the sociology of knowledge: the sociology of knowledge should be concerned with the conditions or causes which bring about belief or states of knowledge. Although these conditions are widely varied and just what they are in a particular situation is a contingent matter, it is felt that they are most interestingly cultural and social. The second principle states that all beliefs must be explained regardless of whether they are considered true or false, rational or irrational, successful or unsuccessful. The third principle claims that the same style of explanation should be used for all these beliefs. Finally, the fourth principle states that the strong programme applies to itself; unlike positivism, its presuppositions are open to examination and susceptible to explanation in terms of social and cultural forces.

The strong programme clearly opposes the orthodox conviction of the autonomy of knowledge, i.e. the conviction that those beliefs which are taken to be true, rational, scientific or objective require no explanation except, perhaps, the requirements of reasonableness, logic and rationality. From the perspective of the orthodox position, only those beliefs that are false or irrational have to be explained by sociological or psychological examination.[9] In contrast, the strong programme adopts a position of methodological relativism in which all beliefs are to be explained in the same way regardless of how they are evaluated by a community of scholars. This is not to deny that there may be an absolute truth about an external reality, only to take an agnostic stance towards truth. We might even say that the concept of the autonomy of knowledge has hindered our understanding of what science as a cognitive inquiry is about, i.e. constructing, warranting and criticizing knowledge claims.

---

[7] Bloor, *Knowledge and Social Imagery*, 1976, pp. 3–4.

[8] Bloor, *Knowledge and Social Imagery*, p. 4.

[9] A favourite example of proponents of the strong programme is Lakatos's concept of a scientific research programme, according to which an internal history is selfsufficient and autonomous. In Lakatos's system an external history would, apparently, take care of the irrational residue. See Lakatos, 'History of science and its rational reconstruction', in Buck and Cohen (eds), 1971, p. 9, and Bloor, *Knowledge and Social Imagery*, p. 7.

Once the blinkers imposed by positivism and the orthodox model of knowledge have been removed, it seems a reasonable, if not essential, step to inquire into the knowledge-generation, knowledge-definition and knowledge-legitimization processes associated with the knowledge claims of particular disciplines. Without prejudging the outcome, there seems no reason why we should not focus on the extent to which knowledge claims are socially contingent constructions whose warrant is negotiated and renegotiated over time in specific historical contexts. Instead of defending the proposition that beliefs which are true clearly require no special comment, we should ask what these claims of special privilege are all about. At the very least, we would expect anthropologists to be suspicious of the posture that knowledge — our knowledge — is an autonomous realm immune from anthropological analysis.

Bloor argues that the very fact that science is treated as sacred and that its knowledge claims are 'mystified' and protected from 'pollution' is a sign of its social character.[10] In his words, 'in thinking about knowledge we are thinking about society and society tends to be perceived as sacred; we think about knowledge by manipulating images of society'.[11] We use an 'ideology' to grasp the complexity of society (as we use images to grasp the complexity of nature), and it is these ideologies which control and structure our theories of knowledge. From this perspective, then, 'the character of the epistemological debate (concerning the nature of knowledge) cannot be fully understood without seeing it as an expression of deep ideological concerns in our culture'.[12] Even the tone and style of this debate are an important part of its overall message. Every model of knowledge presupposes a picture of society, people and nature, and these pictures are provided in part by images and metaphors. Familiar examples are Kuhn's holistic and authoritarian 'community of practitioners', Popper's anti-authoritarian and atomistic image of Darwinian struggle and the logical empiricists' image of an oversocialized and overdetermined behaviourist individual.[13]

But to accept all this is not to admit that knowledge in the strong

[10] Bloor, *Knowledge and Social Imagery*, pp. 43−51. The concepts sacred, mystified and polluted are intended to convey the meaning given to them by Douglas, *Purity and Danger*, 1966, and *Natural Symbols: Explorations in Cosmology*, 1970.

[11] Bloor, *Knowledge and Social Imagery*, p. 45.

[12] Bloor, *Knowledge and Social Imagery*, p. 48. Consider also Bhaskar's comment, '. . . if one wishes to understand the mode of production and reproduction of philosophical systems they must be conceived as social objects' (Bhaskar, *The Possibility of Naturalism*, 1979, p. 156).

[13] For a discussion of the underlying social metaphors in Kuhn and Popper, see Bloor, *Knowledge and Social Imagery*, pp. 51−65, and 'Popper's mystification of objective knowledge', 1974, pp. 65−76.

programme is a free creation unconnected with people's experiences. The external world may be hidden from us by our cultural heritage in some important sense, but it is not unknowable, for cultural variation is 'imposed on a stratum of biologically stable sensory capacities'.[14] The following series of quotes capture, I believe, Bloor's position: 'To work with the assumption that the faculty of perception is relatively stable is no retreat from the view that its deliverances do not, and cannot, in themselves, constitute knowledge'; '[an] experience may bring about change [in belief] but does not uniquely determine the state of belief'; 'simply observing the world does not allow men to agree about what is the true account that is to be given' of it'.[15] In other words, since experiences do not determine beliefs, our beliefs or knowledge claims are constituted in part in some non-trivial sense by our social and cultural contexts. As we shall see, this position is not inconsistent with the realist conception of science examined in chapter 7.

The orthodox, weak and strong positions offer a variety of possible explanations as to why New Archaeologists adopted a positivist philosophy. To adopt the orthodox position immediately, however, is to commit the positivist mistake of deciding the issue by fiat rather than by empirical investigation. By adopting the strong programme, at least initially, we subsume what is interesting in the weak position and ask questions of greater risk. If repeated investigations fail to support the strong position, then a retreat to one of the other positions will appear warranted.

Among the questions that the strong programme prompts are the following: What is the relationship between positivism and traditions of ideological dispute? To what extent has the waxing and waning in popularity of positivism been a response to external social or economic factors? What social models and metaphors underlie positivism and what purpose do they serve? To what use is the concept of absolute indubitable truth put in positivist science? What does the tone and style of positivist rhetoric imply? Are there connections between gross social structures, cosmologies and models of knowledge? What was the adoption of logical empiricism by the social sciences a response to? How was it used in various disciplines? Why did some disciplines lag behind others in their acceptance and ultimate rejection of logical empiricism? Is this pattern evidence of a more deep-seated regularity in the acceptance and rejection of other research programmes (say narrow empiricism or structuralism)? Why was logical empiricism most strongly embraced in the United States? Why was Germany so strongly resistant to positivism

---

[14] Bloor, *Knowledge and Social Imagery*, p. 26.
[15] Bloor, *Knowledge and Social Imagery*, pp. 26–7.

and its naturalist pretentions? Why have empirical approaches had a special attractiveness to Anglo-American philosophers?

Before we review answers to a few of these questions, it may be instructive to reflect for a moment on Bloor's fourth principle. Why has there been a 'sociological turn' in assessing models of knowledge in the last several decades? One partial answer may be that 'crisis' periods in academia seem associated with a sense of intellectual crisis in society in general.[16] The result, as in the last decade of the nineteenth century and in the late 1920s and early 1930s, has been methodological dispute, two features of which have been an attack on positivism and controversy concerning the place of cultural values in science. The late 1960s and early 1970s may well have been such a period.

Sociology of knowledge in the two decades following the Second World War was primarily focused on the role of science in democratic societies, on the social settings in which it flourished and on the social responsibility of scientists. Much of this interest can be seen as a response to the role of science in the War, especially in the construction and use of the atom bomb. In hindsight many of these studies appear to praise science and scientists, and to view the 'scientific method' as a paradigm of rational, even reasonable, thought. However, this positive appraisal of the sciences broke down with the crisis of criticism that swept Europe and North America in the last part of the 1960s.[17] New studies moved to explore science, especially natural science, as a social institution with links to cognitive and broader social structures. In general these studies have looked at science as an explicitly value-laden cultural phenomenon and its knowledge as socially produced.[18] If the pattern of response in earlier crisis periods has some substance, it is no surprise that this strong position emerged when it did, and that

---

[16] As Bottomore remarks: 'Very often a crisis in sociology seems to be associated with, and perhaps reflect, a sense of intellectual crisis in the wider sphere of cultural and political life; and this may well have been the case during the 1960s' (Bottomore, 'Competing paradigms in macrosociology', 1975, pp. 191−202, particularly p. 191). For a discussion of cycles in American history that closely approximate the dates given here, see Schlesinger, *The Cycles of American History*, 1986, pp. 23−48. For a different interpretation of the cyclical relation between positivism and realism, see Mackenzie, *Behaviourism and the Limits of Scientific Method*, 1977, pp. 43−53.

[17] As well as criticisms of science and its uses, the value of rationality and the existence of objectivity were also sharply criticized. See, for instance, Nowotny and Rose (eds), 'Counter movements in the sciences', 1979; Roszak, *The Making of a Counter Culture*, 1969, and *Where the Wasteland Ends*, 1972. See also Hollis and Lukes (eds), *Rationality and Relativism*, 1982.

[18] Whitley (ed.), *Social Process of Scientific Development*, 1974; Mendelsohn et al. (eds), *The Social Production of Scientific Knowledge*, *Sociology of the Sciences*, 1977.

the sociological analysis of models of knowledge now seem not only appropriate but even necessary.

It is difficult to say at the present time whether this account is too simple and glib. It may be wrong. Certainly the specific links between crises, models of knowledge and their investigation, and the motivation of individual scholars have not been worked out. However, it does warrant consideration, and it may eventually help us understand the present appeal of the strong programme.

Positivism and American Social Science

The early roots and social history of positivism have been examined in some detail.[19] For example, Hawthorn has remarked on the close ties of Comte's positivism with the religious ideals of the time and its strong reformist intent. An extensive social history of positivism has been provided by Kolakowski, who noted its close correlation with certain social trends, including the association of logical positivism/empiricism (LP/E) with a scientistic defense of threatened civilization.[20]

American social science has been largely positivist from the 1930s to the 1960s,[21] although the roots extend much earlier and the general tradition of thought continues to have staunch supporters today. The early phase in this development, as mentioned in chapter 5, was largely indebted to inductive forms. Even though Feigl, Hempel, Carnap and other logical empiricists fled to the United States with the approach of the Second World War, their deductive programme only began to seep into the social sciences in the 1950s and early 1960s. George Homans is a good example of a social scientist who explicitly adopted 'Hempelian' positivism, which he then used to criticize sociological orthodoxy.[22] The programme, or at least some version of it, played a similar role at about the same time in geography,[23] political science,[24] sociology[25] and

[19] For the early roots and social history of positivism, see Kolakowski, *The Alienation of Reason*, 1968, and Hawthorn, *Enlightenment and Despair: A History of Sociology*, 1976.

[20] The title, for instance, of ch. 8 in Kolakowski's *The Alienation of Reason*, is 'Logical empiricism: a scientific defense of threatened civilization'.

[21] See, for example, Keat and Urry, *Social Theory as Science*, 1975, p. 90.

[22] Homans, 'Bringing men back in', 1964, pp. 809−18.

[23] The references in notes 23−8 are intended to be introductory only, for the literature is quite vast. One of the first books to argue for logical empiricist presuppositions in geography was Haggett, *Locational Analysis in Human Geography*, 1965; see also Harvey, *Explanation in Geography*, 1969. For a review, see Gregory, *Ideology, Science and Human Geography*, 1978. For early roots, see Bunge, 'Fred K. Schaefer and the science of geography', 1968.

economics.[26] Similar forceful statements were made in history[27] and even ecology.[28]

At least in its early phase, the programme seems to have played this polemical role throughout the social sciences. This seems to suggest that the repudiation of 'traditional' social science was performing some kind of unacknowledged function. Consider, for example, the numerous disparaging reviews of traditional research that appear at this time and the overall reactionary style of their delivery. In most cases they appear to be more credo than sound review of an opposing research programme. The distinct impression is given that the new programme must be adopted if the discipline in question is ever to become 'more than narration and chronicle'. A surprising similarity in other phrases is also apparent when these statements are compared. For instance, the discipline (whichever it is) must 'become relevant', 'search for laws', 'be more scientific', 'test hypotheses', and so on.

The style of the debate, the general absence of convincing (as opposed to suggestive) counterexamples and the overall attempt to make traditional practice appear vulgar should not be surprising. As Kuhn has remarked in reference to quarrels resulting from different sets of presuppositions, such disputes 'can never be settled by logic and experiment alone', and 'the competition between paradigms is not the sort of battle that can be resolved by proofs'.[29] As a result, their defence normally quickly falls back on dogma or slides off in an infinite regress of justification. It is for this reason that research programmes are perhaps best regarded as heuristic tools of the trade, rather than statements of 'absolute, indubitable truth'.[30]

Two reasons are often given for the adoption of positivist philosophy and formalism in general in the social sciences. The first views it as part of a broader tendency, especially marked in the United States, to turn

[24] For a review, see Gunnell, *Philosophy, Science and Political Inquiry*, 1975.

[25] Keat and Urry, *Social Theory as Science*; Friedricks, *A Sociology of Sociology*, 1970; Halfpenny, *Positivism and Sociology*, 1982; Tudor, *Beyond Empiricism: Philosophy of Science in Sociology*, 1982; Gouldner, *The Coming Crisis of Western Sociology*, 1971. See also Benton, *Philosophical Foundations of the Three Sociologies*, 1977.

[26] Caldwell, *Beyond Positivism: Economic Methodology in the Twentieth Century*, 1982; and 'Positivist philosophy of science and the methodology of economics', 1980, pp. 53–76.

[27] For an introduction, see W. H. Dray (ed.), *Philosophical Analysis and History*, 1966.

[28] Fretwell, 'The impact of Robert MacArthur on ecology', 1975, pp. 1–13.

[29] Kuhn, *The Structure of Scientific Revolutions*, 1970, pp. 94, 148.

[30] Freundlich, 'Methodologies of science as tools for historical research', 1980, pp. 257–66.

the 'soft' disciplines into simulacrums of the 'hard' sciences in the hope of sharing their prestige.[31] The second points to the relative immaturity of the social sciences. From this view, the adoption of positivist philosophy was a conscious attempt to gain a foothold on maturity by assimilating as rapidly as possible the core of scientific theory as it was being revealed by logical empiricists at the time. Hempel, Feigl and other logical empiricists were vigorous proselytizers of their programme, and their prose, especially that of Hempel, was remarkably clear and lucid. Furthermore, although their programme was being vigorously attacked from within philosophy, much of their most popular writings intended for a general audience appeared around the early 1960s. For example, Hempel's *Aspects of Scientific Explanation and Other Essays in the Philosophy of Science* appeared in 1965 and his more programmatic *Philosophy of Natural Science* in 1966; Ernest Nagel's *The Structure of Science* was published in 1961, and John Kemeny's *A Philosopher Looks at Science* in 1959. The style of these works was authoritative and assured, leaving no doubt that this was what science was about.

But are these sufficient reasons for the widespread adoption of the logical empiricists' programme by the social sciences in the early 1960s? Why should there be a perception of lack of prestige? Why was there a broad tendency toward formalism, abstractness and the subsumption of the individual to systems of one kind or another just at that time? Why did logical empiricism itself find the United States such a receptive setting for its development? On the immaturity issue even a cursory review of the sources shows that the social sciences are not exactly new; anthropology, sociology, history, psychology, geography and political science have been with us in some form or other for a long time. What accounts, then, for the apparent (or the appearance of) immaturity in the social sciences? Since it is a characteristic of the history of the sciences that the roots and pattern of development of disciplines can be read in different ways depending upon the research programme adopted, it is not inappropriate to ask whose criterion of maturity we should accept and why.

There are a variety of tacks that one can choose from in trying to answer questions like these while remaining true to the intent of the strong programme. That chosen here views positivism, like formalism in general and some forms of empiricism, as an expression of a deep-seated ideological tradition in western thought that has waxed and

---

[31] This argument has been applied to philosophy itself to account for its slide into formality and abstractness. See Mitchell and Rosen (eds), *The Need for Interpretation: Contemporary Conceptions of the Philosopher's Task*, 1983, pp. 1–10 (reference is on p. 1).

waned in popularity in response, presumably, to broader social and cultural affairs. The roots of this tradition go back at least to the Greeks and much further back than either positivism or formalism themselves. The tradition has been contrasted with and has often clashed with a Romantic ideology or a Romantic style of thought.[32] After reviewing characteristic features of these two styles of thought, we shall consider some of the reasons given for the shift in popularity from one to the other within the last half century.

The methodological style of Enlightenment thought is associated with a cluster of typical features which stress reason, calculation, simplicity and intelligibility. Among these features are (1) a preference for universal theories, (2) a call for abstract deductivism, (3) a strong prescriptive or moralizing flavour, (4) a marked tendency to divide and distinguish, (5) a stress on the individual rather than on a whole whose properties are greater than the sum of those of its elements and which confers group properties in some sense upon those elements, and (6) the view that the development of knowledge systems (philosophies for example) must be understood in the context of humanity's transition from a mythical to a secular world view.

When in ascendancy this typical grouping of ideas seems to have a predictable affect on scientific practice. For instance, particular historical events and historical variation are routinely treated as unimportant in themselves. What counts is the capture of what is timeless and universal in scientific laws and theories. Particular events, cases of individual behaviour and social phenomena provide the raw material for the formulation of these laws and theories, and are in return illuminated by showing that they are instances of (or covered by) these laws and theories. There is an understandable concern, then, with discovering the general principles of reasoning, abstract deductive or inductive procedures, and other timeless and universal attributes of what we would now call scientific thought and method.

Since effort is being directed at the discovery of a 'suprahuman' universal standard of rational thought (rather than, say, the values of a scientific community or authoritative dogma), there is an accompanying concern for clarity and codification, and a stance of anti-authoritarianism and, often, critical individualism. The gradual emergence of this standard, as mentioned above, is usually regarded as marking the passage from a mythical to a rational, secular and logical style of thought.[33]

---

[32] Bloor, *Knowledge and Social Imagery*, 1976, pp. 54–70; Mitchell and Rosen, *Need for Interpretation*, pp. 2–10. Bloor's interpretation is followed here. My account is necessarily brief and abstract, but it does have the virtue of showing what may be at issue.

[33] Comte's developmental sequence is a classic example.

With the rise of science, secular knowledge itself has come to be epitomized in the natural sciences and so, for the Enlightenment thinker, the social or human sciences (and philosophy) must become cognate with the natural sciences.

The tendency to divide and distinguish in Enlightenment thought has been expressed in the form of many dichotomies which are by now familiar. Examples are the division of values from facts, facts from theories, the rational from the real, the scientific from commonsense, the true from the merely believed and the mythical (*mythos*) from the rational and logical (*logos*). In fact clarification in Enlightenment thought has most often meant boundary drawing and partitioning. This tendency can be seen at work in Enlightenment social theory in the treatment of the structural divisions of society. These divisions are most often broken down into an atomized homogeneity, as in classical structural-functionalism, and the view that the social whole is the mere sum of its parts. The tendency is also expressed in the Enlightenment interpretation of the relationship between societies and people: societies are collections of individuals whose essential nature and individuality are not bound up with society. Societies become, for example, 'superorganic' systems of one kind or another with laws and a movement of their own.

The methodological style of Romantic thought is associated with a quite different cluster of ideas. These stress complexity, wholeness, tradition and concrete individuality. Among these features are (1) a concern for real and concrete action rather than abstract principles and thought, (2) a tendency to see values as blended and united with facts, (3) a call for the study of complex wholes whose properties are greater than the sum of those of its elements, (4) a stress on context, (5) the theme of social cohesion and (6) a tendency to assimilite and unite, not to keep apart.

This typical grouping of ideas seems to have a predictable affect on scientific practice when Romantic ideology is in the ascendancy. For example, the stress on concrete individuality in place of abstract deductive procedures is expressed in a style of analysis in social theory which pays close attention to the social and cultural conditions of different times and places, i.e. analysis that emphasizes 'historical' rather than 'scientific' principles or 'particularizing' rather than 'generalizing' procedures. Indeed, the particular case is thought of as more real than abstract principles, and the concrete and historical as more important than the universal and timeless. As a result, the Romantic tends to pay closer attention to the particularity of features of a society which the Enlightenment thinker would tend to ignore in the search for general principles. These beliefs lead to the replacement of attempts to grasp universal principles of reason and to 'explain' by attempts to 'understand' an individual's point of view or the attributes of a particular society — to a concern in general for the concrete historical individual (whether person or society) rather than the abstract universal principles of reason.

The tendency to assimilate and unite rather than distinguish and divide is reflected in Romantic thought in an emphasis on the social whole, for example, and on holism. A central idea running through this tradition is the view that social wholes have properties of a special kind that require and justify independent study. Since the part or element of a system is in a state of intimate unity with the whole, it can only be fully understood in context. Therefore research must concentrate on overall patterns and their laws, and the Enlightenment's atomistic and individualistic emphasis must be rejected as well as the myth of simplicity. The stress must be on the true complexity of the world, on the wholeness of societies and on the concrete historical individual. This tendency also accounts in part for the Romantic's typical strategy of unifying by analogy as compared with the Enlightenment strategy of distinguishing by naming.

The Romantic thinker is also more likely to see values as blended and united with facts, and to give tradition, dogma and judgement a more prominent role in science. Romantic ideology seems more aware — or at least more willing to admit — that science rests on the collective values of its practitioners, i.e. on prejudice or bias in some sense rather than on some 'suprahuman' objective standard.[34] Since decisions must be made, they are best made and adhered to in an explicit fashion. This position has tended to promote the theme of social cohesion as opposed to the Enlightenment stance of critical individualism. However, it has also tended to promote conservatism and overtones of collectivist paternalist authoritarianism, and to foster a more closed intellectual state within the Romantic tradition. This tendency results in a style of debate quite different from the often devisive individualistic democracy of Enlightenment ideology. Indeed, the Romantic thinker tends to see the desire to criticize, to discuss and to argue about everything as a misfortune.[35]

Finally, the Romantic style of thought commonly views the ideology of atomism as having inhuman mechanical overtones. To embrace a classical structural-functionalism which neglects human agency, for instance, is to lose sight of what it most poignantly means to be

---

[34] For an example, see Kuhn's discussion of the role of dogma in science in Kuhn, *Structure of Scientific Revolutions*, and 'The function of dogma in scientific research', in Crombie (ed.) 1963, pp. 347–69.

[35] Bloor, *Knowledge and Social Imagery*, pp. 58–9.

human.[36] This view is often associated with a 'reactionary scorn' for discovery as such compared with a deeper understanding of a society, people, person, style, tradition or any other historical individual in the broadest sense.

The clash between the Enlightenment and Romantic styles of thought has elicited characteristic responses within universities for more than a century. When Romantic ideology is in the ascendancy, there is a strong commitment, for instance, to intellectual programmes and the 'social' sciences tend to be viewed as the 'human' sciences. This commitment is usually accompanied by a realignment in the links between disciplines, an intellectual milieu and discourse that are strongly resistant to naturalist pretensions and materialism (or at least to what are conceived of as narrow material concerns), a view of science as a process of ever-deeper multifaceted understanding rather than as a linear progressive accumulation of knowledge, and a reward system that favours research or other activities that promote the personal worth of the individual. In research itself there is a tendency to rely more upon reasoned judgement than the evidence of the senses, and a preference for holistic intellectual systems to illuminate the particular.

When Enlightenment ideology is in the ascendancy, in contrast, there is an equally strong commitment to the 'naturalization' of the 'soft' sciences and even the humanities, and the 'human' sciences tend to be viewed as 'social' sciences.[37] This commitment is normally accompanied by a realignment of the interdisciplinary links of the social sciences towards the natural sciences or what are perceived to be the 'hard' sciences, an intellectual milieu and discourse that champion the unity of science, the logic of method, reliance on the senses or observable 'fact' and the eschewal of speculative thinking, a commitment to relevance and technical progress, and a reward system that favours discovery and the accumulation of knowledge. The researcher places value on empirical approaches, abstractness, formality and objectivity, and is

---

[36] A stress in archaeology on artefacts to the exclusion of the 'Indian behind the artefact' is a comparable stance. In North American archaeology this particular Romantic attribute has been expressed, for example, by Robert L. Hall: 'Until as archaeologists we develop more than a little empathy for the prehistoric Indians we presume to understand, prehistory may never be more than what it has become, the soulless artifact of a dehumanized science' (Hall, 'Ghosts, water barriers, corn, and sacred enclosures in the Eastern Woodlands', 1976, pp. 360–4, quotation on p. 363).

[37] The terms social and human reflect, of course, the emphasis in the two styles of thought on the relative importance of the objective impersonal system on the one hand and human agency or the importance of the person on the other. See Polkinghorne, *Methodology for the Human Sciences*, pp. 283–9, for a discussion.

resigned to the often hard-fought and gradual piecing together of fragments of experience. Instead of regarding science as a process of more deeply understanding in some sense what is already known, there is a tendency to see it as a linear homogeneous process whose goal is accumulation of knowledge about an objective reality. There are instructive similarities between the individualistic character of Enlightenment thinking and its model of 'behaviourist man' and classical economics and its model of a rational calculating 'economic man'.

The rhetoric of these two styles of thought is an interesting and instructive cue to their underlying value systems. It is perhaps a truism of anthropology that in examining the rhetoric of a social ideology special attention must be paid to the tone in which it is presented, for tone is an important part of the message of an ideology. This tone is in part provided by the key metaphors and images which are used, and in part by the manner in which the ideology is defended. The universal presence of simplified and simplifying ideologies in human societies is not difficult to understand for a variety of reasons. For example, the limitations of our sense apparatus alone make it impossible to grasp directly the complexity of the world. In addition, simply observing the world does not in itself ensure that people will agree about what they are seeing.

Social ideologies are relatively simple and compelling abstractions from the totality of a society's experience which provide frameworks for understanding and behaviour. They mirror deep-seated and under-lying notions about society, nature and human beings, and are tacitly expressed in metaphors and images. As an ideology becomes deeply ensconced in a cultural tradition, it becomes a social archetype whose metaphors and images come to seem natural and, indeed, are almost impossible to avoid, for thinking and talking presuppose a picture of the world.

From this perspective, the Enlightenment and Romantic styles of thought are social archetypes in our western intellectual tradition with contending images of society, nature and human beings. This divergence in value systems is especially noticeable in the quite different meanings that are attached to shared words, for, as Bloor puts it, 'the meaning of words is inseparably charged with associations and connotations' related to ideologies.[38] We have briefly indicated the different meanings that Enlightenment and Romantic thinkers attach to words like system, knowledge, fact and even science. Bloor uses the word 'culture' and its

[38] Bloor, *Knowledge and Social Imagery*, p. 66.

metaphors to illustrate the embeddedness of these two sets of values in western thought.[39] Since culture is a key word in anthropology, his argument is worth summarizing.

Romantic thinkers tend to provide the word with connotations of tradition, completeness and oneness, or spirituality of some form. A variety of familiar images and metaphors have sprung from this interpretation. For instance, a non-anthropological image, not unsurprisingly, is that of the cultured person. A popular early metaphor was organic growth or, more generally, organism. According to Bloor, 'the metaphor of organic growth with its agricultural overtones made it appropriate for use by the tradition of thought which lamented the growth of industrialism and individualism'. In contrast, Enlightenment thinkers tend to interpret the word as something 'which shatters tradition and stands for change and activity', as something 'which undermines unity, suggesting division, conflict, struggle and atomisation' and as something that must be opposed to spirituality, suggesting instead 'worldliness, practicality, utility, money'. For Bloor, 'this is the image of industrialization, the ethics of capitalism, and *laissez-faire* competition'. The varying uses of the concepts today remain in part, then, a residue of the roles they played in this clash of social values.

It is also instructive, that thinkers in both traditions have tended in their characteristic ways to fend off unwelcome investigation of society by what have been interpreted as 'mystification' procedures. The Enlightenment strategy has been to 'endow logic and rationality with an asocial and, indeed, transcendent objectivity'.[40] The concepts of 'absolute, indubitable truth' and 'the expert' have also played important roles in this strategy. The Romantic strategy has been to stress society's 'complexity, its irrational and incalculable aspects, its tacit, hidden and inexpressible features'. In the view of Mary Douglas, Bloor and others, protective postures like these are a sure sign that a society, whether scientific or otherwise, is being perceived as sacred.[41]

Thus, on this reading, social ideologies provide images, ideals, norms and other intellectual conventions which are taken for granted. These conventions are deeply embedded within a society's world view as a prejudice or bias. Anthropology and comparative philosophy demonstrate that different cultures pay allegiance to different ideological stereotypes. In a complex society like ours, we can expect differences of

[39] Bloor, *Knowledge and Social Imagery*, p. 66. The string of quotes in the following paragraph is from this page.

[40] Bloor, *Knowledge and Social Imagery*, p. 67. The remaining quotes in this paragraph are also from this page.

[41] An instructive example for anthropologists is Luntley, 'Understanding anthropologists', 1982, pp. 199–216.

opinion and a divergence of values into competing ideologies which are widely diffused throughout our culture.

The interesting question remains the relationship between social ideologies and models of knowledge. Bloor and others have suggested that it is an intimate one[42] — that, indeed, a model of knowledge is a projection of a social ideology. However, to say this is not to make an outrageous claim. It is only to claim that in thinking about knowledge and science we cannot help but think with the very ideas with which we have to think — that to project images of society in our models of knowledge is an entirely natural consequence of the way we live and think. This is why, according to Bloor, models of knowledge have the character of 'transfigured conceptions of society'. Constrained by practical utility and open to challenge, methodologies, acceptable results and theories remain social conventions. It is a social norm that the opinion of the 'native' be valued, that knowledge be linked to experience, that creative risk taking be praised and so on.

It is a hypothesis, then, that social ideologies control and structure models of knowledge — that there is an indissoluble union between society and knowledge. If the hypothesis is correct, then the 'character of an epistemological debate cannot be fully understood without seeing it as an expression of deep ideological concerns in our culture'.[43] At the very least, it allows us to predict that the popularity of models of knowledge in the social sciences will rise and fall with the varying fortunes of their corresponding ideology. From this view, the Enlightenment and Romantic stereotypes are two basic responses to war and to other upheavals in our society.[44] Either one or the other is appealed to 'to explain the experiences which men are undergoing and to justify the positions in which they find themselves or the actions they are inclined to take'.[45] Given the nature of the dialectical relationship between these

[42] Bloor, *Knowledge and Social Imagery*, p. 65. See also, for example, the discussions in Scharfstein et al., *Philosophy East/Philosophy West: A Critical Comparison of Indian, Chinese, Islamic, and European Philosophy*, 1978.

[43] Bloor, in *Knowledge and Social Imagery*, p. 66, concludes: 'What may feel to the philosopher like a pure analysis of … concepts or a pure appeal to their meaning, or the mere drawing out of their logical entailments, will, in reality, be a rehearsal of the accumulated experiences of our epoch'. He clarifies this statement by adding that it is social ideologies and not the totality of social experiences which control and structure models of knowledge (p. 46). To illustrate his point he contrasts the methodological stances of a Romantic and an Enlightenment thinker, of Kuhn and Popper (pp. 51–3, 61–5). While Kuhn stresses social solidarity, holism, authority, conservatism and the images of the 'community of practitioners' and 'revolution', Popper is anti-authoritarian and atomistic, and promotes the images of Darwinian 'struggle' and individual risk taking.

stereotypes, we should anticipate that when one is established, it will be attacked by some variant of the concepts of the other.[46]

This picture of two contending models of knowledge fluctuating in predictable popularity with the rise and fall of their corresponding social ideologies is attractive because of its simplicity, ease of exposition and naturalist overtones. However, it is deceptively simple and too abstract. Real-life fluctuations are more complex, multifaceted and messy. At best, it only alerts us to what may be at issue in an epistemological

---

[44] Although extremely interesting and informative, a consideration of why one stereotype or the other has been more strongly expressed in some western countries than in others cannot be included for reasons of space. However, it is worth noting that Germany has continued to foster an intellectual milieu strongly resistant to positivism and to naturalist pretensions. The Frankfurt School is a modern example. Discourse in German Idealism is marked by a profound antinaturalism and anti-materialism. France has also tended to be more rationalist than empiricist. In contrast, Anglo-America has tended to find empirical approaches, whether logical empiricist or other empirical perspectives, especially attractive. Some authors have seen these preferences as responses to broader social concerns. For instance, German Idealism is connected with the illumination of a purely German *Geist* which intellectuals 'saw emerging out of the precariously reunited fragments of the Empire', and Anglo-American empirical preferences with emerging capitalism and *laissez-faire* (Mitchell and Rosen (ed.), *The Need for Interpretation*, Preface). Here methodologies are seen as intellectual justifications for precisely those conditions which favoured capitalism, free trade etc. If true, this raises interesting questions about the kind of social order which seeks the justification of one type of ideology or another. See Douglas, *Natural Symbols*, for an attempt to grapple with this problem from an anthropological perspective.

[45] Bloor, *Knowledge and Social Imagery*, pp. 57–8.

[46] Bloor, *Knowledge and Social Imagery*, suggests that this explains why the student 'radicals' of the 1960s 'could subscribe to Kuhn's conception of science despite its profoundly conservative overtones' (p. 69). In addition, he concludes that the differential tendency to treat knowledge as sacred and beyond the reach of scientific study can be explained by the strength of the variable of perceived threat (pp. 68–70). Thus a threatened established group will tend to mystify their values and standards, while those 'complacently unthreatened' will treat them as naturalistic, i.e. as open to investigation. This is a primary reason why the tone and style of an epistemological debate should be attended to: it gives warning of the nature of the clash. It should also be apparent that the connection between individuals and the ideas of a model of knowledge is not necessarily simple, for individuals may have sudden conversions or gradually shift from one position to another creating a kaleidoscopic mixture of fundamentally inconsistent notions along the way (which, ironically, is often labelled 'progress'). An example of this 'aren't we making wonderful progress' approach is Couclelis and Golledge, 'Analytical research, positivism, and behavioral geography', 1983, pp. 331–9. A similar mood is expressed by Watson, 'Archaeological interpretation, 1985', in Meltzer et al. (eds), 1986, pp. 439–57. As Bloor, *Knowledge and Social Imagery*, p. 65, notes, 'it is the mechanics of the transfer of the ideas from the one realm to the other which remains to be examined'.

debate and provides us with a schema with which to approach the sociological (or anthropological) analysis of the debate.

With this in mind, how, then, can we account for the rapid spread of logical empiricism in the social sciences in the early to mid-1960s? My hypothesis is that it was part of a broad response, especially marked among the 'softer' social sciences, to faltering financial support and a perceived loss of prestige near the tail-end of the boom years of the late 1940s to the 1970s.[47] The primary, though largely unconscious, purpose of this response was to 'mystify' entrenched positivist social science by making it appear 'harder', i.e. more 'scientific', objective, rigorous, relevant and so forth.

Although the distinguishable movements within this response have different sources, they are interrelated and in keeping with Enlightenment thinking.[48] These include the quantitative revolution, the 'behavioural' turn and the adoption of logical empiricism itself. Logical empiricism, let us remember, was not a break with earlier tradition, but a newer and more sophisticated extension of it. Its sophisticated form, abstract nature, claim of objectivity and relatively clear set of procedures and standards made it an ideal weapon of defence. The quantitative revolution also gave the impression that 'variables' were being manipulated in a perfectly objective and sophisticated manner.

The ire of this defence was initially turned against traditional practice and older practitioners for several reasons. First, although the threat was perceived as real enough, its source remained vague and difficult to pinpoint. Who specifically, for example, could be blamed for the widespread faltering of financial support that marked the tail-end of the boom years? Worse, perhaps the apparent loss of prestige was not undeserved. Second, it seems a normal response in situations like these to blame older practitioners for failing 'properly' to develop and protect the general epistemological position, whether Enlightenment or Romantic. A group that feels complacently unthreatened, as social scientists did during the peak decades of the boom years, tends to treat its values and standards as naturalistic, i.e. as in need of exposition but not of special defence. When the heirs of the group feel threatened and begin to mystify their model of knowledge, the absence of similar

---

[47] The multifaceted nature of this response can be represented by the 'panic' that followed the launching of Sputnik in 1957 and the resulting spur given to the pursuit of science in the US (if only in granting institutions).

[48] To claim that the primary purpose of this response was to protect positivist social science by mystification is not to say that no substantive contributions resulted from this response.

earlier efforts tends to be viewed as a serious defect. The active imagin-ation can easily supply the details of this scenario.

It is particularly revealing that many of the changes that occurred at this time prevailed in the face of telling criticism, often seem poorly understood and resulted for the most part in very meagre results. For instance, the controversy surrounding logical empiricism was largely ignored, and only a handful of seriously intended deductive theories, laws and explanations conforming to the covering-law model were actually attempted. For the most part, the tenets of logical empiricism were used as rhetoric in statement papers and theory books, where illustrative examples could be given without any pretence that they were being seriously proposed or, at least, where their proof was not of immediate concern.[49] In a parallel manner very damaging criticism of various aspects of the use of statistical inference was ignored.[50] In addition, it did not seem to matter at all that some of the conceptual systems being used, such as structural functionalism and logical empiri-cism, were inconsistent with each other.[51] Equally telling, it did not seem to matter that clearly defined concepts in the logical empiricist program, such as hypothesis, theory and explanation, were ignored in most substantive research for other definitions.

It has become common practice in recent years to attribute the failure to fulfil the logical empiricists' research programme to its lack of adequate development,[52] and to explain inconsistencies in the use of concepts or the adoption of conceptual systems as lapses in judgement. However, to say this is to play the positivist game by evaluating research complexes within disciplines solely in terms of rational, objective and internal criteria. From the perspective advanced here, it is to miss the point that it did not particularly matter whether there were internal

[49] The books on theory construction in sociology mentioned in chapter 5, n. 2, are of this nature.

[50] See, for example, Morrison and Henkel (eds), *The Significance Test Controversy*, 1970 and Danziger, 'The methodological imperative in psychology', 1985, pp. 1–13.

[51] Although inconsistent, they still remained compatible with the Enlightenment style of thought. Structural functionalism, for instance, continued to play a key role in archaeology and other social sciences despite criticism by logical empiricists. See Hempel, 'The logic of functional analysis', Gross (ed.), 1959, pp. 271–307, and Bottomore, 'Competing paradigms in macrosociology', pp. 191–202.

[52] Sabloff, 'When the rhetoric fades: a brief appraisal of intellectual trends in American archaeology during the past two decades', 1981, p. 2, argues that New Archaeology failed because of the lack of a rigorous methodology. In contrast, the logical empiricist base of New Archaeology was undoubtedly the most complete and sophisticated philosophy of science yet developed. Lack of 'rigour' of its methodological base was hardly the reason for the failure of New Archaeology.

inconsistencies or that the substantive results actually flowing from that philosophy were meagre indeed. Logical empiricism, like the quantitative revolution, was primarily a weapon. Although proponents of the philosophy may have deeply believed that it would produce the results promised, its main role was not to produce substantive internal results, but to protect externally, i.e. to mystify.

Even though contending positions in the Romantic style of thought were always present, they remained largely muted in the social sciences until the Vietnam War, which was itself, perhaps, a sign of decreasing US power, and the resulting chaos that shook the universities in the last half of the 1960s. The clash between social images and metaphors was particularly severe at this time, but by the mid-1970s Romantic ideology with its corresponding model of knowledge had clearly become dominant.[53] Enlightenment ideology and positivism had been vanquished once and for all, or so it has been argued, and a sweeping conversion made to Romantic ideology and a postpositivist philosophy of science.

Logical Empiricism and New Archaeology

Why did New Archaeologists adopt a logical empiricist philosophy of science? There is little to add to what has already been said except to draw the obvious conclusion. A concerted effort to 'harden' the social sciences was made in the early 1960s. The quantitative revolution was an integral part of this process, as was the adoption of neoclassical economic models, logical empiricist philosophy of science, the 'behavioural' turn and other conceptual tools solidly within the Enlightenment style of thought. This 'revolution' has usually been interpreted as a spirited break with traditional practice and a major, if ultimately flawed, step forward to a new era in the social sciences.

---

[53] As we saw in chapter 3, there are severe problems with logical empiricism as a philosophy of science. However, as Bernstein demonstrates, there seem to be problems with every major contemporary research programme (Bernstein, *The Restructuring of Social and Political Theory*, 1976). Once problems are identified, a patching-up process normally occurs; the shift from logical positivism to logical empiricism is an example. If there is any substance to this argument, then the 'refutation' of a tradition of research may well herald a shift in popularity of styles of thought, even though proponents of the abandoned style may rightly feel that their position is hardly lost. For instance, most positivists I know remain firmly convinced that, despite the shortcomings of their position, it remains sounder in principle than that of Romantic epistemological systems such as 'interpretative' social science.

The argument developed here interprets this process quite differently. Rather than a step forward to a new era, the attempt to 'harden' the social sciences is seen as an urgent defensive measure to protect entrenched positive social science from real and perceived threats. Public unrest in the late 1960s accelerated the force of these threats and, by the early 1970s, a multitude of new conceptual tools equally firmly planted within the Romantic style of thought had gained widespread ascendancy. Rather than a sharp break with tradition, the early 1960s effort is seen as a last gasp in the attempt to preserve an entrenched position through mystification. What is particularly telling in this process is the almost simultaneous adoption of a similar constellation of ideas throughout the social sciences, the often fuzzy understanding of these ideas as a system of thought and of what was involved in their substantive application, and the meagre substantive contributions made within the confines of logical empiricism itself. However, these are not surprising outcomes of a mystification process. This scenario was also played out in North American archaeology. Logical empiricism was just one of a number of conceptual tools adopted and adapted at this time.

Is this account true? Is it what really happened? Maybe. And then maybe not. Whatever the answer may be, it is a contingent matter. It must be capable of testing. To decide a priori that the history of archaeology, or for that matter any other discipline, can be understood primarily in terms of internal intellectual developments is to decide the issue before it is joined. It is to refuse to apply the standards of science and, more specifically, anthropology to ourselves and our own institutions. The suggestion made here — that the adoption of logical empiricism in the early 1960s throughout the social sciences was primarily a reaction to real and perceived threats to an entrenched Enlightenment position — is a hypothesis. It may seem bizarre and even far-fetched to some readers, although it is no different in nature from other attempts in anthropology to explain social change. But then these are changes, for the most part, in foreign cultures — and no raw Anglo-American nerve has been touched.

Conclusion

The internalist—externalist dispute raises difficult if fascinating questions for historians and methodologists of archaeology and of the social sciences in general. Of course, few persons consider research programmes or models of knowledge as only disembodied intellectual abstractions or as the epiphenomenal and implicitly mechanical responses of social conditions. Therefore the questions that we might want to raise about

New Archaeology include both internal questions about what happened where and when, what was and what was not meant, what the social conventions of expression were and so forth, and external questions about the sociocultural context of the discipline and its practitioners and the nature of its change.

The sheer empirical complexity of the provenance of ideas involved is staggering when viewed in this manner. Here we can only say that the role of external factors in the origin and development of New Archaeology remains unresolved. In so far as they operated, they influenced an ongoing and progressive intellectual tradition. Given the general lack of interest in archaeology in external factors that might have significantly shaped archaeological practice, we cannot expect answers to emerge for a considerable time. In fact it might prove difficult to resolve some of the key issues as we work our way back through the history of archaeology. The social context of the origins of archaeology and the ethos within which important figures worked, for example, may prove difficult to reconstruct. Even so, confidence in the necessity of some kind of external history can be retained. There are many questions which cannot be treated by an internal account and which demand systematic explanation. For instance, the social and temporal distribution of the seminal figures in New Archaeology cannot be fully explained by that history. Neither can the parallel and widespread changes occurring in several branches of knowledge at the same time be left as a matter of coincidence, especially when some of these changes occurred against an internal context of knowledge and technique which had changed little or caused little dissatisfaction for a considerable preceding period – even despite sharp internal criticism, such as that by W. W. Taylor and others in archaeology. Such a constellation of changes invites explanation in terms of some large-scale shift in social ideology. However, to say all this is still only a contribution to the posing of questions about the nature of the discipline. The hard work of rolling up our sleeves and getting down to closely examined case studies has hardly begun.

7

Realist Archaeology

If we accept the weight of the arguments in chapters 3 and 5, then positivism and positivist archaeology, at least in their standard forms, are seriously flawed if not discredited research programmes. The essential question, of course, is whether viable options exist. Must we patch up positivism or are there alternatives to positivist science and archaeology?

A variety of conceptions of the human sciences that achieved some prominence with the demise in popularity of positivism were mentioned in chapter 3. Here we concentrate upon one of these, realism, for a variety of reasons: (1) it is an influential contemporary perspective in the philosophy of science, (2) it has deep roots in both anthropology and archaeology, and (3) it seems particularly appropriate as a heuristic for contemporary archaeology, in that (4) it balances a recent fascination with meaning and symbols with mundane observational data.[1] Given the subject matter of archaeology and its special interpretative difficulties,

---

[1] Manicas and Secord, 'Implications for psychology of the new philosophy of science', 1983, p. 394, refer to 'the emergence of an extraordinary convergence on a new heuristic for the human sciences' in Anglo-American social science 'firmly grounded in the fundamental insights of' realism. Harré, *The Principles of Scientific Thinking*, 1970, p. 15, considers at least some of the insights of transcendental realism to comprise a Copernican revolution in the philosophy of science. On its balance between a focus on observational data and a focus on symbols, Runciman, *A Treatise on Social Theory 1: The Methodology of Social Theory*, 1983, p. 144, remarks that it steers a course 'between the Scylla of positivistic empiricism and the Charybdis of phenomenological hermeneutics'. Several reviewers of this book in manuscript form have misinterpreted my intention in this chapter. I am neither promoting realism nor supporting the Harré–Bhaskar realist perspective but merely illustrating one alternative to logical empiricism. Indeed, as is implied in chapter 6, it is as important to ask why realist philosophies of science supplanted logical empiricism in the 1960s and 1970s, as it is to ask why logical empiricism was the standard interpretation of science in previous decades.

this attempt warrants, in my opinion, close scrutiny. Besides demonstrating that a non-positivist archaeology is possible, the chapter will, I believe, further illustrate the implications and inadequacies of both inductive and deductive forms of positivist archaeology.

The realist theory of science is briefly introduced in the first section, and a few of its implications as a heuristic for the social sciences are explored in the second. Its potential as a conceptual framework for archaeology is discussed in the final section.

The Realist Theory of Science

Like other postpositivist conceptions of the social and natural sciences, the realist theory of science has only fully emerged as a constructive alternative to the standard positivist view within the last three decades.[2] Although they are antagonistic and their origins lie in different philosophical traditions, realism and positivism share a number of features in common. These include the following assumptions: (1) science is an objective, rational inquiry; (2) science aims at true explanatory and predictive knowledge of an external reality; (3) scientific theories must

[2] The earliest anticipations of modern realism are to be found in the various writings of Michael Scriven (1956, 1962, 1964) and Michael Polanyi (1964, 1967), and in Bunge (1959), Bohm (1957) and Toulmin (1953, 1961): Scriven, 'A possible distinction between traditional scientific disciplines and the study of human behaviour', in Feigl and Scriven (eds), 1956, pp. 330–9; 'Explanations, predictions, and laws', in Feigl and Maxwell (eds), 1962, pp. 170–230, and 'Views of human nature', in Wann (ed.), 1964, pp. 163–83; Polanyi, *Personal Knowledge*, 1964; and *The Tacit Dimension*, 1967; Bunge, *Causality*, 1959; Bohm, *Cause and Chance in Modern Physics*, 1957; Toulmin, *The Philosophy of Science*, 1953 and *Foresight and Understanding*, 1961. The decisive advance was taken, by general agreement, by Rom Harré (1970, 1972) and Harré and Madden (1975), and as influenced by Harré and others, by Roy Bhaskar (1975, 1978, 1979, 1982): Harré, *The Principles of Scientific Thinking*, and *The Philosophies of Science*, 1972; Harré and Madden, *Causal Powers*, 1975; Bhaskar, *A Realist Theory of Science*, 1975, 'On the possibility of social scientific knowledge and the limits of behaviorism', 1978, pp. 1–28, *The Possibility of Naturalism*, 1979, and 'Emergence, explanation and emancipation', in Secord (ed.), 1982, pp. 275–310. General accounts can be found in Manicas and Secord, 'Implications for psychology', Keat and Urry, *Social Theory as Science*, 1975, McMullin, 'A case for scientific realism', in Leplin (ed.), 1984, pp. 8–40, and Stockman, *Antipositivist Theories of the Sciences*, 1983. The picture of realism presented in this chapter relies heavily upon Bhaskar's interpretation, which he has called transcendental realism (1979) or simply the realist theory of science (1975). Realism, like positivism, has a long history in science and philosophy. For example, an emphasis on causal explanation through the discovery of essences goes back to Aristotle.

be objectively assessed by reference to empirical evidence; (4) there are 'objects', in the broadest sense of the term, which exist independently of our beliefs and theories about them; (5) there is a general 'logic' to scientific method shared by the social and natural sciences. Realists, however, interpret these shared assumptions — and concepts like objective, empirical, cause and reality — in a manner consistent with another set of presuppositions. A feeling for what these presuppositions may be can be gained by considering realist conceptions of knowledge, objects of knowledge, explanation and prediction, and the research process.

Scientific knowledge and the objects of knowledge

Realists distinguish between two dimensions of knowledge: (1) scientific knowledge or the *transitive* facts and theories, paradigms and models, and methods and techniques of enquiry available to the science of the day, and (2) the *intransitive* objects of knowledge, the real things and structures, mechanisms and processes, events and possibilities of the world which are for the most part quite independent of us and invariant to our knowledge of them.[3] The aim of realist science is the production, with the cognitive tools at its disposal, of knowledge of the kinds and ways of acting of the unknown (but knowable) intransitive objects of the world. According to this interpretation, science is a social activity and the transitive objects of science are social products like any other. Since experiences and the facts that they generate are social products (and therefore socially changeable), scientific knowledge must be viewed as the fallible body of accepted science. Still, it can be and is corrected, and our knowledge of the real things and structures of the world can and does grow over time.

For the realist, there are three domains (rather than one) of interest to the scientist: those of the real, the actual and the empirical. The domain of the real consists of the often 'hidden' or unobservable structures and processes of the world. These intransitive objects of scientific enquiry endure and act quite independently of humans. Familiar

---

[3] Bhaskar calls these the transitive and intransitive dimensions, or the transitive and intransitive objects of knowledge. On the transitive objects of knowledge, see Ravetz, *Scientific Knowledge and Its Social Problems*, 1971, pp. 116–19. For a similar line of argument, see Keat and Urry, *Social Theory as Science*; because the objects of knowledge are 'intransitive', Keat and Urry (p. 44) are able to argue that science 'is descriptive, and not constructive, of the nature of that which exists'. Bhaskar, *A Realist Theory of Science*, 1978, p. 61, considers the establishment of an intransitive dimension as a second Copernican revolution in the philosophy of science. Subsequent references to Bhaskar's *Realist Theory* in these notes refer to this second edition.

examples from modern science include electrons, protons, quarks, genes and magnetic fields. It is the task of science to identify, define and explain the natural kinds of 'real things' that exist in this domain. Real things are often complex stratified composites. A familiar if simple example may be helpful in visualizing their composite nature. Ordinary table salt can be conceived of at a number of levels, each of which has its own properties. Examples are actual salt with all its impurities, the compound NaCl, the constituent elements sodium and chlorine with their own causal properties, and the complexes of electrons, neutrons and so forth which form these elements. Establishing the existence and properties of these novel 'things' − the theoretical things of science − is the objective of theoretical and experimental work in science.

The effects of the activity of real things combine to generate the flux of phenomena that constitute the actual states and happenings − the events or phenomena − of our ordinary observable world. This is the domain of the actual. These 'ordinary things' and events can be conceived of as phases or levels of real things which occur within the domain of normal human perception; like structures at other 'hidden' levels, they are compounds formed by the effects of a multitude of structures at more remote levels of reality, often operating according to principles of relatively different kinds.[4]

The concepts 'sense experience' and 'empirical' belong to the domain of the empirical and to the social world of science. Events and ordinary objects are the objects of our perception, but the experiences and facts our perception generates remain interpreted social products; perception does not provide 'pure' facts. Still, the theory ladenness of perception does not imply that an event or ordinary thing can be seen in any way at all, for perceptions are rooted in the 'material' of 'reality'. For this reason, perception remains our primary source of information about the 'transfactually' active machinery of nature which is the object of scientific knowledge.[5]

This realist view presents us with a very different sort of relationship of knowledge to the world than that posited by positivism: for the positivist, knowledge is passively (or 'objectively') reported, while, for the realist, knowledge plays a much more active role in creating the world we are studying in our minds. Since the domain of the actual

---

[4] The view that ordinary things and events may be (and usually are) compounds generated by the affects of different real things 'allows us to make sense of the *individuality* of historical particulars; just as the conception of ordinary events as "conjunctures" allows us to make sense of the uniqueness of historical events' (Bhaskar, *Realist Theory*, p. 227).

exists independently of our interpretations of it, experiences are often
'out of phase' with actual events and entities. Similarly, real structures
exist independently of and often out of phase with the actual patterns
of events. As a result, we may be mistaken about what is 'there', and
what is 'there' may be the muddled manifestation of the activity of
multiple 'hidden' structures.

On first reading, the notion that the objects of scientific knowledge
are neither experiences (the domain of the empirical) nor the objects of
which they are the experiences (the domain of the actual) may seem
somewhat peculiar. According to realists, however, the class of things is
far wider than that of material objects; we must learn to divest the
concept 'thing' of its normal material object connotations. In fact it is a
serious error even to think of 'things' as necessarily like material objects.
Obvious counterexamples are fluids and gases, but powers, forces,
fields, complex structures and sets of relationships may also be things.
In committing this error, we constrain a priori the possible forms of
reality.

The realist is perfectly willing to regard terms such as electronic
structure, genetic code, molecule and atomic structure as referring to
real entities in the world, in much the same manner as 'non-theoretical'
terms like iron and wood do.[6] Indeed, the things posited by science in
its investigations are more often than not quite unlike the things of our
ordinary experience. The causal criterion for the ascription of reality to
a posited object is the capacity of the object whose existence is in doubt
to bring about changes in material things, i.e. to act back as a causal
agent on the materials out of which it has been formed.[7] It is precisely
because of this transfactual (non-empirical) activity and their persistence,

[5] The use of the term 'real' in the 'domain of the real' does not imply that
experiences are less real than events, or that events are less real than structures; all
can be conceived of as different kinds of real objects. For a review of the role perceptions play in postpositivist science, see Brown, 'Perception and meaning', 1972,
and *Perception, Theory and Commitment: The New Philosophy of Science*, 1977,
pp. 81–94. What is important here is the view that the objects of perception, the
events and ordinary things of the domain of the actual, limit the class of possible
constructs without dictating a specific percept. Therefore, the theory ladenness of
perception (which remains a thesis) does not imply relativism, although what is
'empirical' remains relative and theory dependent; that is, 'there are no absolutely
privileged statements' (Bhaskar, *Realist Theory*, p. 189). It should be recalled here
that positivists did not necessarily argue that there were not 'hidden' causes of
phenomena or a nature of things in themselves – just that they, if they did exist,
were inaccessible to the human mind; claims to their existence were meaningless.
Realism is based, then, on an ontology of structures and transfactually active things
that positivists find nonsensical.
[6] Bhaskar, *Realist Theory*, p. 226.

that the structures in the domain of the real can be regarded as real things.

Causal laws are simply descriptions of the way that the structures in the domain of the real act and interact.[8] The ways in which these structures act combine to generate the flux of phenomena that constitute the actual states and happenings of the world.[9] Not all properties of a structure are equally important, however, and it is by reference to some but not others that its causal powers, its characteristic ways of acting, are defined and explained. In general, it is those properties which are most basic in the explanatory sense — without which it would not be the kind of thing it is — that constitute its identity and allow us to talk of the intrinsic structure, real essence or essential nature of a thing and fix it in its kind.[10]

It is also these same core properties that allow us to talk of the same thing persisting through changes. For example, the essence of hydrogen is its electronic structure, because it is by reference to this structure that its powers of chemical reaction are explained. Similarly, if theoretical salt, $NaCl$, is put in theoretical water, H_2O, then it must dissolve, because this is a causal property of the combined constituent elements

[7] Bhaskar, *Realist Theory*, p. 113: 'Whatever is capable of producing a physical effect is real and a proper object of scientific study'. Popper adopts a somewhat similar criterion in his definition of an objective object.

[8] For Bhaskar, causal laws do not express conjunctions of events as in positivism; in fact, 'a constant conjunction of events is no more a necessary than a sufficient condition for a causal law' (Bhaskar, *Realist Theory*, p. 10). Furthermore, a causal law as a way of acting of a transfactually active thing must be distinguished from a statement of a law; the first is a concept in the intransitive dimension, the second a concept in the transitive dimension. While causal laws do not change, our statements about them may and do. It should be added that transfactually active things would act and interact in a world without humans and their perceptions.

[9] Since structures generate the flux of phenomena, Bhaskar usually refers to them as generative mechanisms. The generative capacities of things have also been called powers. On powers see Harré, 'Powers', 1978, p. 85, and *Principles of Scientific Thinking*, p. 270, and Harré and Madden, 'Natural powers and powerful natures', 1973, pp. 209–30, and *Causal Powers*; see also Smart, 'Dispositional properties', 1961–2, pp. 44–6, and Armstrong, *Belief, Truth and Knowledge*, 1973, particularly pp. 11–16.

[10] There is, then, a concept of natural kinds of things whose naturally occurring behaviour takes place independently of our definitions and statements of causal laws. The key idea here is structure, i.e. the system or set of relations between the constituent elements of the core of the theoretical entity. The structure of an entity consists of given, patterned and relatively enduring relationships. Of course, the constituent elements themselves can be seen as composed of sets of relations at a deeper level of reality. See Bhaskar, *Realist Theory*, p. 171, and Smith, *Realism and the Progress of Science*, 1981, p. 10. See Keat and Urry, *Social Theory as Science*, pp. 121–37, for a comparison of positivist and realist conceptions of 'structure'.

sodium and chlorine (and of H_2O). A stuff remains hydrogen or the compound NaCl only as long as its nature (or real essence) remains unchanged. In this sense not all ways of classifying things identify natural kinds or taxa because not all sets of properties represent features of the essence of a single natural kind, i.e. do not individuate just one and only one kind of real thing.[11] Tables and chairs, for example, have no real essence, but water, hydrogen and salt do.

To suppose that things have real essences is not to suppose, however, that the real essence of those things cannot be explained in terms of more fundamental structures and processes. For the realist, the world is not only differentiated into different kinds of natural things, it is also stratified. The world consists not only of things which are already complexly structured and preformed wholes, it consists of things which may be simultaneously constituted at different levels and simultaneously controlled by different principles. Consider again, for example, actual salt with all its impurities, the compound NaCl, the constituent elements sodium and chlorine with their own causal properties and the still more basic complexes of electrons, neutrons, quarks and so on.[12] Each stratum has its own real essence and is capable as a causal agent of acting back on the materials out of which it is formed. Thus the behaviour of a thing on one stratum or level is not solely determined by more basic laws of animate things, for instance, by physical laws alone. Since no end to the existence of ever deeper and explanatorily more basic strata can be envisaged, the world is seemingly characterized by an open-ended stratification.

The realist is committed, then, to the view that the world is differentiated, structured and stratified, and that the particular things it contains and the ways in which it is differentiated are matters for substantive scientific investigation. The process of science is a continuous dialectic between taxonomic and explanatory knowledge, between knowledge of what kinds of things there are and knowledge of how these things behave. It aims at real definitions of the things and structures of the world as well as statements of their characteristic and essential

---

[11] Because of the existence of the intransitive dimension of the world and the transitive dimension which represents our knowledge of it, it is necessary to distinguish between real and nominal definitions (Bhaskar, *Realist Theory*, p. 211). Nominal definitions are our fallible attempts to capture in words the real definitions of things. As so conceived, they may be true or false, fruitful or misleading. As we learn more about the real definition of a thing, we change our nominal definition. Therefore changes in nominal definitions are a normal part of the ongoing social activity of science.

[12] The example is from Manicas and Secord, 'Implications for psychology', p. 401.

behaviour. Even though science is a social activity and scientific knowledge a fallible social product, there is, none the less, a truth about the world; science changes and grows as it attempts to bring scientific knowledge and the objects of knowledge into accord.

Explanation and prediction

In the positivist research programme the logical form of deductive—nomological explanation ensures that explanation and prediction are symmetrical: if an event has already occurred, then the formal structure of sentences 'explains' the event; if the event has yet to occur, then the structure of sentences 'predicts' the event. For the realist, however, there is a radical asymmetry between explanation and prediction. The essence of science lies in the movement at any one level of reality from knowledge of manifest phenomena at that level to knowledge of the structures or 'things' that generate them. Science explains the properties of things identified at any one level of reality by reference to their intrinsic structures, or the structures of which they are an intrinsic part. Thus, according to Bhaskar,[13] 'the dispositional properties of, say, nickel, e.g. that it is magnetic, malleable, resistant to rust, melts at 1445 °C and boils at 2900 °C are explained, in the context of post-Daltonian atomic theory, by reference to such facts about its intrinsic structure as that its atomic number is 28, its atomic weight is 58.71 and its density is 8.90'. The atomic constitution of nickel is its real essence. It is the powers or ways of acting of this essence that explains these dispositional properties. Such continuing activity is in turn referred back for explanation to the essential nature of nickel.

In contrast with the closed world of the positivist, the world of the realist is open. A closed system is one in which a constant conjunction of events obtains, i.e. in which an event of type A is invariably accompanied by an event of type B. An open system is one in which expected conjunctions do not necessarily occur, owing to the operation of intervening mechanisms or countervailing causes. This mesh of influences and cross-influences causes an instability of empirical relationships in open systems in space or over time. It is characteristic of open systems, then, that two or more generative mechanisms, perhaps of radically different kinds, act together to produce effects. A complete account of

---

[13] Bhaskar, *Realist Theory*, p. 210. The dispositional properties of a thing are called its nominal essence by Bhaskar (p. 211). Dispositional properties are those properties that serve to identify a thing in general; the real essence of a thing is formed by its basic properties. On structural explanation, see also McMullin, 'Structural explanation', 1978, pp. 139—47.

an event or a sequence of events would, as a result, be a description of all the different principles involved in its generation.[14]

Closed systems are rare in nature and must, in general, be experimentally established. In fact, the intelligibility of experimental closure in science itself is accounted for by the ubiquity of open systems.[15] Experimental closure enables scientists to establish closed systems and therefore a one-to-one relationship between a causal law and a sequence of events. The purpose of an experiment is to produce a predicted pattern of events; the process identifies a causal law and gives us access to the intransitive structures that exist independently of us. By isolating the effects of a single generative mechanism or transfactually active thing, we are able to make statements about its nature and its characteristic way of acting. It is through this process that the theoretical scientist attempts to identify the real things in the world and their modes of operation. It is this characteristic pattern of activity or mode of operation that is described in the statement of a causal law.

In realist science phenomena are not explained by showing that they are instances of well-established regularities, for, as we have already mentioned, realists argue that there is an ontological distinction between causal laws and patterns of events. An adequate causal explanation requires the discovery not only of regular relations between phenomena but of some kind of mechanism or process that links them. The presence of a regular relationship between two kinds of phenomena only gives us reason to believe that they are causally related − that there is some intervening mechanism which links them together. It is the scientist's task to discover and analyse the natural connections that exist in the physical world. As the world is open, there will be necessary connections between some but not other matters of fact; i.e. we can and must distinguish between necessary and accidental sequences or connections between events. To say that a connection is necessary is to say that there is a generative mechanism at work such that when one event

---

[14] Because of these multiple influences, 'most events in open systems must thus be regarded as "conjunctures"' (Bhaskar, *Realist Theory*, p. 119). We can see the general weakness of the Humean concept of laws here: it ties laws to closed systems, i.e. systems where a constant conjunction of events occurs. Once we allow for open systems, laws can only be universal if they are interpreted in a non-empirical (transfactual) way, i.e. as designating the activity of generative mechanisms and structures independently of any particular sequence or pattern of events.

[15] See Bhaskar, *Realist Theory*, pp. 33−5, and *Possibility of Naturalism*, pp. 11−14, on the relation of experiments and closed systems. It is just because the things to which laws are ascribed go on acting in their normal way independently of whether or not a closure obtains that the scientific investigation of nature is possible.

occurs the other will also occur in the absence of intervening causes.[16]

Explanation in realist science, then, involves reference to underlying mechanisms and structures, and to the manner in which they generate or produce phenomena in the domain of the actual. In the deductive–nomological model, the behaviour of gases can be completely explained by using the laws that relate their temperature, volume and presure; a satisfactory realist explanation requires that we make reference to their essential natures and powers, i.e. to the molecular theory of gases. While this may seem a more satisfactory account of scientific explanation, it generates its own problems. Since causal laws are manifest in open systems, for instance, they need not, and in general will not, be reflected in an invariant pattern or regularly recurring sequence of events; there will not be a one-to-one relationship between a causal law representing the characteristic mode of operation of a transfactually active thing and the particular sequence of events that occurs. Therefore, law-like behaviour has to be interpreted 'normally', i.e. as involving the exercise of tendencies which may not be realized. Statements of laws in realist science make a claim about the activity of a tendency, about the way of acting or powers of a thing that would, if undisturbed, result in the tendency's manifestation in a regular sequence of events. Such statements do not specify the conditions under which the tendency will be exercised, since the operation of the generative mechanism does not depend upon the closure or otherwise of the system in which the mechanism operates. While scientists are interested in both causal laws and the conditions in which they are manifest, then, the two must be kept distinct, for things may endure even when not active and act in their normal way even when the consequences of the law-like statements they underlie are, owing to the operation of intervening mechanisms or countervailing causes, manifest in a modified form.

Still something does happen, and the tendency, as one of the influences at work, helps to explain what. The task of the applied scientist is to untangle the web of interlocking influences, to identify the conjuncture of causes in which an event occurred. For the realist, predicates like natural, social, human, physical, chemical, aerodynamical, biological

---

[16] According to the realist, then, scientific explanation is not a form of logical argument that establishes relations of logical necessity between premises and conclusions as in the deductive–nomological model. As Keat and Urry, *Social Theory as Science*, p. 27, argue, 'to show that the truth of the conclusion follows necessarily from that of the premises is no substitute for describing the necessary, causal connections between things in nature'. The concept of natural, or causal, necessity is a non-Humean view of causal relations; see Harré, *Principles of Scientific Thinking*, pp. 105–6.

and economic do not differentiate distinct kinds of events, but distinct kinds of mechanisms that generate (if unhampered) events. In the generation of an open-systemic event, several of these predicates may be and usually are simultaneously applicable. Even though the same mechanism may be active in two separate events, the effects produced can be quite diverse because of the differing combinations of mechanisms that conjoin in each case.[17]

There are four stages in the explanation of an open-systemic event.[18]

(1) The first is the causal analysis or resolution of the event to be explained into its components. By definition, all events in open systems are a 'condensation' or 'distillation' of the effects of multiple causal mechanisms; they should, then, be separable into their component 'parts'. For example, we might begin our explanation of the observable reaction in chemistry between the substances called sodium and hydrochloric acid by simply identifying these two substances.

(2) The second involves the theoretical redescription of these component parts, so that theories of the various kinds of mechanisms at work in the generation of the event can be brought to bear on its explanation. In our example the two substances and their observable reaction when brought together can be redescribed as $2Na + 2HCl \rightarrow 2NaCl + H_2$.

(3) The third stage involves the process of retroduction in which inferences are made to the possible causes of the redescribed components via normic statements. Our chemical reaction has been explained, for instance, by reference to the atomic hypothesis and the theory of valency and chemical bonding, and to the essential properties or powers of sodium (Na), hydrogen (H) and chlorine (Cl).

(4) The final stage is a vigorous attempt to eliminate alternative causes. Since each determinate effect may have a plurality of possible causes, the process of retroduction alone cannot be decisive. Scientists must gather independent evidence to determine which of several possible causes actually produced the effect on the occasion in question.

In actual practice scientists concentrate upon only one or two of the many mechanisms that may network together to cause an event. As a

---

[17] This accounts for the uniqueness of historical events and is the reason why the individual case merits attention in the social sciences.
[18] Bhaskar, *Realist Theory*, p. 125.

simple example, we assume that we can refer to the gene pool of a particular life form to explain its species-specific behaviour without having to make reference to physical laws, such as that of gravity. Arguments in the transitive dimension of science that certain mechanisms are less decisive than others (and may even be ignored) are instructive in illuminating present and past conceptions of the essential nature of things.

It should be clear by now why realists regard explanation and prediction as radically asymmetrical. Most real things in the world are complex objects, by virtue of which they possess an ensemble of powers or ways of acting. It is by reference to the exercise of these powers that the phenomena of the world are explained. Such continuing activity is in turn referred back for explanation to the essential nature of things. Now it is characteristic of open systems that the events that constitute them are produced by the combined effect of two or more generative mechanisms, perhaps of radically different kinds. Since we do not know *ex ante* which mechanisms will actually be at work, future events are not deductively predictable. It is for this reason also that the explanation of events in open systems normally requires retroduction, i.e. a posteriori thinking (in this case inferences from present effects to prior causes via the application of normic statements).[19]

Since by definition normic statements are statements of tendency as far as the domain of the actual is concerned, it is even possible to give complete explanations of events without being in a position to deduce them. In fact, we may be incapable of any but the most tentative of predictions. The acid test of a theory cannot, then, be its predictive power, for we are normally only justified in predicting an event deductively if the system in which the mechanism acts is closed.[20] Realists argue, for this reason, that science is primarily concerned with what kinds of things there are and what they tend to do − and only derivatively concerned with predicting what is actually going to happen.

It should, perhaps, be emphasized that what are explained are never 'pure' phenomena, but always phenomena read in a certain way, i.e. the 'facts' of science at any one moment. By clearly distinguishing between an intransitive dimension in which real things do cause phenomena and a transitive dimension consisting in part of current claims in science as

---

[19] Another criticism of the Popper−Hempel theory of explanation is apparent here. As we have seen, a closure is necessary to satisfy the conditions for the covering-law model, for it is only under conditions of a closure that, given the antecedent, the deduction of the consequent event is possible. But if this is so, then closure is necessary for a symmetry between explanation and prediction to obtain. See Bhaskar, *Realist Theory*, p. 103.

to what these things are, realists are able to maintain the possibility of a rational criticism of current knowledge claims in a way quite foreign to positivism.

The research process

Unlike positivists, realists argue that there is a logic of discovery in science, that this logic is imposed by the multitiered stratification of reality and that the research process is constructed in an essential sense around this logic.[21] Three stages of research can be distinguished at any one level of reality in this process.

1   In the first we identify something, say a segment of experience, as an interesting focus of investigation. This segment consists of our perception of some apparent event or pattern, sequence or regularity in an open system, or of the invariance of an experimentally produced result in a closed system.[22] There is no doubt in our mind that something produced the effect; our only doubt is over what it was.

---

[20] It is only rarely, and normally under conditions which are artificially produced and controlled (experimental closure), that scientists can predict what is actually going to happen; so '. . . theory is never disconfirmed by the contrary behaviour of the uncontrolled world, where all our predictions may be defeated' (Bhaskar, *Realist Theory*, p. 119). This points to yet another difference between explanation and prediction: explanation proceeds by way of normic statements and prediction by way of empirical statements. The first set of statements concerns the way of acting of a real thing or phenomenon (if not disturbed by other generative mechanisms); the second concerns our expected perceptions in the domain of experience. This difference is based on the ontological distinction between causal laws and patterns of phenomena, the mechanisms of nature and the events they generate, the domain of the real and the actual. Bhaskar (*Realist Theory*, p. 135) distinguishes between two kinds of prediction (my emphasis): '*practical predictions* of categorical form which are rarely made in science but which are important in some of its practical applications in open systems and about which the applied scientist can never be deductively certain; and *test predictions* of hypothetical form made under effectively closed conditions in order to test a theoretical hypothesis or putative law'. According to Bhaskar, the aim of prediction, incidentally, is that of only a few sciences such as astronomy and terrestrial mechanics.

[21] See Bhaskar, 'Forms of realism', 1975, particularly pp. 108–14, and *Realist Theory*, particularly pp. 15, 172. See also Harré, 'Blueprint for a new science', in Armistead (ed.), 1974, pp. 240–59.

[22] Bhaskar, *Realist Theory*, pp. 91, 145, differentiates between a result which is an invariant pattern of events produced by experiment and a regularity which is a noninvariant pattern of events produced by tendencies. A realist science must take as its starting point the regularities observed within a particular subject of study (see, for example, Harré, 'Blueprint for a new science').

2   In the second stage we attempt to construct and test explanations for this interesting segment of experience. This step involves creative model building, in which plausible generative mechanisms are imagined to produce the 'phenomena' in question.[23] We ask: What unobservable operative mechanisms could have produced and so explain the events we think we saw? Which structure or combination of structures possesses mechanisms that would tend to produce something like what we think we saw? Here it is important to remember that the 'things' which are the objects of our models are not necessarily the same 'things' whose behaviour we are trying to understand.[24] We might, for example, postulate the existence of a genetic code to explain in part some observed behaviour of an animal. While the animal is the object of our investigation, the objects of our model are species-specific genes, for it is this 'hidden' stratum, or so we believe, that explains in large part the animal's behaviour.

Since the structural entities and mechanisms or processes that scientists postulate are nearly always unobservable in a normal sense, they are generally given analogical definitions; that is, their meaning is related analogically to some already understood term or terms. Thus a theoretical entity might be defined as 'small', a 'particle', 'charged' or 'like an organism', and a model of an atom based upon an analogy with the solar system (the solar model), a model of the movement of light and sound based upon an analogy with the behaviour of water (the wave model) or a model of gases based upon an analogy with billiard balls in a container (the molecular model).[25]

Now it is not usually obvious what these structures and processes are. As a result, just what they are must be discovered as part of the

[23] The subject of such models is the unknown but knowable intransitive structures of the world; the models themselves are part of the transitive dimension of science. On the use and importance of models in realist science, see Bhaskar, *Realist Theory*, pp. 148–63; Keat and Urry, *Social Theory as Science*, pp 32–6; and Harré, *Principles of Scientific Thinking*, ch. 2.

[24] A distinction can be drawn in realist science between a model, the sources of a model and the subject of a model. A model is an attempted representation of the nature of that which is the subject of the model. It is analogically related to its source, which is a phenomenon that is already understood. Models are of a subject, and are modelled on a source. Thus the subject of a model might be the structure of an atom and its source the solar system. Here the model is a representation of this subject — an atom — and analogically related to a source — the solar system. See Keat and Urry, *Social Theory as Science*, pp. 32–6, for these distinctions, and the role abstraction and idealization play in model building in realist science.

[25] Postulated entities need not be smaller in size than actual entities, although this is normally the case in physics and chemistry; see Schlesinger, 'The prejudice of micro-reduction', *British Journal for the Philosophy of Science*, 1961, pp. 215–24.

social activity of science. We may, for instance, propose that copper (Cu) has a certain atomic or electronic structure, and then attempt to deduce its dispositional properties or powers from a statement of that structure. We could then postulate that it is this structure and these powers that account for at least some of the behaviour of the actual copper wire (with all its impurities and imperfections) which is the focus of our investigations. Again, although the event we are investigating is assumed to be the compound product of the effects of multiple generative mechanisms, the experimental or pure scientist character-istically focuses upon and only builds models for one or, at most, a few of these mechanisms at a time.

3 The third stage in the research process, according to realists, is the moment of theory construction. It is here that the reality of the postulated structures and powers is checked, and an attempt is made to give the structures real definitions and to describe the ways that they act in statements of causal laws. During this process, precision in definition or meaning rather than accuracy in measurement becomes the a posteriori arbiter of theory; in fact, precise measurement of the structures that the theory proposes is generally impossible at this stage, for they are in the process of definition.

This process does not, however, guarantee that mistaken reconstruc-tions will not be made. We are by now familiar with and in general accept the fact that metals have specific electronic structures and life forms specific genetic codes. However, scientists could have and at one time did refer to other imaginary structures to explain many of the characteristic features of metals and of animals and plants.[26] Since it is relatively easy for scientists to propose models of hypothetical structures, models tend to proliferate and compete. It is much more difficult, however, to construct theories, for theories are models with existential commitment, i.e. models whose hypothetical structures and powers are conceived of as and empirically demonstrated to be real.[27]

There are several ways of testing a model. A familiar procedure is to identify some of its consequences that are open to empirical test. For instance, a scientist might postulate the existence of entities such as genes or electrons, and then attempt to develop instruments like electron microscopes or cloud chambers that are capable of observing them if

---

[26] As the history of science amply demonstrates, many novel structures and mechanisms have been proposed (and accepted) that are now considered mistaken; we would now say that the terms used failed to refer to or have an extension in reality. Darwin's homunculus comes immediately to mind. Other favourites include phlogiston, vital forces, the caloric, magnetic flux and the luminiferous ether.

they actually exist. It is in this movement from suggestive model to empirically 'confirmed' theory that experimental closure plays its crucial role in science. The task of the experimental scientist is to trigger a mechanism and to isolate its effects, so that its characteristic activity can be established without interference from other mechanisms.[28]

Once this activity has been experimentally established, the scientist is able to attempt a real definition of things like copper, hydrogen and water, and to describe the ways that they characteristically act in statements of causal laws. Once their real definitions have been satisfactorily established, it is no longer just contingent that hydrogen, for instance, is a gas with a particular atomic structure; now anything possessing that structure is hydrogen, and it will remain hydrogen as long as its nature (or real essence) remains unchanged. Furthermore, the criterion for the application of that concept has changed; it has now become its intrinsic structure rather than its observable behaviour, for given that hydrogen has the structure it does, it is necessary that it behaves the way it does and produces (if unimpeded) the effects it does.

To ascribe a law to explain an event, however, we need a theory, for it is only if it is backed by a theory, containing a model of a natural structure and its mode of operation, that a law can be distinguished from a purely accidental pattern of events. The theory allows us to distinguish between a purely accidental pattern of events and events produced by a causal law. It should be noted that there is an element of

---

[27] According to Bhaskar (*Realist Theory*, pp. 191–3), some sciences have lagged in development because they have not been able to establish theories, only propose models. In realist science criteria like rational connection, explanatory scope and efficiency of explanation are still retained as standards by which a choice can be made between competing models to establish a theory. This does not mean that the model chosen as a theory is necessarily or really true; scientists may be mistaken, even though an accepted theory satisfies most criteria for a 'true' theory. A classic example of a postulated theory that proved very fruitful in research is the concept of phlogiston. In its earlier stages the theory proved very fruitful in generating explanations and new avenues of research. It was recognized, however, that the precise nature of the postulated entity required further specification. It was eventually shown through experiment that the predicted results did not occur or could otherwise be explained, and the concept was abandoned. An example of an entity that was successfully postulated is the notion of 'gene' used to explain Mendel's laws of inherited characteristics.

[28] It is only under closed conditions that there will be a one-to-one relationship between causal laws and patterns of events, and it is normally only in the laboratory that these enduring mechanisms of nature, whose operations are described in the statements of causal laws, become manifest and empirically accessible to scientists. Consistency with the 'facts' in an open system is neither necessary nor sufficient for a theory to be demonstrated to be true.

natural necessity here which is entirely lacking in a positivist view of causality.

We cannot imagine that the research process is now completed, for the three-step dialectic discussed above has in principle no foreseeable end. A new level or stratum of reality has been identified and must itself now be explained. For example, the stratum I chemical reaction $2Na + 2HCl \rightarrow 2NaCl + H_2$ was explained earlier by the stratum II theory of atomic number and valency. This structure and its powers has in turn been explained by the stratum III theory of electronic and atomic structure, and at present competing models of subatomic structures are attempting to provide a stratum IV explanation of this theory itself.[29] There is, presumably, no end to this process of discovery and description of new and ever deeper, and explanatorily more basic, strata. If correct, this means that there are no basic explanations, only more basic ones; there are no ultimate explanations in science.

This process has several implications for our understanding of the nature of science as viewed from a realist perspective. First, there is a clearly definable difference between the goals of the experimental and applied scientist. The experimental scientist is concerned with the process of discovery discussed above; it is his or her task to discover the different levels of real objects and their causal connections. The applied scientist uses the theories of the experimental scientist, as in the engineer's use of the laws of physics and chemistry to build a bridge.

Second, science is hard work that requires creative intelligence; the scientist is not the passive observer of events and constant conjunctions of positivism. The experimental scientist must design new experimental techniques to bring about closure and invent new sense-extending equipment.[30] The applied scientist must learn to analyse a situation as a

[29] As another example, geometrical optics has been explained in terms of Young and Fresnel wave optics, which has been explained in terms of the electromagnetic theory of light, which can be explained in terms of the quantum theory of radiation. Both examples are provided by Bhaskar (*Realist Theory*, pp. 168–9).

[30] Since causal laws, patterns of events and experiences are categorically independent, an 'enormous effort − in experimental design and scientific training − . . . is required to make experience epistemically significant in science' (Bhaskar, *Realist Theory*, p. 35). Examples of theoretical entities may be known to exist indirectly through the perception of their effects, e.g. the detection of radioactive materials by a geiger counter, of electricity by an electroscope or of a magnetic field by a compass needle. For the realist, the image of the scientist is not the positivist's 'man of logic', but the 'person of practical wisdom' who has sufficient experience and training to be able to weigh information, to make decisions on the basis of insufficient information, to deliberate and to 'see' the results of experiments for what they are. See Brown, *Perception, Theory and Commitment*, pp. 148–51, for the notion of the 'man of practical wisdom'.

whole, to think on several levels at once and to be aware of the normic statements of a range of different disciplines in order to explain, predict, construct and diagnose the phenomena of the world.[31] Even though the skills of the experimental and the applied scientist are characteristically different, with the one deliberately attempting to exclude and the other always to accommodate the effects of multiple mechanisms and intervening levels of reality, both must be trained and theoretically informed. As a simple example, the ability to recognize such objects as a cathode-ray tube or electrons crossing a screen requires a great deal of highly specialized knowledge; simple passive observation is not enough to see these objects for what they are. In this sense there is an important respect in which the layperson and the physicist see different things when they observe, say, the same experiment.[32]

Third, it is to be expected that with the discovery of structures on deeper levels of reality we shall learn to see and understand structures on less fundamental levels (a table or an atom, for instance) in new ways. The normal result is change in some part of our formally accredited stock of knowledge. Corrections in our understanding of these 'objects' can be made, the contours of the terrain of reality redrawn and the history of science rewritten from the vantage point of this new perspective.

Finally, it should be clear why the realist views explanation and prediction as radically asymmetrical. Accurate prediction is normally possible only under carefully controlled experimental conditions.

The New Heuristic in the Human Sciences

Is naturalism possible? Can the realists' conception of science be applied to the human sciences? If it can, what kinds of enduring and transfactually

---

[31] The pattern of explanation in applied science is characteristically different from that in experimental science, for known theories concerning the structures of the world and their tendencies are being applied rather than constructed. The applied scientist is therefore concerned with questions like: Is there evidence that a mechanism is present or that a structure is active? What are the conditions under which a mechanism operates and is manifest? The applied scientist is concerned with the actual outcome of the activities of multiple mechanisms on particular occasions; the experimental scientist is concerned, in contrast, with the activity of a particular structure, but not the conditions under which the mechanisms operate and hence not the results of its activity except within the confines of closure. See Bhaskar, *Realist Theory*, p. 252.

[32] For a review of 'seeing' in science and a general discussion of how two perceivers can gain different information from a single perceptual situation, see Brown, 'Perception and meaning', and *Perception, Theory and Commitment*, pp. 81–94.

active social 'things' are there and what do they tend to do? What properties do societies and people possess that might make them possible subjects of scientific knowledge?

One substantial barrier to the possibility of naturalism comes immediately to mind. In fields such as history and the human sciences, experimental activity is impossible, for the conditions for even a restricted closure (of a non-trivial kind) can neither be naturally nor experimentally satisfied. If a realist science of society is to be possible, then some kind of surrogate of closure must be devised or identified to permit confirmation and falsification of explanatory models. Bhaskar has argued that such a surrogate is present precisely in those properties peculiar to social objects, and proposes a new 'critical naturalism' which entails a transformational model of social activity and a causal theory of mind. This model imposes a series of limitations on a naturalistic science of society, however, and necessitates a relational conception of social objects.

For the realist, a society exists as a real object — a complex structure irreducible either to its effects or to people. It is a real object irreducible to simpler ones because it satisfies the causal criterion; that is, but for the relatively enduring relations presupposed by its structure and sub-structures, certain physical actions would not be performed. By definition, then, a society is a social structure consisting of the sum of the relations within which individuals (and groups) stand. The task of theoretical social science is to illuminate these relations and 'the relations between these relations (and between such relations and nature and the products of such relations)'.[33] Since the relations between the relations that constitute the proper objects of knowledge in the social sciences may be internal, social life must be grasped as a totality whose 'various moments may be asymmetrically weighted, primed with differential causal forces'.[34]

However, unlike natural structures, social structures cannot exist independently of their effects or of people. While societies do not consist of people (or their actions or thoughts as social actors), they exist only by virtue of the intentional activity of people. It is not necessary that societies should exist and endure, but if they are to do so people must reproduce them. Similarly, the existence of a society may be irreducible to its effects, but like charged clouds, magnetic fields and radio stars it can only be detected through its effects. In Bhaskar's words, it can 'only be known, not shown, to exist'.[35]

[33] Bhaskar, *Possibility of Naturalism*, p. 36.
[34] Bhaskar, *Possibility of Naturalism*, p. 55.
[35] Bhaskar, *Realist Theory*, p. 195.

It is these two features of social structures that provide the surrogate for experimental closure in the social sciences. A social structure generates social life and its products. However, it (or at least some part of it) exists only as long as it is being exercised and then in the last instance only via the intentional activity of people. If a social structure exists, its effects are being manifest in social behaviour and products, and conceptualized in the experience of those who are its bearers. The essential movement of theory in the social sciences consists, then, in the movement from the manifest phenomena of social life, especially as conceptualized in the experience of the social agents concerned, to the essential relations that necessitate them.

According to realist naturalism, the objects of knowledge in social science are the relatively enduring relations presupposed by particular social forms or structures. These relations include but do not entirely consist of interpersonal relationships. They also include relationships between people and nature or social products like arrowheads and sweat lodges. Such products are social forms rather than just material objects precisely because they depend on (and in a sense consist of) the relationships mentioned above. They represent the material presence of society as much as does the social behaviour of people.[36] The material presence of society can be recognized, then, in patterns of interpersonal relationships (which presuppose the existence of a tacit set of rules that govern social behaviour in much the same manner as our tacit knowledge of grammar governs speech), in a property of the behaviour of people as they interact with nature or in material objects such as tables and chairs.

Now such relations must be conceptualized as holding between positions and practice, not between the individuals who occupy or engage in them. On the transformational model, the very existence of social activity presupposes that such relations have a life prior to, and independent of, any particular individual. According to Bhaskar, 'people, in their conscious activity, for the most part unconsciously reproduce (and occasionally transform) the structures governing their substantive activities of production'.[37] This has certain implications for the nature of social relations and change that will be elaborated upon below.

Let us pause for a moment before we look more closely at theory

[36] '. . . the material presence of social effects consists only in changes in people and changes brought about by people on other material things — objects of nature, such as land, and artifacts, produced by work on objects of nature. One could express this truth as follows: *the material presence of society = persons and the (material) results of their actions*' (Bhaskar, *Possibility of Naturalism*, p. 37).

[37] Bhaskar, *Possibility of Naturalism*, p. 44.

construction in the social sciences and review a few of the characteristic features — from a realist perspective — of social structure and its relationship with human agency that affect the nature of social science theory. Since a social structure cannot exist independently of its effects and of people, it has peculiar features that differentiate it from a natural structure. For instance, though social relations must be exercised in time, they need not be localized at any point in space as are social activities. Simple examples are relations such as those of kinship or economic reciprocity which endure through time, have causal effects and are manifest in social behaviour and products, but have themselves no position in space. Another peculiar feature is the relative degree of sharpness that may characterize a set of rules that governs behaviour. Some rules of interaction and production, say, might have fuzzy boundaries (such as taking a walk) while others sharp ones (like traffic light behaviour). The former leave space for individual decision and 'capriciousness' that the latter fill.

Both these peculiar features of social structure may make it more difficult to recognize and define the essential nature of social rules and relations, especially if they have been fuzzily conceptualized by the social agents concerned. This points in turn to another peculiarity — the concept dependence of social objects in their mode of operation: social relations are conceptualized in the experience of social agents and are already named in one form or another. Finally, societies are being continuously transformed in practice and thus may be only relatively enduring. Therefore, unlike the vast majority of natural structures, they are irreducibly historical.[38]

A perennial problem in the social sciences is the link between human agency and social structure. There is general agreement that a social structure is ultimately a human product which in turn shapes individuals and influences their interaction with each other and with nature. Through the years methodologists have tended to emphasize either one or the other as the more important.[39] Bhaskarian realists, however, argue that

[38] For Bhaskar (*Realist Theory*, p. 196), 'the Newtonian revolution in social science consists in coming to see that it is not necessary to explain society as such; but only the various structures responsible for different societies and their changes'.

[39] Structural functionalism and structural Marxism have tended to de-emphasize human agency, while some schools of phenomenology (ethno-methodology, interactionism and interpretative sociology in general) have weakened the role of social structure. Weber and Durkheim are good examples of two extreme camps, with the former viewing social objects as the results of (as constituted by) intentional or meaningful human behaviour, and the latter regarding the same objects as possessing a life of their own, external to and coercing the individual.

both are indispensable in explaining human behaviour and social products; neither can be excluded nor collapsed into the other.[40] Even though society would not exist without human activity and a society is a necessary condition for any intentional human act at all, both social structure and human agency — as well as people themselves — are radically different kinds of things.[41]

For the realist, the causal power of social forms is mediated through human agency and social forms are a necessary condition for any intentional act. However, this does not mean that human behaviour is determined by or can be completely explained by reference to some framework of social rules.[42] The properties possessed by people and which characterize human actions, like purposefulness, intentionality and a degree of self-consciousness, are very different from those possessed by social forms. In fact people and societies make very poor models for each other. Therefore, according to Bhaskar, we must 'distinguish sharply, then, between the genesis of human actions, lying in the reasons, intentions and plans of people, on the one hand, and the structures governing the reproduction and transformation of social activities, on the other; . . . between the domains of the psychological

---

[40] Attempts to reunite structure and agency emerged like so many other movements in the late 1960s following the collapse of logical empiricism. Examples in sociology are the 'general' functionalist, 'humanistic' Marxist and interactionist movements. The most detailed argument for the indispensability of both structure and function is given by Cohen, *Modern Social Theory*, 1968. See also Blau (ed.), *Approaches to the Study of Social Structure*, 1976, and Blau and Merton (eds), *Continuity in Structural Inquiry*, 1981. A recent influential attempt to collapse structure and action is Anthony Giddens's concept of 'structuration', which has its roots anchored in the newer linguistic structuralism, semiotic studies and hermeneutics (Giddens, *Central Problems in Social Theory*, 1979). See also Margaret Archer's comments on the effect of this collapse in Archer, 'Morphogenesis versus structuration', 1982, pp. 455–83, and 'The myth of cultural integration', 1985, pp. 333–53.

[41] 'People and society refer to radically different kinds of things — they are not related "dialectically," not two moments of the same process' (Bhaskar, *Possibility of Naturalism*, p. 42).

[42] 'Most social life occurs within a framework of rules but what happens within (and outside) the framework, though still social, is, rather like the moves in a game of chess (and the off-stage play), not determined by, and hence cannot be completely explained by reference to, the framework' (Bhaskar, *Possibility of Naturalism*, pp. 182–3). Grammar and speech provide another example (Bhaskar, *Possibility of Naturalism*, p. 45): '. . . we can allow that speech is governed by the rules of grammar without supposing either that these rules exist independently of usage (reification) or that they determine what we say. The rules of grammar, like natural structures, impose *limits* on the speech acts we can perform, but they do not *determine* our performances'.

and the social sciences'.[43] Intentional human behaviour is always caused by reasons, but these may be psychological and physiological, for example, as well as social; people act in open systems co-determined by the effects of a variety of mechanisms of which the social is just one.[44]

Even this brief review should be sufficient to show that, from a realist perspective, there are significant differences between the subject matter — and the methods appropriate for their study — of the social and natural sciences. Ontological, epistemological and relational considerations all qualify the form that the scientific study of social life must take. Still, for the Bhaskarian realist, there remains an essential unity of purpose and approach. For instance, the goal of each is to reveal real transfactually active structures; both use the same form of retroductive reasoning (a tentative working back from observed effect to unobserved cause) and structural explanation, and the causal laws of each must be expressed in terms of tendency or normic statements because they act in systems that are always open (or nearly always so in the case of the natural sciences).

To explain human activity, the social scientist must, in a manner analogous to her or his counterpart in the natural sciences, take into consideration a wide variety of usually radically different kinds of structures, such as social, psychological, environmental, biological and physical. As the natural scientist learns to identify and focus upon the effects of a single natural structure, so the social scientist must attempt to isolate just the social component or some aspect of it, and to explain it by reference to its essence, i.e. by reference to the structure whose presence means that this activity must tend to occur.

According to Bhaskar, the explanation of social phenomena proceeds by the same general process as in the natural sciences.[45]

(1) First, the activity or human product to be explained is resolved into its components. Like natural events, social events must be viewed as conjunctural, i.e. as the result of the combined affect of a wide variety of active structures, only some of which are social. Because

---

[43] Bhaskar, *Possibility of Naturalism*, pp. 44–5.

[44] Since reasons can be causes and affect states of the material world, their reality is established (as with social forms) by their causal efficacy (Bhaskar, *Possibility of Naturalism*, p. 102). Therefore people possess properties irreducible to those of matter for the same fundamental reason that societies possess properties irreducible to those of people. For Bhaskar (*Possibility of Naturalism*, p. 103), 'mind is a *sui generis* real emergent power of matter, whose autonomy, though real, is nevertheless circumscribed'.

[45] Bhaskar, *Possibility of Naturalism*, p. 165.

of the activity-dependent nature of social structures and the content-dependent nature of social activities, the elements of the social component are generally already named in one form or another and therefore are open to the skilled observer.

(2) These elements are redescribed in the language of the social science involved.

(3) A (retroductive) attempt is made to lay out the structural conditions that must have existed for them to be present. Because the human agents involved could have acted otherwise, the causal laws describing the way that the social structure acts must be analysed as tendencies.

(4) Finally, an attempt is made to eliminate alternative possible causes of the elements, for it is always possible that we have misidentified the social structure involved or at least some of its properties.

Because social structures are only ever manifest in open systems, decisive test situations are in principle impossible in this process. It follows, then, 'that criteria for the rational appraisal and development of theories in the social sciences ... cannot be predictive and so must be exclusively explanatory'.[46] Thus real definitions of capitalism, segmentary lineage, city and other apparent social forms must find their ultimate confirmation in their capacity to 'render intelligible' a certain domain of phenomena.[47]

The social sciences also have their theoretical and applied aspects. The task of the theoretical or pure social scientist is to reveal the transfactually active forms of social life. He or she struggles to develop and employ suggestive models and metaphors with the goal in mind of arriving at real definitions or theories of social forms. It is these models, metaphors, definitions and theories that others apply in a manner analogous to their counterpart in the natural sciences. They have also learned to regard inconsistencies in the manifestations of social structures as the perfectly normal outcome of the activity of opposed tendencies in complex social structures and the interference characteristic of open systems. Humans live in open systems co-determined by the activity of complex psychological, social, biological, environmental and other structures. Applied social scientists therefore know, that, while their explanations of human activity and its products must refer to relatively

---

[46] Bhaskar, *Possibility of Naturalism*, p. 27.
[47] Bhaskar, *Realist Theory*, p. 246.

enduring social relations, they must make reference to other kinds of structures as well. For instance, since subjective meanings or reasons may be causes of human actions, the applied social scientist must also make reference to or at least take into consideration an individual's or group's own intentions, purposes and theories about the social and natural world.

The social scientist is also concerned with those conditions that tend to preserve or change societies. Since societies are themselves ultimately social products, they are possible objects of transformation and so may be only relatively enduring. Among the many possible causes of change in the nature of social life are internal inconsistencies in or elaboration of the social structure, and the dialectical interplay between components of the structure and those of human agency, the natural environment or the biological basis of the population. Because of the presence of material continuity – because changes are transformations, not replacements – the social sciences can sustain a genuine concept of social history and identify a clear criterion of a historically significant event: an event that initiates or constitutes a rupture or other transformation of a social form to the extent that it ceases to be of that kind.

In summary, the realist theory of science provides an alternative interpretation of what it means to do social science. Social scientists have both taxonomic and explanatory objectives. They are as interested in what social forms there are as with how they act. From this perspective much of social science can be seen as an attempt to identify and produce real definitions of forms of social life. Since the point of contact or link between social structures and individuals are positions (with functions, rights, duties, tasks and other practices attached), the social scientist tries to discover what these positions are. The characteristic mode of reasoning in this process is retroductive, i.e. an argument from manifest (and usually named) phenomena to possible (hidden) causes. The goal of retroductive reasoning is to lay out those structural conditions that make human social activity intelligible. Because social structures only ever manifest themselves in open systems, hypotheses about these conditions can only be assessed by their explanatory fruitfulness or power. It is this criterion rather than predictive accuracy that decides which of a set of competing models becomes theory. Finally, like the natural scientist, trained judgement is required: the application of statements of causal laws, the correct identification of social situations and other activity in the social sciences are never automatic.

Practising Archaeology on Realist Assumptions

What would a realist archaeology be like? How would it differ from positivist archaeology? The elements of a realist archaeology seem fairly clear. It would be an archaeology concerned with both taxonomic and explanatory objectives, as interested in what social forms once existed as with how they 'behaved'. Above all, it would be concerned with relations — relations between people, between people and nature, and between relations themselves — as they are manifest in the material aspect of social life. The characteristic mode of reasoning would be retroductive; an argument from manifest (and, in historical archaeology, usually named) phenomena to possible (hidden) causes. The goal of this reasoning process, as in the natural and social sciences in general, would be to lay out those structural conditions — social, transformational and physical — that would have meant that the social activities encapsulated in the archaeological record must have occurred. Because social structures only ever manifest themselves in open systems, causal laws about these structures would have to be expressed in the form of normic or tendency statements. These definitions and statements of causal law would be considered a model until explanatory fruitfulness convinces archaeologists to accept them as theories, i.e. as probably true, although there is never any guarantee that the 'right' or even best commitment has been made. Most of these theories would be about historically developing social totalities whose mode of transformation and eventual change into other kinds of societies is an object of study. Finally, unlike the natural sciences, a realist archaeology would combine both theoretical and applied interests: most archaeologists would be as concerned with the interplay between social, environmental, biological and other structures that affected humans, their behaviour and the formation of sites, as with social relations alone.

Examples of realist archaeology are not difficult to find in North American archaeology. Deetz's *In Small Things Forgotten*, for example, is a particularly appropriate example, for it suggests how a small number of principles could have generated social relations and activities that are expressed in house form, type of burial and other social forms preserved in the archaeological record. Other examples include attempts to show that historic settlement—subsistence systems are fruitful analogues for some prehistoric settlement—subsistence systems in similar environmental zones, and Flannery's system model of internal elaboration resulting from the adoption of limited maize horticulture. Even classic New Archaeology exemplars, such as Longacre's attempt to identify kinship rules in the American Southwest, provide suitable examples.[48]

Each of these examples is concerned with identifying the presence of a specific social form, with showing how the generative mechanisms of a particular historically situated society were manifest in the archaeological record, with constructing suggestive models of past social relations (and their change) that might have generated in part the archaeological record and with other characteristic tasks of the realist archaeologist. There are no attempts in these examples to build axiomatic theories, to discover universal conjunctions among the 'facts', to assume system closure or to achieve the other core goals of positivist archaeology.

However, archaeology remains a unique social science with its own strengths and limitations. The locus of this uniqueness is, of course, the archaeologists' subject matter — the material aspect of social life as viewed through the archaeological record. A Winchian social scientist and some social anthropologists would see this as a reason for despair, for social life is to be explained by either rendering it intelligible in the terms that the agents under study do or by identifying the social rules that govern social interactions. However, the realist argues that social behaviour has both a conceptual (or 'inner') component and a material (or 'outer') component, and that it cannot be reduced to its conceptual component alone, for the material component may interact with and constrain or transform the conceptual component.[49] It is for this reason that the social sciences are (or should be) concerned not only with agents' conceptualizations and actions but also with what they do and make. They are as concerned with the practical skills, competences and social interactions that transform nature, as with doing which is signifying or expressing. While the designator of archaeological analysis remains the totalizing social whole, it is the material substrate or (physical)

[48] Deetz, *In Small Things Forgotten*, 1977; Flannery, 'Archeological systems theory and Early Mesoamerica', in Meggers (ed.), 1968, pp. 67–87. The classic New Archaeology exemplars referred to could just as easily be interpreted as explorations of the manner in which social rules were instantiated in archaeological assemblages rather than attempts to provide positivist 'operational definitions'. More recently, Ian Hodder's 'interpretative' approach to archaeology is a particularly vigorous example of a realist position. See, for example, Hodder, *Symbols in Action: Ethnoarchaeological Studies of Material Culture*, 1982, and 'Postprocessual archaeology', in Schiffer (ed.), 1985, pp. 1–26.

[49] For Winch and other interpretative social scientists, it is always the interpretation of the bearers of a culture that is to be considered correct or most important. What counts as praying, for instance, can only be settled from *within* a form of life. While Winch argues for the conceptual nature of social reality, Bhaskar (*Possibility of Naturalism*, pp. 173–95) maintains that social reality is not exhausted by such conceptualizations, and that such conceptualizations are not incorrigible, for people can and do make mistakes, act irrationally, do not comprehend a situation and so forth.

aspect of this doing and making which, by definition, archaeologists study.

Archaeologists use the features of this material aspect of social life as a basis for building models of the structural conditions that caused it. The prehistoric archaeologist searches the archaeological record for patterned residue and artefact types that may point to the presence at one time of strongly patterned conduct. The task is made easier for the historical archaeologist, who is normally working with named artefacts, activities, institutions and other kinds of evidence more familiar to the cultural anthropologist and historian.

Still, model building in archaeology is not a simple straightforward process for a number of reasons. There are the normal problems that arise from working with a resource that is finite and rapidly disappearing, and that is nearly always difficult, expensive and very time consuming to recover and process for analysis. However, there are other problems that arise because archaeologists (with historical archaeologists often being exceptions) must study the material aspect of social life without access to human agency. For this reason, prehistoric archaeologists have tended to concentrate on the reconstruction of natural environments and changes in those environments as primary causes of sociocultural change. But these efforts will prove fruitless in those instances where the explanation of visible changes in the archaeological record is rooted in the causal effects of human interactions or purposes and therefore is not visible to archaeologists.

Another example is provided by the fact that human activities as well as archaeological sites are the product of both a plurality and a multiplicity of causes. Apart from the effect of what Schiffer[50] has called C-transforms and N-transforms, the realist archaeologist, unlike the Humean, cannot suppose that there is a unique set of antecedent conditions to which any given event is constantly conjoined. For instance, the same bodily movement can be used to perform different actions, and the same action can be performed with different bodily movements. (A simple example is raising our hand and doing something to inform the teacher that we really just have to leave the classroom. Raising our hand may indicate that we would like to leave the room, just as we may indicate that we would like to leave the room by raising our hand. But raising our hand may also indicate that, 'I have the answer!', while a squirm or two may just as well inform the teacher of our desire.) Since the same causal law may be manifested in both the material 'face' of society and in the archaeological record in a number of different ways, the archaeologist cannot rely upon statistical measures of association or

[50] Schiffer, *Behavioral Archeology*, 1976.

other quantitative techniques for its identification. These problems and others may cause archaeologists to have less confidence in the explanatory efficacy of their models and make theory construction more difficult.

However, there is no reason to believe that archaeologists cannot in principle discover the structures and activities that produced archaeological sites. For example, there is no reason why archaeologists must assume that the social relations that social anthropologists concentrate upon are any more important than other social forms which are more accessible to the techniques of archaeology. A simple example illustrates the point. Some archaeologists have adopted the premise of historical materialism, i.e. the assumption that it is material production that ultimately determines the rest of social life.[51] Like other presuppositions, this one has been subject to many interpretations. Here we shall assume that it means that the mode of production − the economy − dominates the development of social, political and intellectual life. By identifying the essential nature of the mode of production, which is usually manifest in ways more accessible to archaeologists than are many other social forms, archaeologists would have an advantage in model building denied them by the assumption, say, that all social forms were equally autonomous or dominated instead by ideational factors. We could probably agree that material production is a necessary condition for social life, but still be no more able to prove that it is the ultimately determining one than we could prove that it is not. The point remains that historical materialism points down a path with rich modelling possibilities for archaeology. Like other research programmes, it must be justified by its fruitfulness.

Finally, we should note the implication of Bhaskar's assumption that the realist theory of science is true and not merely a research heuristic. It should, if true, make the history of North American archaeology

---

[51] Julian Steward's concept of a culture core based upon modes of production that strongly influence other social forms in a hierarchical manner has been familiar to North American archaeologists for some time, as are V. G. Childe's extensive writings; see, for example, Steward, *Theory of Culture Change*, 1955, and Childe, *Piecing Together the Past*, 1956. More recently, this added premise has been most vigorously explored in an explicit manner by Marxist archaeologists; see, for example, Spriggs (ed.), *Marxist Perspectives in Archaeology*, 1984. On historical materialism, see Harris, *The Rise of Anthropological Theory*, 1968, and *Cultural Materialism: The Struggle for a Science of Culture*, 1979, Althusser, *For Marx*, 1969, and Althusser and Balibar, *Reading Capital*, 1970. Althusser argues that it is the economy that determines which relatively autonomous structure is dominant. Currently, there is disagreement about whether this premise is applicable to all societies or only to some, especially less complex ones like hunter−gatherer and simple agriculturalist. On Marx's attempt to found a science of historical materialism, see Keat and Urry, *Social Theory as Science*, pp. 96−140.

more intelligible than New Archaeology, which could only reject it. There are a number of arguments that could be used in favour of this interpretation. Three will be mentioned here. First, there are numerous slippages into realist strategems in New Archaeology. Some of these have already been mentioned in chapter 5. This could be interpreted as a 'correct' practice asserting itself despite the constraints of a false ideology. Second, realists could argue that their interpretation of the strong interdisciplinary nature of archaeology is more satisfying than that of positivism. Positivists tend to identify each science as different, holding that within each there are sets of given and potentially discoverable general laws. In archaeology laws of closed systems buffered by external forces would be an example. A realist would emphasize the artificial character of these disciplinary distinctions, and argue that we must analyse the causal interrelations between the different orders of reality.

A strong argument could also be made that the pattern of development of North American archaeology supports a realist interpretation. The long initial period of exploration was as concerned with the explanation of archaeological units as with their identification (remember the Mound Builders?) Although in the late 1930s and the 1940s archaeologists were primarily concerned with the taxonomic arrangement of these units, and in the 1950s with their firm anchorage in time following the discovery of radiocarbon dating, examples of analogical model building, based principally upon the concepts of diffusion, migration and independent invention, are easy to find. It should hardly be regarded as a 'revolutionary' shift in 'paradigms', then, when the various 'hidden' structures and processes involved in the formation of archaeological sites – social, environmental and transformational – emerged as an increasing focus of study in the 1960s, a period when our spatial–temporal charts were more or less complete. It could easily be argued that the main contribution of the 1970s and 1980s has been an increasingly sophisticated understanding of the generative mechanisms responsible for the formation of archaeological sites, rather than the identification of universal Humean laws or the construction of axiomatic positivist theories.

Conclusion

No attempt has been made in this chapter to develop a systematic realist research programme for archaeology. Our task has been the simpler one of merely showing that an alternative to positivist archaeology is possible. Many of the assumptions of such a programme are fairly clear and can be quickly summarized: the world consists of enduring and transfactually active structures; science is a social activity and knowledge is a social product; causal laws must be analysed as tendencies; knowledge is about intransitive objects existing and acting independently of it; societies are irreducible to people; the objective of science is to discover the often unobservable structures and mechanisms which causally generate observable phenomena; models and analogies are essential features of theories, which enable us to represent unobservable structures and mechanisms intelligibly; there exists a mind-independent material world which is the object of scientific theories and which plays a crucial role in determining what is observed; sense data cannot be the primary objects of scientific knowledge; we have no direct access to the intransitive world of real things; scientific reasoning is retroductive; scientific knowledge is the fallible body of accepted science; no finite procedure can prove a scientific theory true; the concepts of structure and structural explanation are central to any science.

Should archaeologists adopt a realist research programme? Questions and problems remain. Is the version of realism discussed in this chapter even an approximately true account of science? Can archaeologists develop an adequate theoretical account which treats simultaneously with human agency and social structure? How successful can archaeologists be in distinguishing between those cases of social behaviour which are strictly rule governed (such as traffic light behaviour) from those which are not (such as going for a walk)? What are the conditions for the identification of causal laws in archaeology? What criteria can we use to detect the empirical presence of specific theoretical entities in archaeological materials? If we adopt the premise of historical materialism, how do we reconcile the thesis of the relative autonomy of the superstructure with that of its determination in the last instance by the economic base? Will realism, like positivism, eventually collapse under the weight of internal contradictions and inconsistencies with the history of science and nature itself?

Whatever the answers to these questions may be, a few conclusions seem certain: there are viable alternatives to a positivist archaeology, at least some of these alternatives seem more tenable reconstructions of the history and practice of archaeology than that provided by positivism; and postpositivist archaeology will lack even the illusion of concreteness briefly enjoyed by New Archaeology.

Archaeology, Philosophy of Science and the Anthropology of Knowledge

What are the implications for archaeologists of working within the context of postpositivist conceptions of science? Perhaps the most fundamental concerns our understanding of the nature of knowledge. The positivist attempt to establish a foundation of indubitable facts and a set logic of science has proved illusory. At best we seem capable of assertoric knowledge — knowledge claims that are acceptable by a community and that we do not know to be false. It is such an understanding that is the base from which archaeologists must work.

If this claim is correct, interesting questions can be asked about the enterprise we call archaeology. For instance, if there is no objective foundation to guide research, what is our authority for experimenting with one research programme rather than another, and for accepting one set of criteria for a proper explanation, a fruitful theory or a genuine science? If forms of knowledge are grounded in social practice, what becomes of objectivity, the authority of science and the evaluation of different claims to knowledge? It seems clear that our choices may be difficult to defend without succumbing to dogma, an infinite regression of justification or an appeal to cultural interests and standards.

To conclude this exploratory analysis of the relationship between positivism and the New Archaeology, two issues raised by questions like these are briefly reviewed. The first concerns the proper role of the philosophy of science in a substantive discipline like archaeology, and the second the types of questions we might consider in pursuing the cultural underpinnings of archaeology.

Can the Philosophy of Science help Archaeology?

It may seem somewhat brash to ask whether philosophy of science can help archaeology and, more broadly, the social sciences. But what are we to make of the contentious debate briefly summarized in earlier chapters between realist and positivist philosophers of science? Who is right? Is there a right?

Part of the root of the problem is the lack of an agreed conception of the philosopher's task in current Anglo-American philosophy.[1] It is no wonder, then, that archaeologists and other social scientists receive confusing and often conflicting signals from reading philosophy of science. How this confusion might arise becomes obvious when different conceptions of the philosopher's task are compared. One scheme for systematizing these conceptions divides them into two great streams of thought which roughly correspond to the Enlightenment and the Romantic or Understanding styles of thought mentioned in chapter 6.[2]

The Enlightenment conception of philosophy includes positivism, formalism and some forms of empiricism. For many Enlightenment philosophers, rational secular knowledge is epitomized in the natural sciences, and philosophy itself should be cognate with the sciences. Either it should be a branch of science or function as an aid to science, preparing the conceptual ground for the edifice of science. In a 'weak' view the philosopher serves as an 'underlabourer' or occasionally as the 'midwife' of science, clearing away obstacles like logically inconsistent assumptions that lie in the path of knowledge. In a 'strong' view the philosopher is a system builder whose goal is the construction of a philosophy *for* science. In the latter view methodological issues cannot be resolved without substantial philosophical treatment of, for example, the philosophy and methodology appropriate for the social sciences.[3] Positivism is a classic expression of this 'strong' view.

The second view, the Understanding conception of philosophy, does not restrict philosophy to the role of 'underlabourer' or 'midwife' to the sciences, but assesses it more broadly in terms of the contributions it makes to human understanding in general — to our ability to find the world and our deeds in it intelligible. In this view philosophy is concerned

---

[1] See, for example Mitchell and Rosen (eds), *The Need for Interpretation: Contemporary Conceptions of the Philosopher's Task*, 1983. For a frequently quoted discussion of the relationship between philosophy and the social sciences, see Benton, *Philosophical Foundations of the Three Sociologies*, 1977, ch. 1. On the positivist influence on our conception of this relationship, see Giddens, 'On the relation of sociology to philosophy', in Secord (ed.), *Explaining Human Behaviour*, 1982, pp. 175–87.

[2] See Mitchell and Rosen, *Need for Interpretation*, pp. 1–10.

[3] For the concept of the role of the philosopher as 'underlabourer', see Locke, *Essay Concerning Human Understanding*, 1959, p. 14. Bhaskar is another system builder; his purpose is 'to develop a systematic realist account of science' (Bhaskar, *A Realist Theory of Science*, 1978, p. 8).

with constructing the whole of human knowledge into logically connected systems. This 'master scientist' conception of philosophy is
exemplified by the writings of the great metaphysical systems builders
like Descartes, Leibnitz and Hegel.

Proponents of each of these views — underlabourer, systems builder
and master scientist — have made unique contributions to the social
sciences, but the very diversity of their goals and styles (for instance,
philosophers in the Enlightenment stream have tended to be more
prescriptive while those in the Romantic stream are more 'critical') can
be confusing to non-philosophers lacking time to digest the literature of
another discipline.

A few additional problems that the non-professional commonly en-
counters in reading philosophy of science should illustrate why this
body of literature cannot be casually approached as seems to have been
the case in New Archaeology.

(1) A conception of science like that developed by Hempel, Popper,
    Kuhn or Lakatos may simply be defective in the same manner in
    which a theory of the origins of domestication may be defective. As
    a result, social scientists who adopt this conception will be working
    with a defective conceptual tool which may retard their research.[4]

(2) Philosophers of science are no more impartial judges of their own
    ideas than are other scholars. The image of the detached thinker calm-
    ly reviewing and discarding conceptual systems without emotional
    attachment is as misleading as the positivists' image of the white-
    coated scientist objectively recording the facts of nature.

(3) Philosophers of science, for understandable reasons, generally write
    as if their views rather than those of their antagonists are correct.
    Indeed, if they are firmly committed to the view that there is a
    'truth about the matter', then they have every reason to write
    as if their proposed methodology, problem resolution and the like
    is correct or true until proved otherwise.[5] As a consequence, an
    unwary archaeologist who only reads Hempel's *Aspects of Scientific
    Explanation*, for instance, will normally be left quite unaware of the
    storm within which his efforts occurred unless she or he also reads
    Feyerabend or Scriven.

[4] Bhaskar (*Realist Theory*, p. 260) writes, 'ideologies derived from defective
conceptions of these sciences (i.e., the experimental, physical sciences) weigh like a
dead hand, heavily on the shoulders of many of the other sciences, particularly, of
course, the proto-sciences of society and man'.

(4) Philosophers of science, particularly of a positivist persuasion, have been reluctant to acknowledge the metaphysical base of their own programmes. The result is a posture that philosophical thinking occupies a privileged position not significantly influenced by cultural factors.[6]

(5) Philosophers of science frequently talk in terms of ideal or imaginary constructions and not in terms of the imperfect conditions of real practice. As a result, the games being played by archaeologists and philosophers of science are different. Thus positivist-inclined social scientists trying to apply the covering-law model of explanation or the hypothetico-deductive approach find that they lack a real guide. While the construction of 'fantasy science' may have its uses in philosophy of science, it is opposed to real-life messier social science. This tendency reaches its peak when, as in positivism, philosophers claim that their fantasies are real and that real-life practice is misguided at best.

(6) The philosophy of science is dominated by the analysis of a science of the past, by the conception of science of a Mach or an Einstein for example, and not of contemporary insights by their successors. Contemporary physicists, for instance, pay little attention to philosophers' criteria of what is or is not observable. They even distinguish between which 'unobservable' entities have been observed and which have not.[8] If we are searching for a guide, what are we to make of these discrepancies?

(7) We might ask who philosophers of science are writing for? Bhaskar's *A Realist Theory of Science* was presumably intended to explain

[5] Bhaskar tells us that social science is impossible without philosophy, for philosophy establishes the criteria for social science: 'philosophy is essential if we are to situate the possibility of any social scientific criteria of understanding at all (Bhaskar, *The Possibility of Naturalism*, 1979, Preface); and 'Philosophy, indeed can neither anticipate the results nor guarantee the success of a naturalistic science of society; what it can do is to specify the (ontological) conditions that make and the (epistemological) conditions that must be satisfied for such a project to be possible' (Bhaskar, *Possibility of Naturalism*, p. 4). He also provides us with a second Copernican Revolution in the philosophy of science and tells us what the Newtonian insight in the social sciences is. These comments are not intended as criticism of Bhaskar, but merely indicate the style in which his ideas are presented.
[6] An instructive example for anthropologists is Luntley, 'Understanding anthropologist', 1982, pp. 199–216.
[7] Was Hegel exaggerating when he said that 'philosophy always comes on the scene too late'? (Hegel, *Philosophy of Right*, 1952, p. 12).
[8] For instance, see Shapere, 'The concept of observation in science and philosophy', 1982, pp. 485–526.

science to scientists, but its style and assumed background knowledge require a level of philosophical sophistication beyond that of most already overstressed research scientists. Contemporary philosophers are members of a rich historical tradition which has accumulated problems, attempted resolutions, well-demarcated positions and acceptable solutions, as well as a massive literature. Like any cultural tradition, it is no easy matter to comprehend its language, background presuppositions and nuances.

(8) Finally in mainline Anglo-American philosophy of science, there is what appears from an outsider's view to be an inordinate interest in logical matters of evaluating and criticizing theories, and much less interest in their empirical validation − an interest in the ideal rather than in problems of working with incomplete and often imperfect data. It would not be improper to ask why the structure of an idea, and the arrangement of its premises and of the contentions derived from or otherwise built upon them, should be more fundamental than its content − if the philosophy of science is to be shared with scientist. Presumably, these interests are a result in part of this tradition's long-term commitment to the power of reason and the existence of indubitable truth rather than to the practical problems involved in grappling with knowing as a never-ending process.

While acknowledging all these difficulties, the thesis that philosophy does have a role to play in the human sciences is easy to defend. Only a few of the ways in which this role can be and is fulfilled are mentioned here.[9] Perhaps the most obvious way that philosophy can contribute to the human sciences, including archaeology, is by questioning methodological presuppositions such as the propriety of applying presuppositions first developed in the natural sciences to the human sciences. Second, philosophy can help to define the phenomena that archaeologists study. Questions in archaeology are often framed in ordinary pretheoretical language. Philosophers can serve to explicate the expressions being used and to suggest more precise ways of describing the observational domain; linguistic analysis of this sort strengthens our capacity to address substantive issues. Third, philosophy may also aid in subjecting commonsense concepts to philosophical analysis in order to determine whether they could become good scientific concepts. For example, are our ordinary concepts of meaning, cause and process the right kinds of concepts to enter into scientific explanations? Fourth, philosophers still provide arguments which show what theories or explanations in the

[9] For a more extended discussion, see Kirsh, 'The role of philosophy in the human sciences', in Mitchell and Rosen (eds), 1983, pp. 11−32.

human sciences ought to be like. Although our encounter with positivism has taught us to be wary of such received views of science, they merit at least close attention. Fifth, philosophers are skilled at raising awkward questions which may provoke us into re-examining our basic conceptual presuppositions. For example, the presence of a philosophical problem is evidence that there is some difficulty in our own received way of thinking about our subject matter. Perhaps a popular research programme generates inconsistencies and paradoxes.

Finally, philosophy has a role to play in archaeology if for no other reason than that 'substantive' discipline are by their very nature philosophical pursuits. The assumption that philosophical speculation is a separate and distinct enterprise from substantive science is a prejudice of positivist philosophy that cannot be sustained.[10] The sociocultural systems which archaeologists study are so complex that there is no shared view of goals and methods for us to appeal to in times of dispute and conflict. At these moments scientific argument becomes so abstract as to be indistinguishable from philosophical argument, and the two disciplines, philosophy and archaeology, merge. In tackling these questions we are engaged in a dispute centred on a point where philosophy and archaeology meet in mutual satisfaction and possibly collaborative advancement.[11]

Archaeology and the Anthropology of Knowledge

Among the many questions briefly raised about New Archaeology in earlier chapters are those that we can call for convenience historical, philosophical and anthropological. Historical questions concern the who, when, where and how of New Archaeology. How and when did positivist concepts infiltrate the discipline? What impact did they have on daily practice? How were they integrated into ongoing archaeological practice? How and when did New Archaeology fade in popularity?

---

[10] For an attempt to do just this, see Runciman, *A Treatise on Social Theory 1: The Methodology of Social Theory*, 1983.
[11] The contributions of philosophers of science, such as Merileee Salmon and Alison Wylie, aptly illustrate the nature of philosophers' contributions to archaeology. See, for example, Salmon, 'Confirmation and explanation in archaeology', 1975, pp. 459–64, '"Deductive" versus "inductive" archaeology', 1976, pp. 376–80, 'What can systems theory do for archaeology?' *American Antiquity*, 43, pp. 174–83, 1978, and *Philosophy and Archaeology*, 1982; and Wylie, 'Positivism and the New Archaeology', 1981. Of course, these contributions are not 'objective' reflections on the state of archaeology, but are delivered from the bastion of entrenched positions within philosophy.

The answers to these and similar questions raise still broader questions about the nature of archaeology. Some of these are philosophical and relate to idealized conceptions of the task and general procedures of archaeology and the human sciences in general. For instance, what are the epistemological foundations of various research programmes in archaeology? What are the ontological foundations of these programmes? What do theories in archaeology look like? What should they look like? What is an adequate explanation in archaeology?

One clear benefit of the New Archaeology movement has been a heightened awareness of the importance of these and similar philosophical questions. Indeed, from a purely philosophical point of view, New Archaeology is an interesting and immediate instance of the working out of a set of methodological, epistemological and ontological assumptions in a substantive discipline.

More fascinating, from an anthropological perspective at least, is yet another set of questions which concern archaeology as a social practice. For example, what is epistemological discourse in archaeology – in any science – really about? Why do we choose one ontological foundation, or one epistemology, rather than another? How are reason and logic really used in archaeology? Are archaeological theories culturally biased and, if so, how and why? Are historical (as compared with 'anthropological') investigations alone capable of providing us with an understanding of the diversity and plurality of cultural forms in archaeology, such as North American, British, Russian and Chinese? Why *was* a logical empiricist philosophy of science adopted when it was in North American archaeology? Why was it only partially adopted and then in the form or forms it was? To what extent is archaeological knowledge 'socially constructed'? How would we know if it was or was not?[12] Finally, if we accept the arguments of chapter 6 for the moment, are these concerns (merely) an expression of the dominance once more of the Romantic style of thought? The stress on the cultural context of

---

[12] A number of recent studies are beginning to demonstrate the lack of force of logic in scientific decision making and, as a consequence, are opening this area of science to sociological investigation. These kinds of studies, which challenge the core of much traditional philosophy of science and, in particular, views on the role of logic of science, are surely one of the most important features of recent sociology and history of science. See, for example, Pinch, 'Theory testing in science – the case of solar neutrinos: do crucial experiments test theories or theorists?', 1985, pp. 167–87. Also of interest in this regard are Rorty, 'Philosophy as a kind of writing', 1978, pp. 141–60, Norris, *The Deconstructive Turn: Essays in the Rhetoric of Philosophy*, 1983; and Unger, *Philosophical Relativity*, 1984.

archaeology, the current blending of fact and value, and the 'interpre
ative' metaphors in play suggest that there is some merit to this view
  Proddings like these raise in turn questions about histories of archa
ology and what they are all about. The neglect until recently of gener
foundation questions in archaeology is magnified by its reluctance t
situate itself historically, or, when it does, its adoption of a ver
selective view of the history of archaeology.[13] In turning its attention t
the past, archaeology has concentrated, for the most part, on its diffe
ences from amateurism and this has given its image of development a
inappropriately rigid perspective. It is as if the alternatives − amateurist
or professionalism − set the limits to the ultimate dimensions of archae
ology's problems. More discriminating attempts to relate archaeolog
to its historical and social contexts are seen as threats to detach it from
its concern with truth and dissolve it into the history of ideas. It mu
be quickly added that these are only tendencies, for, of course, som
conception of the broad course of archaeological history is inseparab
from the practice of the discipline. Still, it is important for us now t
ask what purpose this stunted view of the history of archaeology h:
served? What do the forms and contents of our histories of archaeolog
tell us about the nature of the discipline? Who has benefited from thes
interpretations?
  All this suggests that archaeology is a more uncertain, open, challengir
and perhaps anxiety-ridden enterprise than our positivist heritage ha
indicated. While only a ripple in the history of archaeology, then, it ha
been the thesis of this book that the study of New Archaeology ca
serve as a portal through which to view archaeology writ large.

[13] For a start in this direction, see Trigger and Glover (eds), 'Regional traditions
1981, 1982.

Bibliography

Achinstein, Peter 1968 *Concepts of Science: A Philosophical Analysis.* Baltimore, MD: Johns Hopkins Press.

Achinstein, Peter 1971 *Law and Explanation.* London: Oxford University Press.

Achinstein, Peter and Barker, S. F. (eds) 1969 *The Legacy of Logical Positivism.* Baltimore, MD: Johns Hopkins Press.

Alker, H. 1969 'A typology of ecological fallacies'. In M. Dogan and S. Rokkan (eds), *Quantitative Ecological Analysis.* Cambridge, MA: MIT Press.

Allen, William L. and Richardson, James B., III 1971 'The reconstruction of kinship from archaeological data: the concepts, the methods and the feasibility'. *American Antiquity*, 36, 41–53.

Althusser, L. 1969 *For Marx.* London: Allen Lane.

Althusser, L. 1971 *Lenin and Philosophy and Other Essays*, trans. B. Brewster. London: New Left Books.

Althusser, L. and Balibar, E. 1970 *Reading Capital.* London: New Left Books.

Anscombe, G. E. 1957–8 'On brute facts', *Analysis*, 18, 69–72.

Archer, Margaret S. 1982 'Morphogenesis versus structuration'. *British Journal of Sociology*, 33, 455–83.

Archer, Margaret S. 1985 'The myth of cultural integration'. *British Journal of Sociology*, 36, 333–53.

Armstrong, D. 1973 *Belief, Truth and Knowledge.* Cambridge: Cambridge University Press.

Ashby, R. W. 1967 'Verifiability principle'. In P. Edwards (ed.), *The Encyclopedia of Philosophy*, vol. 8. New York: Free Press.

Austin, J. 1961 *Philosophical Papers* (eds J. Urmson and G. Warnock). Oxford: Clarendon Press.

Austin, J. 1962 *Sense and Sensibilia.* London: Oxford University Press.

Ayer, A. J. 1946 *Language, Truth and Logic*, 2nd edn. New York: Dover Publications.

Ayer, A. J. (ed.) 1959 *Logical Positivism*. New York: Free Press.

Ayer, A. J. 1970 'What is a law of nature?' In Baruch Brody (ed. *Readings in the Philosophy of Science*. Englewood Cliffs, NJ: Prer tice-Hall.

Barnes, Barry 1974 *Scientific Knowledge and Sociological Theor* London: Routledge and Kegan Paul.

Barnes, Barry 1981 'On the conventional character of knowledge an cognition'. *Philosophy of Social Science*, 11, 303–33.

Barnes, Barry 1982 *T. S. Kuhn and Social Science*. New York: Columbi University Press.

Barnes, Barry and Bloor, David 1982 'Relativism, rationalism and th sociology of knowledge'. In M. Hollis and S. Lukes (eds), *Rationalit and Relativism*. Oxford: Basil Blackwell.

Baumrin, B. (ed.) 1962, 1963 *Philosophy of Science: The Delawai Seminar*, vols 1 and 2. New York: Wiley.

Bayard, Donn T. 1969 'Science, theory and reality in the "New Arc haeology"'. *American Antiquity*, 34, 376–84.

Ben-David, Joseph 1971 *The Scientists' Role in Society*. Englewoo Cliffs, NJ: Prentice-Hall.

Bennett, John W. 1943 'Recent developments in the functional interpre tation of archaeological data'. *American Antiquity*, 9, 208–219.

Bennett, John W. 1946 'Empiricist and experimental trends in easter archaeology'. *American Antiquity*, 11, 198–200.

Benton, Ted 1977 *Philosophical Foundations of the Three Sociologie.* London: Routledge and Kegan Paul.

Bergmann, Gustav 1967 *The Metaphysics of Logical Positivisn* Madison, WI: University of Wisconsin Press.

Bernstein, R. J. 1971 *Class, Codes and Control*, vol. 1. London: Rout ledge and Kegan Paul.

Bernstein, R. J. 1976 *The Restructuring of Social and Political Theory* Philadelphia, PA: University of Pennsylvania Press.

Bhaskar, Roy 1975 'Forms of realism'. *Philosophica*, 15 (1).

Bhaskar, Roy 1975 *A Realist Theory of Science*. Leeds: Leeds Books.

Bhaskar, Roy 1978 *A Realist Theory of Science*, 2nd edn. Atlanti Highlands, NJ: Humanities Press.

Bhaskar, Roy 1978 'On the possibility of social scientific knowledg and the limits of behaviorism'. *Journal for the Theory of Socia Behaviour*, 8, 1–28.

Bhaskar, Roy 1979 *The Possibility of Naturalism*. Brighton: Harveste Press.

Bhaskar, Roy 1982 'Emergence, explanation and emancipation'. In P. F Secord (ed.), *Explaining Human Behavior: Consciousness, Behavior and Social Structure*. Beverly Hills, CA: Sage.

inford, Lewis R. 1962 'Archaeology as anthropology'. *American Antiquity*, 28, 217−25.

inford, Lewis R. 1964 'A consideration of archaeological research design'. *American Antiquity*, 29, 425−41.

inford, Lewis R. 1965 'Archaeological systematics and the study of culture process'. *American Antiquity*, 31, 203−10.

inford, Lewis R. 1967 'Smudge pits and hide smoking: the use of analogy in archaeological reasoning'. *American Antiquity*, 32, 1−12.

inford, Lewis R. 1968 'Archeological perspectives'. In S. R. Binford and L. R. Binford (eds), *New Perspectives in Archeology*. Chicago, IL: Aldine.

inford, Lewis R. 1968 'Methodological considerations of the archaeological use of ethnographic data'. In R. B. Lee and I. DeVore (eds), *Man the Hunter*. Chicago, IL: Aldine.

inford, Lewis R. 1969 'Some comments on historical versus processual archaeology'. *Southwestern Journal of Anthropology*, 24, 267−75.

inford, Lewis R. 1971 'Mortuary practices: their study and their potential'. In James A. Brown (ed.), *Approaches to the Social Dimensions of Mortuary Practices*. Washington, DC: Society for American Archaeology, Memoir 25.

inford, Lewis R. 1972 *An Archaeological Perspective*. New York: Seminar Press.

inford, Lewis R. 1977 'General introduction'. In Lewis R. Binford (ed.), *For Theory Building in Archaeology*. New York: Academic Press.

inford, Lewis R. 1978 'On covering laws and theories in archaeology'. *Current Anthropology*, 19, 631−2.

inford, Lewis R. 1980 'Willow smoke and dog's tails: hunter−gatherer settlement systems and archaeological site formation'. *American Antiquity*, 45 (1), 1−17.

inford, Lewis R. and Bertram, Jack B. 1977 'Bone frequencies − and attritional processes', In Lewis R. Binford (ed.), *For Theory Building in Archaeology*. New York: Academic Press.

inford, Lewis R. and Binford, S. R. 1966 'A preliminary analysis of functional variability in the Mousterian of Levallois facies'. In J. D. Clark and F. C. Howell (eds), *Recent Studies in Paleo-anthropology American Anthropologist*, 68, 238−95.

inford, Sally R. and Binford, L. R. (eds) 1968 *New Perspectives in Archeology*. Chicago, IL: Aldine.

lau, P. M. (ed.) 1976 *Approaches to the Study of Social Structure*. London, Open Books.

Blau, P. M. and Merton, R. K. (eds) 1981 *Continuity in Structural Inquiry*.

Bloor, David 1974 'Popper's mystification of objective knowledge'. *Science Studies*, 4, 65−76.

Bloor, David 1976 *Knowledge and Social Imagery*. London: Routledge and Kegan Paul.

Bloor, David 1978 'Polyhedra and the abominations of Leviticus'. *British Journal for the History of Science*, 11, 245−72.

Bloor, David 1981 'The strengths of the strong programme'. *Philosophy of the Social Sciences*, 11, 199−213.

Bloor, David 1984 'A sociological theory of objectivity'. In Stuart C. Brown (ed.), *Objectivity and Cultural Divergence*. Cambridge: Cambridge University Press.

Blum, A. and McHugh, P. 1971 'The social ascription of motive'. *American Sociological Review*, 36, 98−109.

Blumer, H. 1956 'Sociological analysis and the variable'. *American Sociological Review*, 21, 683−90.

Boeselager, Wolfhard F. 1975 *The Soviet Critique of Neopositivism*. Boston: Reidel.

Bohm, D. 1957 *Cause and Chance in Modern Physics*. London: Routledge and Kegan Paul.

Böhme, G. 'Die Bedeutung von Experimentalregeln für die Wissenshaft'. *Zeitschrift für Soziologie*, 3, 5−17.

Bottomore, Tom 1975 'Competing paradigms in macrosociology'. *Annual Review of Sociology*, 1, 191−202.

Braithwaite, Richard 1959 *Scientific Explanation*. Cambridge: Cambridge University Press (first published in 1953).

Braithwaite, Richard 1970 'Laws of nature and causality'. In Baruch Brody (ed.) *Readings in the Philosophy of Science*, pp. 36−63. Englewood Cliffs, NJ: Prentice-Hall.

Bridgman, P. W. 1927 *The Logic of Modern Physics*. New York: Macmillan.

Brodbeck, May (ed.) 1968 *Readings in the Philosophy of Social Science*. New York: Macmillan.

Brody, Baruch (ed.) 1970 *Readings in the Philosophy of Science*. Englewood Cliffs, NJ: Prentice-Hall.

Brown, H. I. 1972 'Perception and meaning'. *American Philosophical Quarterly*, Monograph No. 6.

Brown, H. I. 1977 *Perception, Theory and Commitment: The New Philosophy of Science*. Chicago, IL: University of Chicago Press.

Brown, James R. 1985 'Bloor's strong program'. *Methodology and Science*, 18, 199−224.

Brown, R. 1973 *Rules and Laws in Sociology*. London: Routledge and Kegan Paul.

Buchdahl, Gerd 1982 'Editorial response to David Bloor'. *Studies in History and Philosophy of Science*, 13, 299–304.

Bunge, M. 1959 *Causality* Cambridge, MA: Harvard University Press.

Bunge, W. 1968 'Fred K. Schaefer and the science of geography'. *Harvard Papers in Theoretical Geography: Special Paper A*.

Caldwell, Bruce 1980 'Positivist philosophy of science and the methodology of economics'. *Journal of Economic Issues*, 14, 53–76.

Caldwell, Bruce 1982 *Beyond Positivism: Economic Methodology in the Twentieth Century*. London: George Allen and Unwin.

Caldwell, Joseph R. 1959 'The new American archeology'. *Science*, 129, 303–7.

Campbell, Norman R. 1920 *Physics: The Elements*. Cambridge: Cambridge University Press.

Carnap, Rudolf 1936, 1937 'Testability and meaning'. *Philosophy of Science*, 3, 420–68; 4, 1–40.

Carnap, Rudolf 1937 *The Logical Syntax of Language*, trans. A. Smeaton. New York: Harcourt, Brace (published in German in 1934).

Carnap, Rudolf 1942 *Introduction to Semantics*. Cambridge, MA: Harvard University Press.

Carnap, Rudolf 1942 *Formalization of Logic*. Cambridge, MA: Harvard University Press.

Carnap, Rudolf 1947 *Meaning and Necessity: A Study in Semantics and Modal Logic*. Chicago, IL: University of Chicago Press.

Carnap, Rudolf 1950 *Logical Foundations of Probability*. Chicago, IL: University of Chicago Press.

Carnap, Rudolf 1952 *The Continuum of Inductive Methods*. Chicago, IL: University of Chicago Press.

Carnap, Rudolf 1956 'The methodological character of theoretical concepts'. In H. Feigl and M. Scriven (eds), *Minnesota Studies in the Philosophy of Science*, vol. 1 Minneapolis, MN: University of Minnesota Press.

Carnap, Rudolf 1959 'The old and the new logic', trans. I. Levi. In A. J. Ayer (ed.) *Logical Positivism*. New York: Free Press.

Carnap, Rudolf 1967 *The Logical Structure of the World*. London: Routledge and Kegan Paul (published in German in 1928).

Carnap, Rudolf and Jeffrey, R. C. (eds) 1971 *Studies in Inductive Logic and Probability*, vol. 1. Berkeley, CA: University of California Press.

Cassirer, Ernest 1951 *The Philosophy of the Enlightenment*, trans. F. C. A. Koella and J. P. Pettegrove. Princeton, NJ: Princeton University Press (published in German in 1932).

Chalmers, A. F. 1976 *What is This Thing Called Science?* St. Lucia, Queensland: University of Queensland Press.

Childe, V. G. 1956 *Piecing Together the Past.* London: Routledge and Kegan Paul.

Clarke, David L. 1968 *Analytical Archaeology.* London: Methuen.

Cohen, Percy S. 1968 *Modern Social Theory.* London: Heinemann.

Couclelis, Helen and Golledge, Reginald 1983 'Analytic research positivism, and behavioral geography'. *Annals of the Association of American Geographers,* 73, 331–9.

Danziger, Kurt 1985 'The methodological imperative in psychology'. *Philosophy of the Social Sciences,* 15, 1–13.

Deetz, James F. 1967 *Invitation to Archaeology.* Garden City, NY: Natural History Press.

Deetz, James F. 1970 'Archaeology as a social science'. *Current Directions in Anthropology, American Anthropological Association Bulletin,* 3, 115–5.

Deetz, James F. 1977, *In Small Things Forgotten.* Garden City, NY: Anchor/Doubleday.

De Gré, G. 1967 *Science as a Social Institution.* New York: Random House.

Devereux, George 1967 *From Anxiety to Method in the Behavioral Sciences.* New York: Humanities Press.

Donagan, A. 1966 'The Popper–Hempel model reconsidered'. In W. H. Dray (ed.), *Philosophical Analysis and History.* New York: Harper and Row.

Douglas, J. D. 1967 *The Social Meanings of Suicide.* Princeton, NJ: Princeton University Press.

Douglas, Mary 1966 *Purity and Danger.* London: Routledge and Kegan Paul.

Douglas, Mary 1970 *Natural Symbols: Explorations in Cosmology.* New York: Pantheon Books.

Dray, W. H. 1985 'Narrative versus analysis in history'. *Philosophy of the Social Sciences,* 15, 125–45.

Dretske, F. 1969 *Seeing and Knowing.* Boston: Routledge and Kegan Paul.

Durkheim, E. 1938 *The Rules of Sociological Method.* Chicago: Free Press.

Ezrahi, Yaron 1971 'The political resources of American science'. *Science Studies,* 1, 117–34.

Feigl, H. 1947 'Logical empiricism'. In Dagobert D. Runes (ed.), *Twentieth Century Philosophy.* New York: Philosophical Library.

Feigl, H. 1956 'Some major issues and developments in the philosophy of science of logical empiricism'. In H. Feigl and M. Scriven (eds), *Minnesota Studies in the Philosophy of Science,* vol. 1. Minneapolis, MN: University of Minnesota Press.

Feigl, H. 1969 'The origin and spirit of logical positivism'. In Peter Achinstein and S. F. Barker (eds), *The Legacy of Logical Positivism*. Baltimore, MD: Johns Hopkins Press.

Feigl, H. 1970 'The orthodox view of theories'. In Michael Radner nd Stephen Winokur (eds), *Minnesota Studies in the Philosophy of Science*, vol. 4 Minneapolis, University of Minnesota Press.

Feigl, H. and Brodbeck. M. (eds) 1953 *Readings in the Philosophy of Science*. New York: Meredith Corporation.

Feigl, H. and Maxwell, G. (eds) 1961 *Current Issues in the Philosophy of Science*. New York: Holt, Rinehart, and Winston.

Feyerabend, P. K. 1962 'Explanation, reduction and empiricism'. In H. Feigl and G. Maxwell (eds), *Minnesota Studies in the Philosophy of Science*, vol. 3. Minneapolis, MN: University of Minnesota Press.

Feyerabend, P. K. 1963 'How to be a good empiricist − a plea for tolerance in matters epistemological'. In Bernard Baumrin (ed.), *Philosophy of Science: The Delaware Seminar*, vol. 2. New York: Wiley.

Feyerabend, P. K. 1965 'Problems of empiricism'. In R. G. Colodny (ed.), *Beyond the Edge of Certainty*. Englewood Cliffs, NJ: Prentice-Hall.

Feyerabend, P. K. 1975 *Against Method*. London: New Left Books.

Fitting, James E. (ed.) 1973 *The Development of North American Archaeology*. Garden City, NY: Doubleday.

Fitting, James E. 1977 'The structure of historical archaeology and the importance of material things'. In Leland Ferguson (ed.), *Historical Archaeology and the Importance of Material Things*. Lansing, MI: Society for Historical Archaeology.

Flannery, Kent V. 1967 'Culture history v. cultural process: a debate in American archaeology'. *Scientific American*, 217, 119−22.

Flannery, Kent V. 1968 'Archeological systems theory and early Mesoamerica'. In Betty J. Meggers (ed.), *Anthropological Archeology in the Americas*. Washington, DC: Anthropological Society of Washington.

Flannery, Kent V. 1973 'Archeology with a capital S'. In Charles L. Redman (ed.), *Research and Theory in Current Archeology*. New York: Wiley.

Flew, Anthony 1982 'A strong programme for the sociology of belief'. *Inquiry*, 25, 365−85.

Forman, P. 1971 'Weimar culture, causality and quantum theory, 1918−1927'. *Historical Studies in the Physical Sciences*, No. 3.

Fretwell, S. D. 1975 'The impact of Robert MacArthur on ecology'. *Annual Review of Ecological Systematics*, 6, 1−13.

Freundlich, Y. 1980 'Methodologies of science as tools for historical research', *Studies in the History of Philosophy of Science*, 11, 257–66.

Friedrichs, Robert W. 1970 *A Sociology of Sociology*. New York: Free Press.

Fritz, John M. 1972 'Archaeological systems for indirect observation of the past'. In M. Leone (ed.), *Contemporary Archaeology*. Carbondale, IL: Southern Illinois University Press.

Fritz, John M. and Plog, Fred T. 1970 'The nature of archaeological explanation'. *American Antiquity*, 35, 405–12.

Garfinkel, H. 1967 *Studies in Ethnomethodology*. Englewood Cliffs, NJ: Prentice-Hall.

Garfinkel, H. and Sacks, H. 1970 'On formal structures of practical actions'. In J. C. McKinney and E. A. Tiryakian (eds), *Theoretical Sociology*. New York: Appleton-Century-Crofts.

Gay, Peter 1966, 1969 *The Enlightenment: An Interpretation*, vols 1 and 2. New York: Knopf.

Gellatly, Angus 1980 'Logical necessity and the strong programme for the sociology of knowledge'. *Studies in the History and Philosophy of Science*, 2, 325–39.

Gibbon, Guy 1984 *Anthropological Archaeology*. New York: Columbia University Press.

Gibbs, Jack 1972 *Sociological Theory Construction*. Hinsdale, IL: Dryden Press.

Giddens, Anthony 1976 *New Rules of Sociological Method: A Positive Critique of Interpretative Sociologies*. New York: Basic Books.

Giddens, Anthony 1977 *Studies in Social and Political Theory*. London: Hutchinson.

Giddens, Anthony 1979 *Central Problems in Social Theory*. London: Macmillan.

Giddens, Anthony 1982 'On the relation of sociology to philosophy'. In Paul F. Secord (ed.) *Explaining Human Behavior*. Beverly Hills, CA: Sage.

Giedymin, Jerzy 1975 'Antipositivism in contemporary philosophy of social science and humanities'. *British Journal for the Philosophy of Science*, 26, 275–301.

Giedymin, Jerzy 1976 'Instrumentalism and its critiques: a reappraisal'. In R. S. Cohen, P. K. Feyerabend and M. Wartofsky (eds), *Essays in Memory of Imre Lakatos, Boston Studies in the Philosophy of Science*, 39, 179–207.

Giere, Ronald N. and Westfall, Richard S. (eds) 1973 *Foundations of Scientific Method: The Nineteenth Century*. Bloomington, IN: Indiana University Press.

Godelier, M. 1972 'System structure and contradiction in Capital'. In R. Blackburn (ed.), *Ideology in Social Science*. London: Fontana.

Goodman, Nelson 1965 *Fact, Fiction and Forecast*, 2nd edn. New York: Bobbs-Merrill.

Gould, Richard A. 1978 'The anthropology of human residues'. *American Anthropologist*, 80, 815—35.

Gouldner, A. W. 1971 *The Coming Crises of Western Sociology.* London: Heinemann.

Graham, Gordon 1983 *Historical Explanation Reconsidered.* Aberdeen: Aberdeen University Press, Scots Philosophical monograph No. 4.

Gregory, Derek 1978 *Ideology, Science and Human Geography.* London: Hutchinson.

Grene, M. 1983 'Empiricism and the philosophy of science, or *n* dogmas of empiricism'. In R. S. Cohen and M. Wartofsky (eds), *Epistemology, Methodology and the Social Sciences, Boston Studies in the Philosophy of Science*, 71, 89—106.

Guelke, L. 1971 'Problems of scientific explanation in geography'. *Canadian Geography*, 15, 38—53.

Gunnell, J. G. 1975 *Philosophy, Science and Political Inquiry.* Morristown, NJ: General Learning Press.

Habermas, J. 1971 *Knowledge and Human Interests*, trans. J. J. Shapiro. Boston: Beacon Press (published in German in 1968).

Hacking, Ian 1984 'Experimentation and scientific realism'. In Jarrett Leplin (ed.), *Scientific Realism.* Berkeley, CA: University of California Press (first published in *Philosophical Topics*, 13).

Hage, J. 1972 *Techniques and Problems of Theory Construction in Sociology.* New York: Wiley.

Haggett, P. 1965 *Locational Analysis in Human Geography.* London: Edward Arnold.

Halfpenny, Peter 1982 *Positivism and Sociology: Explaining Social Life.* Boston: Allen and Unwin.

Hall, Robert L, 1976 'Ghosts, water barriers, corn, and sacred enclosures in the Eastern Woodlands'. *American Antiquity*, 41, 360—4.

Hamlyn, D. W. 1971 *The Theory of Knowledge.* London: Macmillan.

Hanfling, Oswald 1981 *Logical Positivism.* New York: Columbia University Press.

Hanson, N. R. 1958 *Patterns of Discovery.* Cambridge: Cambridge University Press.

Hanson, N. R. 1969 *Perception and Discovery* (ed. W. C. Humphreys). San Francisco, CA: Freeman, Cooper.

Hanson, N. R. 1971 *Observation and Explanation.* New York: Harper and Row.

Harré, R. 1970 *The Principles of Scientific Thinking.* Chicago, IL: University of Chicago Press.

Harré, R. 1970 'Powers'. *British Journal for the Philosophy of Science*, 21, 81–101.

Harré, R. 1972 *The Philosophies of Science*. Oxford: Oxford University Press.

Harré, R. 1974 'Blueprint for a new science'. In N. Armistead (ed.), *Reconstructing Social Psychology*. Harmondsworth: Penguin.

Harré, R. and Madden, E. H. 1973 'Natural powers and powerful natures'. *Philosophy*, 48, 209–30.

Harré, R. and Madden, E. H. 1975 *Causal Powers*. Totowa, NJ: Littlefield Adams.

Harris, Marvin 1968 *The Rise of Anthropological Theory*. New York: Crowell.

Harris, Marvin 1979 *Cultural Materialism: The Struggle for a Science of Culture*. New York: Vintage Books.

Hart, H. L. A. 1961 *The Concept of Law*. Oxford: Clarendon Press.

Harvey, D. 1969 *Explanation in Geography*. London: Edward Arnold.

Hawthorn, Geoffrey 1976 *Enlightenment and Despair: A History of Sociology*. Cambridge: Cambridge University Press.

Hegel, G. W. F. 1952 *Philosophy of Right*, trans. with notes by T. M. Knox. Oxford: Oxford University Press.

Hempel, Carl G. 1942 'The function of general laws in history'. *Journal of Philosophy*, 39, 35–48.

Hempel, Carl G. 1943 'A purely syntactical definition of confirmation'. *Journal of Symbolic Logic*, 8, 122–43.

Hempel, Carl G. 1945 'Studies in the logic of confirmation'. *Mind*, 54, 1–26, 97–121.

Hempel, Carl G. 1958 'The theoretician's dilemma: a study in the logic of theory construction'. In H. Feigl, M. Scriven and G. Maxwell (eds), *Minnesota Studies in the Philosophy of Science*, vol. 2 Minneapolis, MN: University of Minnesota Press.

Hempel, Carl G. 1959 'The logic of functional analysis'. In L. Gross (ed.), *Symposium on Sociological Theory*. New York: Harper and Row.

Hempel, Carl G. 1962 'Deductive–nomological vs. statistical explanation'. In H. Feigl and G. Maxwell (eds), *Minnesota Studies in the Philosophy of Science*, vol. 3. Minneapolis, MN: University of Minnesota Press.

Hempel, Carl G. 1963 'Reasons and covering laws in historical explanation'. In S. Hook (ed.), *Philosophy and History*. New York: New York University Press.

Hempel, Carl G. 1963 'Explanation and prediction by covering laws'. In Bernard Baumrin (ed.), *Philosophy of Science: The Delaware Seminar* vol. 1. New York: Wiley.

Hempel, Carl G. 1965 'Explanatory incompleteness'. In C. Hempel, *Aspects of Scientific Explanation and Other Essays in the Philosophy of Science*. New York: Free Press.

Hempel, Carl G. 1965 *Aspects of Scientific Explanation and Other Essays in the Philosophy of Science*. New York: Free Press.

Hempel, Carl G. 1966 *Philosophy of Natural Science*. Princeton, NJ: Prentice-Hall.

Hempel, Carl G. 1970 'On the "standard conception" of scientific theories'. In M. Radner and S. Winokur (eds), *Minnesota Studies in the Philosophy of Science*, vol. 4. Minneapolis, MN: University of Minnesota Press.

Hempel, Carl G. 1970 'Studies in the logic of confirmation'. In Baruch Brody (ed.), *Readings in the Philosophy of Science*. Englewood Cliffs, NJ: Prentice Hall first published in 1945).

Hempel, Carl G. and Oppenheim, Paul 1948 'Studies in the logic of explanation'. *Philosophy of Science*, 15, 135−75.

Heritage, J. 1978 'Aspects of the flexibility of language use'. *Sociology*, 12, 79−103.

Hill, James N. 1966 'A prehistoric community in eastern Arizona'. *Southwestern Journal of Anthropology*, 22, 9−30.

Hill, James N. 1968 'Broken K Pueblo: patterns of form and function'. In Sally R. Binford and L. R. Binford (eds), *New Perspectives in Archeology*. Chicago, IL: Aldine.

Hill, James N. 1970 *Broken K Pueblo: Prehistoric Social Organization in the American Southwest*, Anthropological Papers of the University of Arizona, vol. 18. Tucson, AZ: University of Arizona Press.

Hill, James N. 1971 'Summary of a Seminar on the Explanation of Prehistoric Organizational Change'. *Current Anthropology*, 12, 406−8.

Hill, James N. 1972 'The methodological debate in contemporary archaeology: a model'. In D. Clarke (ed.), *Models in Archaeology*. London: Methuen.

Hill, James N. and Evans, R. K. 1972 'A model for classification and typology'. In D. Clarke (ed.), *Models in Archaeology*. London: Methuen.

Hindess, Barry 1977 *Philosophy and Methodology in the Social Sciences*. Atlantic Highlands, NJ: Humanities Press.

Hintikka, J. (ed.) 1975 *Rudolf Carnap, Logical Empiricist*. Dordrecht: Reidel.

Hodder, Ian 1982 *Symbols in Action: Ethnoarchaeological Studies of Material Culture*. Cambridge: Cambridge University Press.

Hodder, Ian 1985 'Postprocessual archaeology'. In M. B. Schiffer (ed.), *Advances in Archaeological Method and Theory*, vol. 8. Orlando, FL: Academic Press.

Hollis, Martin 1977 *Models of Man: Philosophical Thoughts on Social Action.* New York: Cambridge University Press.

Hollis, Martin and Lukes, Steven (eds) 1982 *Rationality and Relativism.* Cambridge, MA: MIT Press.

Homans, G. C. 1964 'Bringing men back in'. *American Sociological Review*, 29, 809–18.

Hooker, C. A. 1973 'Empiricism, perception and conceptual change'. *Canadian Journal of Philosophy*, 3, 59–75.

Hookway, C. 1978 'Indeterminacy and interpretation'. In C. Hookway and P. Petit (eds), *Action and Interpretation*, Cambridge: Cambridge University Press.

Howson, Colin (ed.) 1976 *Method and Appraisal in the Physical Sciences.* Cambridge: Cambridge University Press.

Huff, Toby E. 1984 *Max Weber and the Methodology of the Social Sciences.* New Brunswick, NJ: Transaction Books.

Hughes, John 1980 *The Philosophy of Social Research.* New York: Longman.

Hume, David 1975 *A Treatise of Human Nature*, (ed. L. A. Selby-Bigge). London: Oxford University Press (first published in 1888).

Jobe, E. K. 1967 'Discussion: some recent work on the problem of law'. *Philosophy of Science*, 34, 363–81.

Joergensen, Joergen 1951 *The Development of Logical Empiricism. International Encyclopedia of Unified Science*, vol. 3, no. 9. Chicago, IL: University of Chicago Press.

Keat, R. and Urry, J. 1975 *Social Theory as Science.* Boston: Routledge and Kegan Paul.

Keesing, Roger M. 1974 'Theories of culture'. In Bernard J. Siegel (ed.), *Annual Review of Anthropology.* Palo Alto, CA: Annual Reviews.

Kemeny, J. 1959 *A Philosopher Looks at Science.* New York: Van Nostrand Reinhold.

Kirsh, David 1983 'The role of philosophy in the human sciences'. In S. Mitchell and M. Rosen (eds), *The Need for Interpretation: Contemporary Conceptions of the Philosopher's Task.* Atlantic Highlands, NJ: Humanities Press.

Kluckhohn, Clyde 1939 'The place of theory in anthropological studies'. *Philosophy of Science*, 6, 328–44.

Kluckhohn, Clyde 1940 'The conceptual structure in Middle American studies'. In C. L. Hay et al. (eds). *The Maya and their Neighbors.* New York: Dover Publications.

Kockelmans, Joseph J. (ed.) 1968 *Philosophy of Science: The Historical Background.* New York: Free Press.

Kolakowski, Leszek 1968 *The Alienation of Reason: A History of Positivist Thought.* Garden City, NY: Doubleday.

Kolakowski, Leszek 1972 *Positivist Philosophy*. Harmondsworth: Penguin.

Kraft, Victor 1953 *The Vienna Circle*. New York: Philosophical Library.

Krimerman, Leonard I. (ed.) 1969 *The Nature and Scope of Social Science: A Critical Anthology*. New York: Appleton-Century-Crofts.

Kuhn, T. S. 1963 'The function of dogma in scientific research'. In A. C. Crombie (ed.), *Scientific Change*. London: Heinemann.

Kuhn, T. S. 1970 *The Structure of Scientific Revolutions*, 2nd edn. Chicago, IL: University of Chicago Press (first published in 1962).

Lakatos, I. 1970 'Falsification and the methodology of scientific research programmes'. In I. Lakatos and A. Musgrave (eds), *Criticism and the Growth of Knowledge*. Cambridge: Cambridge University Press.

Lakatos, I. 1971 'History of science and its rational reconstruction'. In R. C. Buck and R. S. Cohen (eds), *Boston Studies in the Philosophy of Science*, vol. 8. Dordrecht: Reidel.

Lakatos, I. and Musgrave, A. (eds) 1970 *Criticism and the Growth of Knowledge*. Cambridge: Cambridge University Press.

Lazarsfeld, P. F. and Menzel, H. 1969 'On the relation between individual and collective properties'. In A. Etzioni (ed.), *Complex Organizations: A Sociological Reader*, 2nd edn. New York: Holt, Rhinehart, and Winston.

LeBlanc, Steven A. 1973 'Two points of logic concerning data, hypotheses, general laws, and systems'. In C. Redman (ed.), *Research and Theory in Current Archeology*. New York: Wiley.

Lenzer, G. (ed.) 1975 *Auguste Comte and Positivism: The Essential Writings*. New York: Harper Torchbooks.

Leone, Mark P. 1972 'Issues in anthropological archaeology'. In Mark P. Leone (ed.), *Contemporary Archaeology*. Carbondale, IL: Southern Illinois University Press.

Leplin, Jarrett (ed.) 1984 *Scientific Realism*. Berkeley CA: University of California Press.

Levin, Michael 1976 'On the ascription of functions to objects, with special reference to inference in archaeology'. *Philosophy of the Social Sciences*, 6, 227−34.

Locke, J. 1959 *Essay Concerning Human Understanding*. New York: Dover Publications.

Longacre, William A. 1964 'Archaeology as anthropology: a case study'. *Science*, 144, 1454−5.

Longacre, William A. 1966 'Changing patterns of social integration: a prehistoric example from the American Southwest'. *American Anthropologist*, 68, 94−102.

Longacre, William A. 1970 *Archaeology as Anthropology: A Case*

Study, Anthropological Papers of the University of Arizona, vol. 17. Tucson, AZ: University of Arizona Press.

Longacre, William A. (ed.) 1970 *Reconstructing Prehistoric Pueblo Societies*. Albuquerque, NM: University of New Mexico Press.

Luntley Michael 1982 'Understanding anthropologists'. *Inquiry*, 25, 199–216.

Mach, Ernst 1985 *Popular Scientific Lectures*, trans. T. J. McCormack. Chicago, IL: Open Court.

MacIntyre, Alasdair 1970 'The idea of a social science'. In B. Wilson (ed.), *Rationality*. Oxford: Basil Blackwell (first published in 1967 in *Aristotelian Society Supplement*, 41).

MacKenzie, B. D. 1977 *Behaviourism and the Limits of Scientific Method*. London: Routledge and Kegan Paul.

Mandelbaum, Maurice 1971 *History, Man, and Reason: A Study in Nineteenth-Century Thought*. Baltimore, MD: Johns Hopkins University Press.

Manicas, Peter T. and Rosenberg, Alan 1985 'Naturalism, epistemological individualism and "the strong programme" in the sociology of knowledge'. *Journal for the Theory of Social Behaviour*, 15, 76–101.

Manicas, Peter T. and Secord, Paul F. 1983 'Implications for psychology of the new philosophy of science'. *American Psychologist*, 38, 399–413.

Martin, Paul S. 1971 'The revolution in archaeology'. *American Antiquity*, 36, 1–8.

Maruyama, Margoroh 1963 'The second cybernetics: deviation amplifying mutual causal processes'. *American Scientist*, 51, 164–79.

McKern, W. C. 1939 'The Midwestern taxonomic method as an aid to archaeological study'. *American Antiquity*, 4, 301–13.

McMullin, Ernan 1978 'Structural explanation'. *American Philosophical Quarterly*, 15, 139–47.

McMullin, Ernan 1984 'The goals of natural science'. *Proceedings and Addresses of the American Philosophical Association*, 58, 37–64.

McMullin, Ernan 1984 'A case for scientific realism'. In Jarrett Leplin (ed.), *Scientific Realism*. Berkeley, CA: University of California Press.

Meltzer, David J. 1979. 'Paradigms and the nature of change in American archaeology'. *American Antiquity*, 44, 644–57.

Mendelsohn, E., Weingart, P. and Whitley, R. D. (eds) 1977 *The Social Production of Scientific Knowledge, Sociology of the Sciences*, vol. 1. Boston, MA: Reidel.

Merton, R. K. 1964 *Social Theory and Social Structure*. London: Collier-Macmillan.

von Mises, L. 1951 *Positivism: A Study in Human Understanding.* Cambridge, MA: Harvard University Press.

Mitchell, Sollace and Rosen, Michael (eds) 1983 *The Need for Interpretation: Contemporary Conceptions of the Philosopher's Task.* Atlantic Heights, NJ: Humanities Press.

Moberg, Carl-Axel 1972 'Review of Lewis R. Binford's *An Archaeological Perspective*'. *Science*, 178, 741—2.

Morgan, Charles G. 1973 'Archaeology and explanation'. *World Archaeology*, 4, 259—76.

Morgan, Charles G. 1974 'Explanation and scientific archaeology'. *World Archaeology*, 6, 133—7.

Morrison, D. E. and Henkel, R. E. (eds) 1970 *The Significance Test Controversy.* Chicago, IL: University of Chicago Press.

Mullins, N. 1971 *The Art of Theory: Construction and Use.* New York: Harper and Row.

Nagel, Ernest 1961 *The Structure of Science.* New York: Harcourt, Brace and World.

Norris, C. 1983 *The Deconstructive Turn: Essays in the Rhetoric of Philosophy.* New York: Methuen.

Nowotny, Helga and Rose, Hilary (eds) 1979 *Counter Movements in the Sciences, The Sociology of the Alternatives to Big Science, Sociology of the Sciences,* vol. 3. Boston, MA: Reidel.

Passmore, J. 1968 *A Hundred Years of Philosophy.* Harmondsworth: Penguin.

Phillips, D. C. 1976 *Holistic Thought in Social Science.* Stanford, CA: Stanford University Press.

Pinch, Trevor 1985 'Theory testing in science — the case of solar neutrinos: do crucial experiments test theories or theorists?' *Philosophy of the Social Sciences,* 15, 167—87.

Pitkin, H. 1972 *Wittgenstein and Justice.* Berkeley, CA: University of California Press.

Plog, Fred T. 1975 'Systems theory in archaeological research'. In B. J. Siegel (ed.), *Annual Review of Anthropology.* Palo Alto, CA: Annual Reviews.

Polanyi, M. 1964 *Personal Knowledge.* New York: Harper and Row (first published in 1958).

Polanyi, M. 1967 *The Tacit Dimension,* London: Routledge and Kegan Paul.

Polkinghorne, Donald 1983 *Methodology for the Human Sciences.* Albany, NY: State University of New York Press.

Popper, K. R. 1959 *The Logic of Scientific Discovery.* London: Hutchinson (published in German in 1934).

Popper, K. R. 1972 *Conjectures and Refutations.* London: Routledge and Kegan Paul (first published in 1963).

Popper, K. R. 1972 *Objective Knowledge*. Oxford: Clarendon Press.

Popper, K. R. 1976 *Unended Quest*. Glasgow: William Collins.

Pratt, V. 1978 *The Philosophy of the Social Sciences*. London: Methuen.

Quine, W. V. O. 1953 *From A Logical Point of View*. Cambridge, MA: Harvard University Press.

Quine, W. V. O. 1960 *Word and Object*. Cambridge, MA: MIT Press.

Quine, W. V. O. 1968 'Ontological relativity'. *Journal of Philosophy*, 65, 185–212.

Radford, Colin 1985 'Must knowledge – or "knowledge" – be socially constructed?' *Philosophy of the Social Sciences*, 15, 15–33.

Ravetz, J. R. 1971 *Scientific Knowledge and Its Social Problems*. Oxford: Clarendon Press.

Rawls, J. 1955 'The two concepts of rules'. *Philosophical Review*, 64, 3–32.

Read, Dwight W. and LeBlanc, Steven A. 1978 'Descriptive statements, covering laws, and theories in archaeology'. *Current Anthropology*, 19, 307–35.

Reichenbach, Hans 1951 *The Rise of Scientific Philosophy*. Berkeley, CA: University of California Press.

Reid, J. Jefferson 1978 'Response to stress at Grasshopper Pueblo, Arizona'. In Paul Grebinger (ed.), *Discovering Past Behavior*. New York: Gordon and Breach.

Renfrew, Colin 1969 'Review of David L. Clarke: *Analytical Archaeology* and, Sally R. Binford and Lewis R. Binford (eds.): *New Perspectives in Archaeology*'. *Antiquity*, 43, 241–4.

Reynolds, P. 1971 *A Primer in Theory Construction*, New York: Bobbs-Merrill.

Robinson, W. S. 1950 'Ecological correlations and the behaviour of individuals'. *American Sociological Review*, 15, 351–7.

Rorty, Richard 1978 'Philosophy as a kind of writing'. *New Literary History*, 10, 141–60.

Roszak, Theodore 1969 *The Making of a Counter Culture*. Garden City, NY: Doubleday.

Roszak, Theodore 1972 *Where the Wasteland Ends*. Garden City, NY: Doubleday.

Rudner, Richard S. 1966 *Philosophy of Social Science*. Englewood Cliffs, NJ: Prentice-Hall.

Runciman, W. G. 1983 *A Treatise on Social Theory 1: The Methodology of Social Theory*. Cambridge: Cambridge University Press.

Russell, Bertrand 1957 'The relation of sense-data to physics'. In B. Russell, *Mysticism and Logic*, Garden City, NY: Doubleday Anchor.

Russell, Bertrand and Whitehead, A. N. 1910–13 *Principia Mathematica*, vols 1–3. Cambridge: Cambridge University Press.

Ryan, A. 1970 *The Philosophy of the Social Sciences*. London: Macmillan.

Sabloff, J. A. and Willey, G. 1967 'The collapse of Maya civilization in the Southern Lowlands'. *Southwestern Journal of Anthropology*, 23, 311–31.

Sacks, H. 1963 'Sociological description'. *Berkeley Journal of Sociology*, 8, 1–19.

Salmon, M. H. 1975 'Confirmation and explanation in archaeology'. *American Antiquity*, 40, 459–64.

Salmon, M. H. 1976 '"Deductive" versus "inductive" archaeology'. *American Antiquity*, 44, 376–80.

Salmon, M. H. 1981 'Ascribing functions to archaeological objects'. *Philosophy of the Social Sciences*, 11, 19–26.

Salmon, M. H. 1982 *Philosophy and Archaeology*. New York: Academic Press.

Salmon, M. H. and Salmon, W. 1979 'Alternative models of scientific explanation'. *American Anthropologist*, 81, 61–74.

Salmon, W. 1966 *The Foundations of Scientific Inference*. Pittsburgh, PA: University of Pittsburgh Press.

Sampson, Geoffrey 1980 *Schools of Linguistics: Competition and Evolution*. London: Hutchinson.

Scharfstein, Ben-Ami, Alon, Ilai, Biderman, Shlomo, Daot, Dan and Hoffmann, Yoel 1978 *Philosophy East/Philosophy West: A Critical Comparison of Indian, Chinese, Islamic, and European Philosophy*. Oxford: Basil Blackwell.

Scheffler, Israel 1963 *The Anatomy of Inquiry*. New York: Knopf.

Scheffler, Israel 1967 *Science and Subjectivity*. New York: Bobbs-Merrill.

Scheffler, Israel 1970 'The fictionalist view of scientific theories'. In Baruch Brody (ed.), *Readings in the Philosophy of Science*. Englewood Cliffs, NJ: Prentice-Hall.

Schiffer, Michael B. 1972 'Cultural laws and the reconstruction of past lifeways'. *Kiva*, 37, 148–57.

Schiffer, Michael B. 1975 'Archaeology as behavioral science'. *American Anthropologist*, 77, 836–48.

Schiffer, Michael B. 1976 *Behavioral Archeology*. New York: Academic Press.

Schlesinger, Arthur M., Jr. 1986 *The Cycles of American History*. Boston, MA: Houghton Mifflin.

Schlesinger, G. 1961 'The prejudice of micro-reduction'. *British Journal for the Philosophy of Science*, 12, 215–224.

Schlick, Moritz 1959 'The turning point in philosophy', trans David Rynin. In A. J. Ayer (ed.), *Logical Positivism*. New York: Free Press.

Schlick, Moritz 1959 'Positivism and realism', trans. David Rynin. In A. J. Ayer (ed.). *Logical Positivism*. New York: Free Press.

Schilpp, P. A. (ed.) 1963 *The Philosophy of Rudolf Carnap, The Library of Living Philosophers*, vol. 11. La Salle, IL: Open Court.

Scriven, M. 1956 'A possible distinction between traditional scientific disciplines and the study of human behavior'. In H. Feigl and M. Scriven (eds), *Minnesota Studies in the Philosophy of Science*, vol. 1. Minneapolis, MN: University of Minnesota Press.

Scriven, M. 1959 'Truisms as the grounds for historical explanation'. 'In P. Gardiner (ed.), *Theories of History*. New York: Free Press.

Scriven, M. 1962 'Explanations, predictions, and laws'. In H. Feigl and G. Maxwell (eds), *Minnesota Studies in the Philosophy of Science*, vol. 3. Minneapolis, MN: University of Minnesota Press.

Scriven, M. 1964 'Views of human nature'. In T. W. Wann (ed.), *Behaviorism and Phenomenology*, Chicago, IL: University of Chicago Press.

Searle, J. 1969 *Speech Acts*. Cambridge: Cambridge University Press.

Sellars, Wilfrid 1963 *Science, Perception and Reality*. New York: Humanities Press.

Shapere, D. (ed.) 1965 *Philosophical Problems of Natural Science*. New York: Macmillan.

Shapere, D. 1966 'Meaning and scientific change'. In R. Colodny (ed.), *Mind and Cosmos*. Pittsburgh, PA: University of Pittsburgh Press.

Shapere, D. 1982 'The concept of observation in science and philosophy'. *Philosophy of Science*, 49, 485–526.

Shapin, Steven 1982 'History of science and its sociological reconstructions'. *History of Science*, 20, 157–211.

Simon, W. M. 1963 *European Positivism in the Nineteenth Century*, Ithaca, NY: Cornell University Press.

Smart, J. J. C. 1961–2 'Dispositional properties'. *Analysis*, 22, 44–6.

Smith, Peter 1981 *Realism and the Progress of Science*. Cambridge: Cambridge University Press.

Spaulding, A. C. 1953 'Statistical techniques for the discovery of artifact types'. *American Antiquity*, 18, 305–13.

Spaulding, A. C. 1973 'Archeology in the active voice: the new anthropology'. In C. Redman (ed.), *Research and Theory in Current Archeology*. New York: Wiley.

Spector, M. 1967 'Theory and observation'. *British Journal for the Philosophy of Science*, 17, 1–20, 89–104.

Spriggs, Matthew (ed.) 1984 *Marxist Perspectives in Archaeology*. Cambridge: Cambridge University Press.

Stanislawski, M. 1973 'Review of *Archaeology as Anthropology: A Case Study*'. *American Antiquity*, 38, 117–21.

Stark, W. 1958 *The Sociology of Knowledge*. London: Routledge and Kegan Paul.

Steward, Julian H. 1955 *Theory of Culture Change*. Urbana, IL: University of Illinois Press.

Steward, Julian H. and Setzler, F. 1938 'Function and configuration in archaeology'. *American Antiquity*, 4, 4—10.

Stinchcombe, A. 1968 *Constructing Social Theories*. New York: Harcourt, Brace and World.

Stockman, N. 1983 *Antipositivist Theories of the Sciences*. Dordrecht: Reidel.

Strong, W. D. 1936 'Anthropological theory and archaeological fact'. In R. H. Lowie (ed.), *Essays in Anthropology Presented to A. L. Kroeber*. Berkeley, CA: University of California Press.

Suppe, Frederick (ed.) 1977 *The Structure of Scientific Theories*, 2nd edn. Urbana, IL: University of Illinois Press (first published in 1973).

Suppe, Frederick 1977 'Critical introduction'. In Frederick Suppe (ed.), *The Structure of Scientific Theories*. Urbana, IL: University of Illinois Press.

Suppe, Frederick 1977 'Afterword'. In Frederick Suppe (ed.), *The Structure of Scientific Theories*, pp. 617—730. Urbana, IL: University of Illinois Press.

Sutton, Michael 1982 *Nationalism, Positivism, and Catholicism: The Politics of Charles Maurras and the French Catholics, 1890—1914*. New York: Cambridge University Press.

Swinburne, R. G. 1971 'The paradoxes of confirmation — a survey'. *American Philosophical Quarterly*, 8, 318—30.

Swinburne, R. G. 1973 *An Introduction to Confirmation Theory*. London: Methuen.

Tarski, Alfred 1956 *Logic, Semantics, Metamathematics*. Oxford: Clarendon Press.

Taylor, Charles 1964 *The Explanation of Behavior*. London: Routledge and Kegan Paul.

Taylor, Charles 1971 'Interpretation and the sciences of man'. *Review of Metaphysics*, 25, 3—51.

Taylor, Walter W. 1948 *A Study of Archeology, American Anthropological Association, Memoir 69*.

Thomas, David 1979 *Naturalism and Social Science: A PostEmpiricist Philosophy of Social Science*. Cambridge: Cambridge University Press.

Toulmin, S. 1953 *The Philosophy of Science*. New York: Harper and Row.

Toulmin, S. 1961 *Foresight and Understanding*. New York: Harper and Row.

Toulmin, S. 1972 *Human Understanding*. Princeton, NJ: Princeton University Press.

Trigg, Roger 1985 *Understanding Social Science*, Oxford: Basil Blackwell.

Trigger, Bruce and Glover, Ian (eds) 1981, 1982 'Regional traditions'. *World Archaeology*, 13, nos 2 and 3.

Tudor, Andrew 1982 *Beyond Empiricism: Philosophy of Science in Sociology*. London: Routledge and Kegan Paul.

Tuggle, H. David 1972 'Review of Patty Jo Watson, Steven A. LeBlanc and Charles L. Redman, *Explanation in Archeology: An Explicitly Scientific Approach*'. *Philosophy of Science*, 39, 564−6.

Tuggle, H. David, Townsend, Alex H. and Riley, Thomas J. 1972 'Laws, systems and research designs: a discussion of explanation in archaeology'. *American Antiquity*, 37, 3−12.

Unger, Peter 1984 *Philosophical Relativity*. Minneapolis, MN: University of Minnesota Press.

Urbach, Peter 1974 'Progress and degeneration in the "I.Q. debate"'. *British Journal for the Philosophy of Science*, 25, 99−135, 235−59.

Walsh, David 1972 'Varieties of positivism'. In Paul Filmer, Michael Phillipson, David Silverman and David Walsh (eds), *New Directions in Sociological Theory*. London: Collier-Macmillan.

Watkins, J. W. N. 1958 'Confirmable and influential metaphysics'. *Mind*, 67, 344−65.

Watkins, J. W. N. 1975 'Metaphysics and the advancement of science'. *British Journal for the Philosophy of Science*, 26, 91−121.

Watkins, J. W. N., Worrall, John, Zahar, Elie, Urbach, Peter and Howson, Colin 1975 'Criteria of scientific progress: a critical rationalist view'. Unpublished position paper, Department of Philosophy, London School of Economics.

Watson, Patty Jo 1986 'Archaeological interpretation, 1985'. In David J. Meltzer, Don D. Fowler, and Jeremy A. Sabloff (eds), *American Archaeology Past and Future*, Washington, DC: Smithsonian Institution Press.

Watson, Patty Jo, LeBlanc, Steven A. and Redman, Charles L. 1971 *Explanation in Archeology: An Explicitly Scientific Approach*. New York: Columbia University Press.

Weber, Max 1964 *The Theory of Social and Economic Organization*, trans. T. Parsons and A. M. Henderson. New York: Free Press.

Weider, D. Lawrence 1974 *Language and Social Reality*. The Hague: Mouton.

Whitley, Richard D. (ed.) 1974 *Social Process of Scientific Development*. London: Routledge and Kegan Paul.

Whorf, Benjamin L. 1965 *Language, Thought, and Reality: Selected Writings of Benjamin Lee Whorf* (ed. J. B. Carroll). Cambridge, MA: MIT Press (first published in 1956).

Willer, D. and Willer, J. 1973 *Systematic Empiricism*. Englewood Cliffs, NJ: Prentice-Hall.

Willey, Gordon R. and Sabloff, Jeremy A. 1980 *A History of American Archaeology*, 2nd edn. San Francisco, CA: Freeman.

Wilson, T. P. 1974 'Normative and interpretative paradigms in sociology'. In J. D. Douglas (ed.), *Understanding Everyday Life*. London: Routledge and Kegan Paul (first published in 1970).

Winch, Peter 1958 *The Idea of a Social Science and Its Relation to Philosophy*. London: Routledge and Kegan Paul.

Winch, Peter 1964 'Understanding a primitive society'. *American Philosophical Quarterly*, 1, 307–24.

Wittgenstein, Ludwig 1968 *Philosophical Investigations*, 3rd edn, trans. G. E. M. Anscombe. New York: Macmillan.

von Wright, Georg H. 1971 *Explanation and Understanding*. Ithaca, NY: Cornell University Press.

Wylie, Margaret A. 1981 'Positivism and the new Archaeology'. Ph.D. Dissertation, Department of Philosophy, State University of New York at Binghamton.

Yolton, John W. (ed.) 1965 *Theory of Knowledge*. New York: Macmillan.

Zahar, E. G. 1973 'Why did Einstein's programme supersede Lorentz's?' *British Journal for the Philosophy of Science*, 24, 95–123, 223–62.

Index